Praise for *The*

The Stepfamily Handbook is a game-thoughtful yet intuitive. As a family law attorney and guardian ad litem who represents the best interests of kids before the court, *The Stepfamily Handbook* gives parents and partners crucial information about expanding families. As a stepmom, it's eye-opening to see the complex dynamics at play of all parties—including co-parents. If you're a parent or considering dating a parent, *The Stepfamily Handbook* should be required reading before that first date!

—Elise Buie, JD, GAL, Principal Elise Buie Family Law Group

The Stepfamily Handbook offers valuable tools, tips, and guidance for parents who are re-entering the dating world and their new dating partners...and eventually hoping to expand their families. This important, well-written and practical handbook should be required reading for parents contemplating dating post-divorce, as well as for therapists, coaches, pastors, and other professionals supporting families.

—Shelley Chambers, MSW, LCSW, Child Psychotherapist and Collaborative Child Specialist

Karen Bonnell and Patricia Papernow have created an essential roadmap for any divorced or separated parent who is dating or re-partnering. Written by experienced professionals, this practical and wise book is a must read for parents stepparents and professionals.

—Robin M. Deutsch, PhD, ABPP, Founder and Past Director of the Center of Excellence for Children, Families and the Law at the William James College

The Stepfamily Handbook is a practical, wise, and helpful. I highly recommend this book to those who are beginning and to those who may be struggling at different stages of stepfamily life.

—Dawn O. Braithwaite, Willa Cather Professor of Communication, University of Nebraska-Lincoln

As a retired judge after 20 years on the bench, I can say that this book goes right to the heart of the matter. This book should be read by every single parent and stepparent.

—Hon. Christina Harms *(ret.)*, Director, Child and Family Psychological Evaluation Service, Center of Excellence for Children, Families and the Law, William James College

The Stepfamily Handbook: There's *a lot* for everyone. Detailed, well-researched and constructive guidance are offered in easily understood language. Parents who read this book will be more sensitive to their children's struggles and strengths and they will be in a much better position to guide them through the shifting waters of family reorganization. Professionals who work with stepfamilies will gain keen insight into the realities of this multifaceted and multi-tiered world.

—Robert L Kaufman, PhD, ABPP, Clinical and Forensic Psychologist, San Rafael, California

Stepfamilies come with unique challenges. Understanding those challenges is the first step toward long-term success. *The Stepfamily Handbook* tackles some of the most common obstacles in a straightforward manner using real-world examples. Every stepfamily will find something of themselves within its pages.

—Kyle D. Bradford, "Chopper Pappa" Blogger for Dads (and Stepdads)

Moving from one relationship to another with kids in tow is a balancing act that requires both patience and insight. *The Stepfamily Handbook* offers guidance for successfully avoiding the many traps that can appear on your way to making your new family work. I highly recommend this book to any person contemplating or currently working in a stepfamily situation.

—Gary Direnfeld, MSW, RSW, Internationally Respected Voice on Parenting

Karen and Patricia have created the quintessential roadmap for helping second (and maybe third) time around couples come together to form a strong base and successfully blend their families. I will be recommending this as essential reading for all my clients.

—Anne Robinson Lucas, MA LMHC, Psychotherapist, Mediator, Trainer, Stepparent

THE STEPFAMILY HANDBOOK

[From Dating, to Getting Serious, to Forming a "Blended Family"]

KAREN S. BONNELL, MS · PATRICIA L. PAPERNOW, EdD

Text Copyright © 2019 by Karen Bonnell and Patricia Papernow
Cover Art Copyright © 2019 by Karen Bonnell

All rights reserved.
No portion of this book may be reproduced or utilized in any form,
or by any electronic, mechanical, or other means, without
the prior written permission of either author.

Cover and Interior Design: Kathryn Campbell

*The Stepfamily Handbook: From Dating, to Getting Serious,
to Forming a "Blended Family"*

ISBN-13: 978-1720855200
ISBN-10: 172085520x

Printed in the United States of America by KDP, an Amazon Company
Published in the United States of America by
CMC Publishers, Kirkland, Washington

www.coachmediateconsult.com

DEDICATION

Karen

To my parents, Ruth and Flip, and my children, Ali, Ardie, and Ben, and to the newest member and first of the next generation, Ariana Ruth.

Patricia

To my husband, my love, and my partner of 23 years, Steve. To my daughter Dina who came from my belly and is always in my soul. To my stepchildren Becky, Jaimi, and Adam and their families, who I love tons; and to my stepdaughters Pam and Phyllis, who remain deep in my heart.

CONTENTS

Foreword ix

Introduction xi

PART I · PARENTING WHILE DATING/DATING A PARENT

Chapter 1   Dating (Again)? 3

Chapter 2   Are You Cut Out for a Stepfamily? 9

Chapter 3   When Is a Relationship "Kid-Worthy"? 19

Chapter 4   Moving Forward? Strengthen Your Relationship Skills! 27

PART II · GETTING SERIOUS: INCLUDING THE KIDS

Chapter 5   Introducing Children and a New Partner:
            A Step at a Time Saves Nine 49

Chapter 6   Children's Responses to a Parent Repartnering 73

Chapter 7   Co-Parents as Allies, Not Enemies 99

Chapter 8   When a Child's Parent Has Died 115

Chapter 9   If Your New Relationship Began with an Affair 125

PART III · BECOMING A STEPFAMILY

Chapter 10 How Stepfamilies Differ from First-Time Families 139

Chapter 11 First Stepfamily Challenge: Children Struggle
            with Losses, Loyalty Binds and Change 151

Chapter 12	Second Stepfamily Challenge: Insider/Outsider Positions	173
Chapter 13	The Third Stepfamily Challenge: Divided Over Discipline	189
Chapter 14	Fourth Stepfamily Challenge: Co-parents Are Part of the Stepfamily	207
Chapter 15	Fifth Stepfamily Challenge: Building a Shared Culture That Respects Differences	227
Chapter 16	A New Wrinkle: Gray Recouplers	243
Chapter 17	Coming Apart with Kids on Board: Thoughtful Endings for Stepfamilies	255

Conclusion: Stepfamilies Over Time 265

• • • • • • • • • • •

Appendix A: My Family 275

Appendix B: Changes in My Life 278

Appendix C: Choosing a Therapist 281

Resources 283

Acknowledgements 290

Author Biographies 292

FOREWORD

The Stepfamily Handbook by Karen Bonnell and Patricia Papernow is, like stepfamilies themselves, a rich and diverse blend. Based largely on developmental psychology and attachment theory, it manages to be that rare thing: a highly researched clinical manual that reads like a thriller! With characteristic warmth and humor, Bonnell and Papernow invite themselves into the readers' world not to lecture or to judge but to sit alongside, sharing the experience, pondering the pitfalls, helping the reader to stay thinking at those moments when reacting comes more naturally. In their skilled hands, the emotions and drives so often felt to be negative—loss, shame, anger, grief, guilt, greed—become the normal stuff of human life, and mistakes become opportunities for learning rather than for recrimination.

This is essentially a book about love at its most stretched and challenged. Not a fantasy hearts-and-flowers love, but a resilient, grown-up version founded on humility and generosity that keeps the needs of others—specifically children—as the key reference point. The stories this book tells are of real and believable people struggling at times with huge pressures and against daunting odds. Like any of us, these anecdotal characters lose faith and lose spirit. They yearn, they regress, they lash out in frustration. And, like the rest of us, they don't always know that these states are normal and recoverable. Karen Bonnell and Patricia Papernow are not only on hand when these crises happen, they help us to see them coming. Most important of all, without talking down or patronizing, they reintroduce us to our children at a critical stage when it might be genuinely hard to know what our children need or how to help them—where kids might be too confused to express themselves clearly, or too frightened that by doing so they will be the cause of more disruption or unhappiness.

For many families facing the trauma of divorce, the notion of a happily "blended family" may be beyond imagining. Yet as a stepparent myself, for whom stepparenting has been life's greatest joy, I warmly applaud the sleeves-up, practical, compassionate approach of this book, not to mention its huge span of wisdom and insight. I have no doubt that *The Stepfamily Handbook* will add greatly to both the thinking about and practice of building successful and healthy stepfamilies so that they become seen not as something second-best, but as the creative and life-enhancing units they can genuinely be if given the right kind of support. Karen Bonnell and Patricia Papernow are that support—the two indispensable stepparent "parents" that the rest of us weren't lucky enough to have!

Christopher Mills
Psychotherapist, Family Consultant, Supervisor, Author
Bath, England
August 2018

INTRODUCTION

THE JOURNEY TO STEPFAMILY

Falling in love can be magical. You feel unbelievably lucky to have found this other person—*your* person.

Falling in love *as* a parent or *with* a parent is amazing, too, but it *isn't* simple. In fact, your life gets complicated pretty fast when you create a family with kids on board. We're here to help.

Whether you're just starting to date, or you've already gotten serious, or you're in the throes of creating a family with kids as part of the picture, here are some things we'd like you to consider.

PACK RIGHT FOR YOUR JOURNEY

You'll definitely need more than a water bottle, protein bars and sunscreen for the trek from getting to know one another, to the adventures of bringing the kids into your relationship, to that hoped-for step of becoming a family, a *"blended family."*

What you really need is a map…but not just *any* map. You need an accurate, detailed, reliable picture of the terrain. You need a map with clearly marked paths and warning signs to help you detour around potential hazards. You need a map that makes clear what's a normal bump in the road and what's a serious pothole that could strand you in a bad place.

The good news is that you're holding that map in your hands right now! *The Stepfamily Handbook* is the culmination of decades of our work guiding people on their journeys from dating, to getting serious, to creating a "blended family," a *stepfamily.*

WE'VE GOT YOU COVERED

No matter how you have come to this point, this book's for you. We wrote this book for long-term singles, for those who were married and now are divorced and for those who have ended a long-term or a short-term relationship. We wrote it for people who chose to be solo parents, for people who always wanted kids, and for people who never wanted to be parents and now find themselves in relationship with a parent—and for people who *still aren't sure* about parenting! We wrote this book for everyone who has kids in the foreground or the background of their dating life.

MEET YOUR GUIDES

In these pages you'll find solid advice, tips that may surprise you and you'll find interesting stories drawn from Karen's many years as a divorce and co-parenting coach, helping parents navigate the tough terrain through separation, divorce and on into stepfamily; and from Patricia's four decades as a therapist working with stepfamilies and her years reading the considerable research we now have about stepfamily dynamics.

We made you this map using evidence-based information, which you can think of as the most up-to-date GPS possible. You'll benefit from our hands-on experience with thousands of people, combined with our knowledge of the most relevant research. We'll serve it up through stories of families who have walked this path before you, with compassion for your particular journey and tools for your immediate use!

Introduction

All the Essentials You Need in One Book

In the following chapters, you'll learn how to manage the unpredictability, stresses and strains of dating a parent and dating while parenting. You'll get tips on how and when to involve children in your relationship. You'll learn how to lay a strong foundation to support a thriving stepfamily.

The Stepfamily Handbook equips you with these essentials:

- Step-by-step guidance on how and when to introduce children into your adult relationship and how to pace the steps to forge positive bonds among everyone.

- A backpack full of solid communication tools for building strong relationships—the foundation of a successful stepfamily.

- Signposts for *five stepfamily challenges*—challenges that will likely grow more intense as your relationship develops—with practical tips for managing each.

- Guidance on how to support children of different ages, with skillful ways to reassure and help them from infancy through adulthood.

- Ideas for how to create and maintain a positive, constructive relationship with a parent's co-parent (the children's other parent).

- Vital information on how to balance hopeful expectations with the reality of building a *next-time* family with kids on board.

DON'T MISS OUT ON THE BIG PICTURE!

Part I of this book focuses on issues around dating. Part II delves into how to include children when the relationship gets more serious. Part III explores the complexities of creating a new family with children in the picture. The end will give you a panoramic view of the journey to create a thriving, long-term stepfamily.

We believe in a one-step-at-a-time approach to building your stepfamily, but this book is for you no matter where you are on the path. If you're well past the dating or getting-serious stages, you might think to skip ahead to part III. Please don't! No matter where you are on the trail, we strongly recommend that you read all three parts of this book so you can look back and see just how far you've come and anywhere you might have lost the path. (And be sure to grab your communication tool kit in Chapter 4—and *refresh* regularly!)

DECIPHERING THE TRAIL MARKERS

Members of a stepfamily often have multiple important relationships that don't fit our conventional labels. It's tricky to figure out what to call everyone.

To make it easier for you, we'll simply use *parent* when we're describing the adult who brings children into the couple relationship and who is also an intimate *partner* in the couple. If you are a child-free partner, then your role is always *partner* (not parent). If you both have kids, when your kids are part of the scene, you're both wearing the parent hat. When children come and go on different schedules, the roles can switch for either of you frequently. Get it?

We will use the term *co-parent* to refer *only* to the children's other parent. (Some people might refer to the co-parent as the parent's "ex.") The child's parents form *the co-parenting team*. Ultimately, over time, in the best of worlds, stepparents may become part of a cooperative parenting coalition along with both co-parents. However, this is a role that must evolve, based on building trust with the child's other parent and with the child.

THE ROAD NOT TAKEN

Throughout this book, we sometimes address partners, and at other times we're talking to parents. That's because the roles are really different. No matter which roles fit you, we suggest you read about them all! To be a good partner in a stepfamily, it helps to learn as much as you can about the road your beloved is traveling. Their journey will often be quite different from yours, with different points of origin and landmarks along the way. The more you understand each other's journey, the more patient, kind and in-step you'll be. The beautiful and challenging thing about this trip you're on is finding a way to be on it together, even when your viewpoints are markedly different. In the end, the best way to walk this path is as allies.

STEPFAMILIES ARE NOTHING LIKE A BANANA-MANGO SMOOTHIE!

You might be wondering about the term "blended family." Is a "blended family" a stepfamily? Yep! Those terms are often used interchangeably. The word "stepfamily" got a bad rap a long time ago. Originally, *steop* was an Old English prefix that referred to an orphaned or ill-favored child. Fairy tales abound with wicked stepmothers and abused and neglected stepchildren—think *Hansel and Gretel, Cinderella, Snow White*. No wonder some people decided to start using a new term!

"Blended family" is a more user-friendly term that bypasses those horrid fairy-tale myths. It certainly captures the longing we all have for closeness and intimacy, especially in a newly formed family.

The problem is that "blended family" suggests we can just blend yours and mine into ours, and, like a dream come true, everyone will feel close and connected. It's a wonderful fantasy. But stepfamilies are nothing like a banana-mango smoothie! Individuals don't just come together and effortlessly swirl into a new flavor of family. Remember *Eight Is Enough*, the late '70s TV drama where two parent-partners came together with a total of eight kids between them—parents wondrously in love and rarely harried? Eight kids were just thrilled to have one another as stepsiblings and all the family dramas neatly resolved in thirty-minute episodes.

Hah! Don't we wish!

You'll notice that we have put "blended family" in quotes throughout the book. That's because *"blended family"* can so easily pull you into the trap of straining to be that banana-mango smoothie when in fact your new family is going to look far more like a salad with lots of different distinct ingredients.

The image we created for the cover of this book is a metaphor for stepfamily. You maintain the individual beauty of bold and unique colors while bringing them together to create a home. Your gaggle of adults and kids don't have to blend to create beauty and harmony together as a family. Honoring your true colors and working to complement each other is key.

TAKE IT STEP BY STEP

If you're the kind of person who flips to the last page of a novel to see how the story ends, then let us help you out here. The main takeaway in *The Stepfamily Handbook* is that the best way to create a thriving, successful stepfamily is to take it *one step at a time*—from dating, to slowly involving kids, to building a life together as a family.

A second-time (or next-time) family is going to need *time* to find its feet. A lot of time. It builds a little at a time toward trust and connection and a sense of "we-ness." This won't happen in the same way a first-time family comes together. We're here to tell you that holding on tightly to those expectations of "blending" is likely to leave you feeling disappointed and worried that you're doing something wrong. We hope that this book replaces those expectations with realistic ideas about the steps it takes to build a thriving stepfamily—a family where differences don't disappear *and* where caring and connection grow and deepen.

KEEPING IT REAL

When kids are part of the picture, a new relationship is likely to be a bit unpredictable for everyone involved. A parent starting to date discovers that when the new romance is heating up, it's much harder than expected to focus on kids, negotiate with the co-parent about carpools and summer camps and also balance work, friendships, health and more. A partner finds it harder than expected sharing a new love with his or her kids (and with the kids' other parent!) and accommodating sudden cancellations and managing the disappointments and frustration of being sidelined.

You both may need to step away periodically to take a breath so you can step back in with a clearer head. *The Stepfamily Handbook* shows you how to move toward each other in the face of these challenges and become tender allies. We will help you learn when to step lightly and when to step deliberately—and when to put your foot down with care and compassion and perhaps, sometimes when to walk away.

You can take a deep breath right now if you want to! Repeat to yourself: *"It's going to be okay. I have the map. I can do this!"*

THE DESTINATION IS WORTH THE TRIP

Don't be surprised if, in the beginning, you step forward only to step back again. Don't worry—that's perfectly normal. Over time, as you get the hang of it, you'll slowly take significant steps forward as you build a family life together that meets the needs of both adults and kids.

That's why we prefer to call your new family a "*step*family." Stepping together, stepping back, stepping away (briefly) only to step back in . . . ultimately, when you learn the right steps, you will move together in a dance that includes and supports all the dancers.

When undertaken deliberately, with knowledge, awareness and some solid communication skills, the one-step-at-a-time approach will help you realize the promise of family expanded and love multiplied. That's the treasure at the end of the journey.

It's time to take the first step!

PART I

Parenting While Dating/ Dating a Parent

*"**News flash:** I have a kid! I can't run off for a long weekend at the drop of a hat."*

—A single parent.

"Fall in love with someone who doesn't make you think love is hard," says blogger Chelsea Walker.

Good luck with that! Love isn't simple or easy. It's marvelous and it's messy as hell!

Before bringing kids into your dating life, you'll want to figure out if there's enough potential with this new person to include kids. Part I will help you sort this out. Are you having a magnetic connection and hot sex? *And*, do you think this is someone you'll want to be with a year, or five years or ten years, down the road? You can save kids a boatload of pain and sorrow if you figure this out *before* involving them in the relationship.

Chapter 1 will take you through the most important questions to ask yourself during the dating stage. You'll discover *five pointers for dating readiness* and *five signs that will help you choose your partner wisely*. Use this information to confirm that you're on the right track.

Chapter 2 introduces you to what's happening in your brain when you fall in love. (Did you know the ancient Greeks saw love as a form of insanity? Seriously!) You'll also learn about the impact of *love hormones* on parenting. You'll explore how the presence of kids in the background of a new relationship affects dating for both people in a couple. The big question to begin asking yourself in Chapter 2: Am I cut out to be in a stepfamily? Just how far do you want to go on this journey?

In Chapter 3, we'll help you figure out whether the new relationship is "kid-worthy." For partners, are you ready, willing and able to go to the next level, which could mean potentially becoming a stepparent? For parents, is this relationship unfolding in a way that makes you feel it's worth involving your kids—worth the risk of their excitement and apprehension about another big set of changes in their lives? How will this new person potentially affect your children's hearts and their day-to-day lives?

Before you leave Part I base camp for the ascent into Part II, you'll need some good tools to help you along the way. Chapter 4 offers you a tool kit of indispensable interpersonal skills that will make this undertaking much easier and more successful.

Chapter 1

Dating (Again)?

"I wish falling in love had traffic lights so I would know if I should go for it, slow down, or just stop."

—Unknown

So you're considering jumping in with both feet, or maybe you're inching in the direction of dating. Perhaps you're the one with kids or you're considering dating someone with children, or you both have kids. Set yourself up for success later by thinking ahead now.

FIVE POINTERS BEFORE DATING AGAIN AFTER A BREAKUP

You may be returning to dating after years of being alone or after a recent breakup. Perhaps you've been looking for a while but haven't met that "someone special." Whatever your specific situation, here are five pointers to consider before moving forward:

1. Finish One Relationship Before You Start Another

No matter how things ended, pausing between significant relationships gives you a chance to center yourself. You and your new potential partner both need to know that you're acting from a place of choice and readiness, not from a place of anxiety and desperation.

2. Figure Out What You've Learned from the Past

People who lurch from one relationship to another without hitting the Pause button tend to repeat their unhelpful patterns over and over again. Reflect on your last relationship. Notice the areas where you felt good about yourself, and the areas where you didn't feel so good. Think about how you want to grow as a person, and as a partner, in your next relationship. For example, "*I don't want to neglect my other interests for the relationship*, as I've done in the past." Or, "*I need to learn to be more vulnerable. I want to be able to share my thoughts and feelings more fully in my next relationships.*" The more you can take responsibility for your part of what went wrong, and right, in past relationships, the more likely you'll succeed next time.

3. Forgive and Let Go to Move Forward

Relationships end for a variety of reasons. In the end, you and your former partners were unable to love each other in the way that you each needed. If you find yourself talking a lot about your ex, or still regretting the end of that relationship, or feeling angry and bitter, then you have some more work to do before you move forward with a new relationship. Remember: The opposite of love is *not* hatred. Hate is just the *other side* of the love coin. You will know you are ready when you stop needing the past to be different from what it was.

4. Check Your Relationship Baggage: Carry-on or Steamer Size?

Humans are messy. We all have histories and places where we feel broken. The goal is getting your relationship baggage down to comfortable carry-on size. Work toward healing old hurts that pop up when you get close to another person. If necessary, get some expert help!

5. Build Your Safe Harbor for Inevitable Dating Storms

A strong network of nurturing friendships and satisfying activities will sustain you through the emotional ups and downs of forming a new relationship, especially as children enter the picture. Maintaining close friendships is not easy in adulthood, especially for busy solo parents, so you may need to get creative. Join a team or find a group that shares your interests or a faith community that fits. These support systems will be especially important if you don't have kids and you're dating someone who does, because there will be times when your new love needs to care for kiddos and won't be available to you.

> ### Are You Ready to Date?
>
> Ask yourself the following questions. If you can answer mostly "yes," then you're ready enough!
>
> - Have I stopped agonizing over my last relationship?
> - Have I let myself grieve the loss?
> - Have I realistically examined my own contributions to the successes and failures of that relationship?
> - Have I separated enough so that my heart is actually free and open to love another?
> - Have I built enough of a supportive network to hold me through the inevitable ups and downs of partnering with—or as—a parent?
> - For parents: Have I built a secure and loving home environment for my children during their residential time with me?
> - Am I developing the healthiest co-parenting relationship with my kiddos' other parent that I can?

COPING WITH LOVE AND LOSS IS HARD

When you find yourself single again, feelings of loneliness can be devastating. You may feel ashamed that you're alone once more, imagining that others judge you for being a failure or a loser. If you're a parent and you're solo now, you may feel overwhelmed at times. No one would blame you for fantasizing about how much easier your life would be if you had another adult to help—a partner who could step in as a supportive, loving companion. These feelings and thoughts could make you desperate to reconnect, resettle and resume the life you once had—or finally create the life you've always wanted.

We all need to be held and loved. Some of us pursue that healthy intimacy with an unhealthy urgency. Desperation *shuts off the critical thinking* you need to make wise decisions. Don't move too fast and settle for a relationship that will not be good for you (or for the kids).

Dating and intimacy bring up a lot of emotions: **anxiety, fear, excitement**, longing, uncertainty and desire. It may take a wellspring of emotional energy to put yourself out there and keep your head about you. Here are some guardrails to help you notice the warning signs, listen to your gut and assess how to pace yourself—slow down or perhaps even pull over and stop for a while.

Look Before You Leap: Five Signs that This Relationship May Not Be "the One"

In the excitement of falling in love, you might ignore or just not see what's really going on. Here are five signs to help you figure out whether it's love, whether it's need, or whether you're being used.

1. **Too much, too fast?** Are either of you falling in love with the *idea* of a perfect partner before you really know each other? Being idealized can be seductive! But did you know that the word "seductive" comes from Greek and means "to lead astray"? Don't be led astray! Pay attention if you have a niggling doubt that either or both of you are *too* certain "you're the one." Understand that it takes time to discover who you both really are behind the rose-colored, lust-tinted glasses.

2. **Codependent no more?** Does this relationship have a subtle, uncomfortable quality of somehow never seeming to be about *you*? Are you listening much more than being listened to? Are you caretaking much more than being taken care of? Caring for another's hurts may make you feel important and even indispensable. But it won't wear well long-term.

3. **Eye candy?** It's one thing to share the excitement of a new love with friends. It's another to feel that your new partner is showing you off as if you're a trophy. Pay attention if the other person is parading your pictures around on social media. Does it feel like too much, or

too fast, or too...*something*? Do you suspect they're trying to get back at an ex or make someone jealous? Red flag!

4. **Too much sex and not enough intimacy?** Sex in the early stages of a relationship is often amazing. It's a chemical thing, like a drug. So ask yourself this: Do most of our dates involve sex and alcohol or drugs? If so, this might be a fun fling, but it may not have the ingredients for a deep and meaningful relationship based on intimacy, mutual trust and respect. If you are a parent, enjoy the fling, but hold off on bringing this person into your children's lives.

5. **Anger, blame and comparisons with former relationships?** It's natural to share your stories while you're getting to know each other. But if someone's stories dominate every conversation, or the stories feel laced with unresolved anger, bitterness or blame, or you find yourself being compared frequently to an ex, consider walking away. This person has their own work to do before they move on. They aren't emotionally ready for a new relationship.

BOTTOM LINE

Listen to all your instincts and keep your eyes wide open.

- - - - - - - - - - -

Nothing works better to reinvigorate all the wonderful aspects of being a teenager than falling in love! Sparked by a new romance, your heart and your body wake up to all things luscious. Enjoy!

Meanwhile, the adult part of you looks ahead to the next turn in the road. You'll now need to ask yourself some key questions: Are you cut out for a stepfamily? Does this new love have the potential to become mature love? Is this new person the one to walk this path with you—*and the kids*?

Chapter 2

Are You Cut Out for a Stepfamily?

"Follow your heart but take your brain with you."
—Alfred Adler, psychotherapist and physician

The early weeks and months of relationships foreshadow what it means when one of you says, *"By the way, I have kids."*

Wait. What exactly *does that mean?* Lots!

If you don't have kids, this chapter will help you understand how much your partner's parenting will regularly impact your new relationship. If you're the parent, you may be surprised just how much being a parent impacts your dating relationship!

FALLING IN LOVE WITH A PARENT / PARENTING WHILE FALLING IN LOVE

You're dating someone and you start to develop those delicious feelings. Your heart quickens when you think about them; you're distracted by thoughts of them. Feeling weak in the knees just thinking about them? Yep—you're falling in love.

Oh, one more thing—your new love happens to be a parent, but you're not. Big deal? Maybe . . . maybe not. Maybe you're thrilled—you've always liked kids and wanted some of your own! Maybe another little voice argues,

"Wait a minute, I still want to travel, stay out dancing when we can; I'm not sure how kids fit into this picture!" For certain, because you've been around the block enough to know, this is more than the average dating situation.

Then you start to witness your new love's wired-in responsiveness to his or her kids, which can be surprising, and it dawns on you: A big difference between dating someone with and without kids starts right here!

For parents, falling in love is complicated right from the start. You have more people's feelings to consider than just yours and your new lover's. A host of brand-new challenges crops up for you at home that signal, *"This is going to be hard!"* You are absolutely correct.

There are at least two hearts of the matter unfolding here: The parent's need to respond to a child's call for attention or parenting. And the newly-in-love couple's intense desire to be together.

THE "CLICK" AND NEUROBIOLOGY OF LOVE

The click: That unmistakable feeling of being drawn to someone, that sense of being seen and reflected back and that sinking into the luscious pleasure of connection. *"I've met someone . . ."* tumbles out as soon as you get on the phone with your best friend. You wonder how you could be so lucky, and you begin to imagine how your life is about to change.

Falling in love changes our brains. With the help of brain scans, scientists have mapped the pathways in the brain as we move from falling in love to deepening, committed loving. By understanding how love starts and progresses on a physiological level, you'll be better able to manage the precariousness of falling "head over heels" while children still need their parents to keep both feet solidly on the ground. We hope that understanding the impact on children when a parent falls in love will make it easier for you to recognize that prudent pacing is a sign of good parenting—something to tell yourselves to help you both to stay on course if you start to feel torn (parents) or sidelined (partners) in the relationship.

In the beginning, there is desire—*and* powerful motivation to satisfy that desire! You don't need brain scientists to explain how amazing this compelling stage of human connection feels. For parents, you need to stay aware of your behavior during this potent time so you don't inadvertently scare your kids.

Love happens in your brain, travels down to your heart, impacts your digestion, disrupts your sleep and creates craving. Can you hear Tina Turner singing to you, "You might as well face it, you're addicted to love"? That's because the initial stage of falling in love affects the part of the brain that's also affected by addictions, the *pleasure center*. They share very similar hormonal pathways. Your normal neurobiology is temporarily hijacked by this rapid-fire, desire-filled process.

You stop thinking clearly. That's why we often say, "Love is blind." The neurochemicals directly impact the functioning of your prefrontal cortex where accurate assessments take place, critical judgments normally occur and good decision-making unfolds. When you're swept off your feet by someone, your assessment and critical-judgment skills go offline. Uh oh!

This could be a recipe for disaster if, as time goes on, your neurobiology didn't return to normal. But it does, and, if things move forward, love calms and deepens; clarity and thoughtful consideration come back online. Phew!

But right now, you want to feed the excitement. You communicate with your love every chance you get—online, on the phone, texting, and of course in person. And, let's be honest, this continual contact alleviates your anxiety. Your head is full of all sorts of clever ways to let your love interest know that they're on your mind and in your heart, and to find out where (or whether) you are in theirs. Nothing much else in your life matters—*not right now*.

Except, *the kids*.

HAZARD ⊘ A parent starting a new relationship is a big change for kids, no matter what their ages. Kids *will likely need their parent even more* when a parent is falling in love. They sense that they don't have their parent's attention and they don't understand why. Kids don't recognize parents in this new state of being in love. It's scary and lonely for kids, which may come out in attention-seeking seemingly "bad" behavior. At the same time, parents (and new partners watching and listening right now from the outside) may feel especially irritated by normal kid antics and typical kid needs.

> ### Helpful Tips to Stay Child-Centered
> ### While You're Falling in Love
>
> The key for both parents and partners is to balance the intense feelings of *falling in love* with the ongoing, day-to-day needs of children. Here's a short list of reminders:
>
> - Enjoy each other fully *during the parent's child-free time* and the partner's free time.
>
> - Parents, when it's parenting time, parent first and be in love second.
>
> - Remember that the chemistry of falling in love makes switching gears to care for children challenging for *both* parents *and* non-parent partners.
>
> - Keep in mind that you're "under the influence" of love hormones, so enjoy yourself but be cautious! No rushing blindly down the path.
>
> - Take your time—*a lot of time*—to assess whether you have a solid, healthy adult partnership before involving kids. To travel the often-bumpy road of coupling when kids are in the picture, your relationship will need considerable bandwidth.

PARENTING THROUGH THE PUSH AND PULL OF DATING / DATING THROUGH THE PUSH AND PULL OF SOMEONE'S PARENTING

Partners, welcome to the world of dating a parent! If you've never been a parent, you may not have much idea of what goes into the day-in, day-out effort of parenting, much less the challenges of helping kids adjust after separation and divorce or loss or trauma. It's no picnic. So, this is another aspect of what it means when one of you says, "Oh, by the way, I have kids."

Managing this push-and-pull can be especially tough on parents, who can start to feel like there's not enough time in a day to respond to everyone's need, never mind their own. Parents, you can easily feel like you're dropping the ball with your new love interest and you might worry about whether they know you're still *there* for them while you're offline parenting kids. For parents struggling to find a way to juggle it all, it is too easy to slip into stealing time and attention from children to feel connected to your sweetie or to soothe and reassure an anxious new romantic partner. It is equally easy to view your partner's loneliness and desire for more of you as yet one more burden. Working through this tension with understanding for yourselves and for each other will help reassure and calm you both.

Parents may have to *force* themselves to focus on their kids. How will you resist the in-love brain's pull? How in the world will you focus on your kids when your smitten cerebral cortex is so offline that you want to grab the phone and send a flirty text instead? Try this: *Put the screens down and give children the attention they need.*

BOTTOM LINE

Start off on the right foot. *The more parents can help their children feel secure and central during this phase, the easier it will be to introduce a new person into the family without children feeling unsettled and lost.*

THE TIME CRUNCH FOR PARENTS

For most parents, especially solo parents, days with kids are filled to the gills. Children want and need their parent's undivided attention, and parenting takes a lot of work: Mealtimes, homework, chauffeuring, shopping, doctor's appointments—the list goes on! For parents, adding a new romantic interest definitely stretches emotional and time resources during their parenting time.

There may not be much time for alone time—for now. If you're a parent, you might have noticed there are only so many hours in the day. Work, children, *plus* relationship will fill them all. Maybe you can squeeze in a yoga class or a beer with a buddy once in a while but be patient with this phase of life.

If both of you are parents, one of you may make a heroic effort to carve out time for the new relationship . . . only to find that your partner is needed by their children. Or, one of you may have ample child-free time while the other doesn't. You may both feel like star-crossed lovers who will never have the time to be together.

HAZARD ⊘ When *both* partners are busy parents and you're both juggling a dozen balls in the air, it's a challenge to find time for everything! One attractive-looking solution may be to bring your children together sooner rather than later so you can be parents and partners at the same time. That might sound logical, but... Caution!! Resist this urge! Keep reading to learn why.

For Nonparent Partners: Coping with Absences While Your New Love Parents

First, know that dating and parenting aren't inherently compatible. If your partner is a parent whose kids share residential time with a co-parent, there will be periods of child-free time to make up for the periods of absence before they go back on parenting duty again. This switching on and off can feel like the relationship is running hot and cold. If your partner has full-time or close to full-time residential time with kids, your time together will be short indeed. It is easy to feel ignored and rejected when your sweetie is less responsive during kid-care time.

Here's where having your own support network to turn to is absolutely critical to making this relationship workable.

Get used to sharing. You may often feel like you're sharing your lover with unseen humans. You are! Especially when your needs and interests are bounced to the back of the line, and your plans play second fiddle to a seven-year-old whose soccer team suddenly made it into the state tournament. Let's be frank: This can be frustrating and lonely. Making space for just the two of you, where you can be fully focused on each other, will always be important. And there are ways in which it may always be harder, because there are kids to consider. *This is not going to change!*

Notice your expectations. Try not to make things a test. Most likely, if your partner has to cancel, it probably doesn't mean lack of interest in you. Sometimes a kiddo just has a stomach virus and a parent is needed. In dating a parent *and* dating as a parent, you'll need to stay flexible because things with kiddos come up unexpectedly and plans have to change.

See your friends and participate in your favorite activities when your partner isn't available. It will be absolutely crucial for you going forward.

Keep your eyes open! This situation is not temporary. The person you love has kids, and will *always* have kids, and those kids will always be important in their life, even if your partner is a part-time parent or a far-away parent.

Learn to state, gently and clearly, what you need. Remember that your desires for more connection, time and attention in the relationship don't make you "needy." Establishing some easy and regular points of connection will help you build trust and ease the reality of sharing your beloved's attention.

HAZARD ⊘ Partners, you are out on thin ice if you find yourself pushing your sweetie to *apologize* for needing to parent. Likewise, if you find yourself calling and texting them during clearly established parent-kid times, you're treading on shaky ground. It's a problem if you're competing with children for their parent's attention. Trust us—this will not work out well for any of you. Better to reconsider: Am I cut out for this?

THE DATING STAGE IS TRAINING WHEELS FOR POTENTIAL STEPFAMILIES

Building a family requires considerably more than the "click" of falling in love. If you're lucky, those intense feelings of desire will transform into the deep thrum of loving, emotional connection and creative compromise.

Compromise Can Be Fun (and Sexy!)

A relationship with kids, even when kids are still in the background, is going to throw you curve balls. Lots of them. Let's look at how James, a dad, and his new partner, Stephanie, were able to shift an unexpected disappointment into an opportunity to get closer.

"Daddy, I Made It!! Can You Come Watch?"

James worked a nine-to-five job, while Stephanie's job required travel that didn't always synch up with James's parenting time. At first, coordinating their schedules was an exciting challenge for them both, with the unpredictability adding intrigue to when and how they'd see each other next. Nights when they were both free and in town were "gold."

After two and a half weeks of waiting and anticipating a romantic dinner and overnight date, James received a call from his daughter, Josie, just as he was leaving work.

"Daddy!!! I made it... I'm on the list for the next round of cheer tryouts *tonight*. Will you please, please, please come watch me?" James froze. This was Josie's time with her mom and James and Stephanie's "gold" time. But as a dad, he needed to be there for his daughter.

A less-grounded couple could have made a mess of it. Very easily. Stephanie might have said, *"How COULD you!"* James might have retorted, *"What's your problem. She's my kid!"* They would have been off and running, and not to a good place.

James Takes a Breath... and Finds a Fun Way Through

James took a breath and called Stephanie. She was clearly disappointed, and she said so. Instead of getting defensive, James responded, "So am I. I definitely owe you one."

He heard her sigh. "You owe me double!" she said, half-serious.

"You've got it!" he said. Then, "I have an idea. How about if I meet you at that fabulous dessert place after the tryouts. If we can't have dinner, at least we can have a romantic dessert together. Then we'll go to your place."

Stephanie thought a moment. "But since you owe me double, how about you come to my office on the way to Josie's tryouts? My office is very private..."

"Yes!" said James. "You've got it!"

Are You Cut Out for the Pushes and Pulls of Stepfamily?

Ask yourself this soul-searching question before you race ahead. Love does *not* conquer all. Successful stepfamilies take grit, commitment, skill and willingness. Your new family will include not only children, but also co-parents (ex-spouses), extended family and more. You are likely noticing the ripples and undercurrents from these relationships. Now is the time to pay attention to how these complexities feel and how they affect your sense of "togetherness." Whether in the parent role or the partner role, ask yourself:

- **Parents: Are you willing and able to hold the intense needs** of (at least) two very important relationships: The one with your kiddos and the other with your beloved? Can you tolerate the competing needs for your love and attention with an open heart? Do you find yourself trying to solve the problem by minimizing the needs of one or the other?

- **Parents: Are you up to the task of coordinating the relationship with your co-parent when you introduce your new partner into the mix?** Will you able to reassure your child's other parent that they will not be replaced as either co-parent with you or parent to their children?

- **Partners: When the children need their parent, can you step back and be supportive?** Can you take care of yourself and not collapse into feeling rejected, angry, unlovable and unimportant? Can you lean into your individual activities and friendships during those times? Can you stop yourself from texting and distracting your sweetie's attention from kids? Can you gently reach for connection when you come back together, and not withhold, withdraw or attack?

- **As a couple: Can you be patient and allow the journey to unfold at a slow, thoughtful pace?** Can you resist the urge to take risky shortcuts?

You may be nursing the hope that things will get easier. *How* you communicate with each other can definitely get easier! But the fact that children and co-parents are part of your relationship *is what it is.*

Here's the beautiful thing to keep in mind: You can get better and better at holding complexity, and you can come to appreciate the ways this helps you grow as a person. A stepfamily has the potential to grow the richest and most rewarding relationships of your lifetime. But, you have to decide if it's the right path for you.

Chapter 3

When Is a Relationship "Kid-Worthy"?

> *"The most difficult part of dating as a parent is deciding how much risk your own child's heart is worth."*
>
> —Dan Pearce, author, blogger and artist

If you've decided you are up for the stepfamily journey, then the next important consideration is determining if your relationship is "kid-worthy."

There is no need to rush to an answer. It's one step at a time to know if you've found the special someone worth introducing to your kids, or if you've found someone whose kids you'd like to get to know.

If your answer is, *"No, this isn't the one,"* you'll have the clarity that it's not right to introduce kids into your relationship. If so, go ahead and have a fun fling and keep it at that!

If your answer is, *"Yes, I think this relationship has potential for something deeper,"* then get ready for an adventure! More choices, opportunities and learning curves ahead for all of you.

> **Special Note for Partners:** *Some of this chapter is addressed more to parents, but it's great information for partners, too. Having a firm grasp of your sweetie's concerns as a parent will be invaluable in forming a solid team.*

PROTECT KIDS FROM THE ADULTS' EMOTIONAL ROLLER COASTER

When you're putting yourself out there in the dating world, it's natural to get your hopes up that this is *the one*, and then, if things don't work out, your hopes get dashed. Euphoria, discouragement, excitement, insecurity, hope, disappointment—the ups and downs of dating can be quite the emotional roller coaster ride. If you're the parent in this relationship, you're feeling so many things, and it's hard to keep what you're going through separate from your home life. You might inadvertently involve the kids in your emotional ups and downs. *Uh-oh. Not good for kids.*

Staying Emotionally Available for Kids

Children need to be able to trust their parent's ability to hold *their* emotional needs, not the other way around. When you involve kids in the dramas of your love life, you can easily lose sight of their vulnerabilities. End result: Kids will struggle when they feel that their parent's emotional requests too often come before their own. Depression, anxiety and somatic complaints (stomachaches, headaches and so forth) are typical responses kids have to an emotionally unavailable parent. Or their distress might come out as sullen behavior, slipping school performance, or angry outbursts. Some seek refuge in their other parent. Others try to fix the problem themselves. These are the children who think it's their job to take care of the parent emotionally, hoping that if they're good enough, things will settle down and the parent will be able to parent again—and then they'll be okay, too.

BOTTOM LINE

Children at all ages may feel heartbroken when they fear they're losing a parent to a new romantic partner.

When You Lose It Emotionally with the Kids

Dating stirs up all kinds of strong emotions. Maybe you snap at a child because you're anxious about being separated from your new love. Perhaps you've been teary because a relationship isn't going well, or you've been feeling rejected because that special somebody isn't returning your text messages. Maybe you lost your temper with your kids because you're mad at your lover.

If you've blown it, *repair* it:

- *"I'm sorry. I was sharp. That must have felt bad. Right?"*

- *"Mommy was in tears. I'll bet that's a bit scary, but I'll be okay. Sometimes moms cry. I have lots of friends to help me when I feel sad. You don't need to worry. Let's go do something fun together."*

- *"Oh, Sweetie, I just lost it. I'm sorry. No excuse. I'll do better."*

Repairing means speaking on kid-level about kid-experience. Explaining what's going on for you in your dating life is *not* on the kid-level (in other words, *it's too much information*). Share the details of your dating life with a grown-up. Meanwhile, return to nurturing and caring for your children.

PROTECT KIDS FROM PREMATURE "WE-NESS"

We know what it's like when the love chemistry starts. The magnetic pull toward "we-ness" with your new sweetie can be very compelling. You may want to be together all the time, and it would make it so much easier and more convenient not to have a split screen between parenting and partnering. But if you rush the process of introducing kids into the relationship, you'll likely be mopping up reactivity and upset for a very long time.

Take it Slow and Really Get to Know Your New Love

Attraction is a powerful potion—a heady elixir! It's hard not to plunge headlong down the path of an intoxicating new relationship. The problem comes when you bring the kids with you on your ride. To make sure you're not bringing your kids along into a hornet's nest or blithely skipping with them into a patch of poison sumac, slow down.

Research tells us that as the amount of family change goes up, children's well-being goes down. Taking it slowly requires relationship muscle—lots of it! When you throw caution to the wind and take that giant leap before you know each other really (really) well, it may take a long time to recover your balance. This can be very, very hard on you and especially hard on kids.

BOTTOM LINE

Holding back can be much more anxiety-provoking than jumping "all in." *Stop yourself and remember what's at stake: The kids. Then before you leave the harbor to sail into the sunset together, truly assess: Is this relationship "kid-worthy"?*

Reassure Kids When They Pick Up on the Fact that You're Seeing Someone Special

Perceptive kids may notice changes in your behavior. *If* you've been exercising your parenting muscles—restraining yourself from rushing things and staying focused—then kids most likely won't feel overly concerned. But they will eventually wonder what's going on. If they ask, you can acknowledge that you've met someone you like. Then reassure kiddos that you want to take time to make sure that this is a good person. *"When the time is right, I'll introduce you!"*

Remember, this information is likely to be both intriguing and anxiety provoking to them. Let them digest the news at their own pace. They'll ask their kid-level questions, and you'll provide them with kid-level answers. Until it's time for introductions, *the less said the better about the new relationship.*

Sneak Peek!

Sneak peeks give partners a chance to meet kids casually, as if by accident. Even though we caution against short-cutting the patient process of getting to know each other before introducing kids, most couples we've met have a really hard time waiting. Even though you *know* it's too soon but you've decided you're going to arrange a way for the partner to check out the kids, please take some precautions!

Consider making this appear to be a chance meeting. It could be setting up a walk-by at the local coffee shop or while standing in line at a movie theater. The new love interest can lay eyes on the kiddos without involving them in the relationship. This should be a very brief interaction—*a drive-by, not a sit-down.*

Critically important: *The adults need to act as if they are colleagues or friends—nothing more. Keep your cool!* If both adults have similar-aged kids, it might be natural to show up at the playground or basketball court at the same time. These casual-seeming meetings will help you feel like you're moving forward, without rushing the process of introducing children before the time is right.

Co-Parents Can Help Normalize Dating for Kids

Although not always possible, ideally, you and your co-parent have a mechanism in place to alert each other that you're dating (even though you are not introducing kids yet). The fact that a parent is dating will travel quickly across your two-home family as the children *share the news*. Better that the parent inform a co-parent respectfully, adult-to-adult first, than inadvertently put kiddos in the position of the surprise messenger.

"After Divorce, Sometimes Parents Date"

Levon and Zoe had both accepted that, now that their divorce was nearly complete, either one of them might begin dating. Neither of them wanted this to be upsetting for the kids.

A few months later, Zoe heard through the grapevine that Levon was seen having a glass of wine with a gal in a nearby restaurant. She called Levon and suggested it might be time to discuss dating with the kids. Zoe knew how quickly this news could travel in their small community. Levon was certain he had been discreet, but he acknowledged that Zoe was right; it was time. They agreed it would make dating seem more normal and okay if Zoe was the one to talk with them about it.

At breakfast the next morning, Zoe talked over their waffles with the kids. "You know guys, now that we are all settled, Dad and I wanted you to know that there might be a time when he or I would meet another grown-up for coffee or a bite of dinner when we're not taking care of you. Dad and I have discussed that those kinds of meetings are perfectly OK." Her six-year-old son squished strawberries with his fork and piped up, "You mean like *going on a date?*"

"Well, yes, kind of like going on a date," Zoe echoed.

Her nine-year-old remained silent. No questions from her.

And that was that. Zoe had provided enough kid-level information to normalize parents dating and then allowed the children to lead regarding their questions and concerns. That was the end of the conversation. For now. She followed up with Levon by email about the exchange.

Providing information in a matter-of-fact way that is appropriate to their kid-level supports children through this new stage of their family life.

IMPORTANT INFORMATION FOR PARTNERS WHEN IT'S *ALMOST* TIME TO MEET THE KIDS

If you're a partner without children of your own, you may feel confident that you've assessed and vetted your new relationship. You may realize that you'd have no hesitations at all . . . *if* your sweetie didn't have kids. Kids are a big, scary unknown. You may be trying to sort out your feelings about having kids in your life. It's normal to wonder, *"What will it mean to this relationship if the kids don't like me, or if I don't like them?"*

You may be feeling anxious about how you'll fit into your new love's busy parenting life. And you're likely sorting through your feelings about having to share your love's attention with a long list of other priorities: kids, the children's other parent, work, friends, extended family, favorite pastimes.

If you've hit the wall in your dating life and can't move forward until you sort this out a bit more, here are questions to help you make your *best guess* about whether your relationship has what it takes to be kid-worthy. Of course, there's no way to be certain without actually meeting the kids, but these questions will help you determine when and if to move forward. Please consider them carefully, not just for your own sake, but also for the kids' sake.

Is Our Relationship Strong Enough to Handle More Complexity?

These five questions shine a light on relationship skills that help stepfamilies thrive. These questions help you assess your current "relationship-muscle" strength. You may benefit from discussing these with your partner.

- How do we each deal with disappointment? Do we let each other know with kindness and tenderness when we're hurt or disappointed? Or do we lapse into blame and criticism?

- How do we each handle differences between us? Do we stay curious and interested in each other's needs and points of view? Or do we fall into the blame game and argue about who is right and who is wrong?

- How do we want to create separate parenting time and relationship time so we can maintain our connection? However difficult, can we both remain respectful and kind rather than sharp or dismissive?

- Can we tell each other we miss each other without pressuring the one who is the parent to turn away from the kids?

- Can the "partner who feels lonely, needy or "want-y" ask for comfort instead of whining, attacking or withdrawing? Can the other partner provide comfort and reassurance without blaming, shaming, defending or withdrawing?

Chapter 4 will outfit you with really helpful tools to give your relationship the best chance of success. It's the gear you'll be grateful to have as you venture into some potentially challenging territory.

* * * * * * * * * * *

Deciding whether a new relationship is "kid-worthy" takes time. If you're a relationship sprinter, you might want to start training instead for a marathon! A successful stepfamily grows best in the soil of patience, mindfulness and lots of pauses to catch your breath.

Chapter 4

. . . .

Moving Forward?
Strengthen Your Relationship Skills!

> *"If we could look into each other's hearts and understand the unique challenges each of us faces, I think we would treat each other much more gently, with more love, patience, tolerance, and care."*
>
> —Marvin J. Ashton, American author

For lots of reasons, building a good relationship turns out to be challenging. You may have the best intentions in the world, but you may not have the skills. Even if you do have the skills, we have never met a soul who couldn't up their game!

Here's a fact that might surprise you: Research suggests that thriving stepfamilies face *the same challenges* that struggling stepfamilies do. But successful stepcouples have much better interpersonal skills. They have the strength to turn toward each other when they want to turn away; they have the persistence to listen deeply when they want to shut down or fight.

Here you are, contemplating a new, exciting relationship. Practicing these **five skills** can give you the power to land squarely in the success category down the road:

1. Calm yourself in the storm

2. Listen to understand

3. Switch out of defensiveness
4. Balance five positives for one negative
5. Repair the hurts

Before we dig into strengthening your relationship skills, let's look at why intimate partnership gets so tricky. How do our powerful human emotions lead us to love each other so fully, but also hurt each other *big-time?*

WHY LOVING SOMEONE WELL TAKES MUSCLE

The more we love and care about another person, the more vulnerable we become to feeling upset, threatened and misunderstood. That's a normal part of the territory for two people in an intimate relationship. But the tenor changes dramatically when one (or both) of you has children. Now you're looking at emotions and dynamics that include relationships between partner and kids, parent and kids, co-parents with each other, co-parents with partner, and—when both of you are parents—interactions among your kids. The challenges can escalate exponentially even in the dating and getting-serious stages of your couple relationship. Indeed, as you are likely experiencing, even when you're in the dating phase and kids are *in the background,* there can be a fair amount of relationship commotion.

Humans have a built-in emergency response system when faced with the danger of being *left* or hurt or frightened. This internal defense defaults to three typical reactions: fight, flight or freeze. Physiologically, these three options were designed to protect our ancestors when they were confronted by life-threatening situations, like crossing paths with a lion or a bear in the wild. Today, a wild beast is not likely to be a problem, but our defense system still gets triggered by perceived emotional threats. The problem is that fight, flight and freeze, up close in an intimate relationship, can all cause considerable emotional damage when regularly deployed to protect your heart. These responses have an impact on your beloved's heart.

The part of our brain that switches to autopilot when it perceives a life-threatening situation is the amygdala. It was originally designed to kick in before the thinking part of the brain could come online. Cascading neurochemicals hijack the body *and* the brain. In a split second you *react*. Concentration narrows, blood flow shifts, heartbeat races and your most automatic, protective mechanisms take charge. Your thoughtful self goes offline.

"*I was so mad, I could hardly think!*" Yep—that was the amygdala taking over.

"*I just* lost *it with my kid this morning!*" There it was again—the amygdala taking charge.

We all have parts of our personalities that were created a very long time ago, when we were small, vulnerable and scared. The young person you once were came up with strategies to try to keep you safe, keep you loved, and keep you *alive* when the amygdala sounded the alarm. You might have had to learn how to fight, or strike out, or desperately try to control others. Or maybe you learned to withdraw and shut down to take care of yourself.

These protective mechanisms developed when you faced overwhelming experiences as a child without enough adult support. Most of us default to those old, automatic responses when we feel threatened. But, especially as adults, they're rarely, if ever, necessary to ensure our survival. Often, however, they come on so quickly we don't see the destruction coming; they all too often derail problem-solving, prevent closeness and disrupt intimacy. Wait a second . . . that's not what you want!

BOTTOM LINE

When something upsetting happens, it takes mindfulness and skill to override your most tried-and-true coping strategies and replace them with more effective approaches.

The first step is to recognize when the amygdale has taken charge. Take a moment to think about how you respond when you feel disappointed, or when someone does something you don't like, such as cutting you off in traffic, or when you're treated unfairly? Do you:

- Attack, become defensive and fight back?

- Take control or demand resolution?

- Withdraw or shut down?

- Smooth over the edges and maybe pretend nothing happened?

***Or*, do you have ways to calm yourself**? Can you take a breath, listen to yourself, and to those around you, and re-engage with problem-solving in mind? If you do, that's wonderful. Being able to center yourself (calm down) while you're in a heated exchange with your loved one (or children) will make all the difference in your relationships.

For this journey, you're going to need to outfit your backpack with a good survival kit. The more you practice using each of these relationship-saving measures, the more easily you'll be able to scramble over some of the rocky passages in the path ahead. So let's take them out one at a time and learn how they work.

Tool #1: Calm Yourself in the Storm

"You can't calm the storm. … What you can do is calm yourself. The storm will pass."

—Timber Hawkeye, author of *Buddhist Boot Camp*

Why It's Important

Self-regulation—the ability to calm down in the face of anger, threat and unpleasant surprise—is one of the most important skills for a successful relationship. Why? Without the capacity to calm down, those protective childhood responses take charge. When they're in charge, the chances that you will respond constructively go down, down, down.

Conversely, especially with emotionally charged problems, your calmed mind will help you articulate your needs clearly, listen fully, and respond in ways that make resolution possible.

Calming yourself down *before* you try to communicate is crucial to the outcome. When you bring calm to a complex problem, you make it easier for the others involved to do the same. And when the other is your beloved, you *both* generally reap the rewards!

How to Do It

The first step is to notice that you're getting upset, triggered or scared. Most likely, you'll first recognize the onslaught of neurochemicals by the sensations in your body.

Try to notice and remember the physical signs that your nervous system (the amygdala) has stepped in and is ready to fight, flee or freeze. For example, are you tense? Are you clenching your teeth? Is your belly tight? Do you feel like lashing out? Have you stopped breathing? Are you starting to hunch over or shrink away from others? Or maybe you're feeling kind of numb and spacey? These are all signs that your amygdala has stepped in and you're now in "reaction" mode. Time to take a breath, take a break . . . and calm down.

> ### Helpful Tips on How to Take a Breath and Take a Break
>
> Some storms are almost predictable. Tensions been building with a tough work project, you skipped lunch and traffic was particularly heavy on the drive home. Doesn't take much to know you might arrive home with some dark clouds hanging over you, right? Other storms unfold more like a tornado touching down out of nowhere! Are you tuned into your emotional weather report? And how can you shift from dark clouds to gentle winds and mostly clear skies? Well, here are a few ideas:
>
> - **Breath in slow and deep:** As soon as you notice yourself starting to tense, train yourself to take a breath. Pause. Take another slow, deep breath. On the in-breath, say to yourself, "I am breathing in peace." Say, "I am breathing out calm" on the out-breath
>
> - **Take a self-care break:** If breathing deeply doesn't help, take a break. Read something enjoyable for at least twenty minutes. (NOTE: This does *not* mean playing video games, which is not soothing to the brain.) If exercise helps you get centered, go for a walk or a run. If petting the dog chills you out, give Rover a belly rub.
>
> - **Enjoy creature comforts:** Maybe a cup of warm tea calms you down, or *a* relaxing shower, or ten minutes curled up in a favorite chair listening to a favorite song. Find what works to get you back into your body in a calm and centered way.

It helps to keep in mind that we *all* have inside us young parts of ourselves who fear being left or hurt or shamed—*including your partner*. Get to know those young parts of your loved one. When you need to take a break, try to reassure them that you're not rejecting them. *"I'll be back"* sends a clear message that you have no intention of *leaving-leaving*. You are stepping away temporarily, and that is ultimately good for the relationship.

Being able to calm and center yourself is the foundation of every other important relationship skill. It is the first step in protecting your relationship from the harmful effect of repetitive knee-jerk reactivity. It's the first step in breaking down adversarial escalations during conflict. With this skill, you'll be treating each other more often as partners and less often as enemies!

BOTTOM LINE

Take a breath. Take a break. This is your first relationship mantra! Make this your personal self-management strategy. If only for a single moment of pause, you invite the possibility of choosing skillful responses over knee-jerk reactions.

Tool #2: Listen to Understand

"Seek first to understand, and then to be understood."

—Steven Covey, author of *Seven Habits of Highly Effective People*

Why It's Important

The emerging field of neurobiology tells us that feeling heard and "gotten" is a remarkably calming and connecting experience. Your *understanding* is a powerful salve in your relationships with friends, coworkers and even enemies. Understanding is about gaining knowledge about how the other person sees the situation. It's related to empathy, which is connecting with how others feel. Understanding and empathy are the best medicine for upset children and a distressed partner.

How to Do It

Feelings connect us. When you listen deeply, you can understand your partner's feelings about whatever they're struggling with. When we listen with not only our ears but also our hearts, we can do the most good for others. Often, we get into the habit of hearing without really listening. We're busy worrying about how we can fix it or coming up with what we're going to say next, or we're having judgmental or critical thoughts. Empathy and understanding arise when we're fully present, taking in what the other is saying and holding it with full attention and compassion. You'll know you're truly listening when your partner's expression softens and their shoulders drop a bit, and when they say, "I feel like you *understand*."

You may not *agree* with what they're saying. Understanding doesn't need to equal agreement. Understanding is the bridge that helps all of us to calm down, to feel safe enough to connect, to trust enough that we'll find our way through a problem or a situation. Sometimes having a good listener is all we need.

When you offer to listen with empathy to one another, you're often able to solve struggles in surprisingly creative ways. Such a valuable gift in a partnership.

While feelings connect us, facts often divide us. But that doesn't mean facts are irrelevant. Later, if the facts are really that important, you can go back and talk about them. But that comes *second*. The first task is to understand your partner's feelings so they'll be more open to hearing perspectives that might untangle the knots of misunderstanding between you. Besides, until you understand why the other person is upset, they're probably not letting go of their "facts" without a fight!

Listening Can Be Hard!

The ability to listen is key to understanding. We inadvertently create all sorts of barriers to listening without even knowing it. Here are questions to help you identify what might get in your way:

- **Do I allow myself to be distracted?** When your mind wanders, so does your ability to listen. Steam is likely to start coming out of a partner's ears! If you need a moment to focus, say so.

- **Am I stuck on "sticking to the facts"?** When it comes to talking to each other, facts can be highly overrated. In an intimate conversation, everyone's feelings matter *much* more than facts! It turns out that "sticking to the facts" often leads to more frustration and less understanding.

- **Do I find myself holding on to preconceived ideas and thoughts?** When your partner starts sharing, do you think, "*Here we go again!*"? If so, this is likely dumping you right off a communication cliff into disconnection or attack mode (or both).

- **Do I talk too much, too often? Do I interrupt?** Interrupting is often the young self in each of us impatiently wanting to grab the attention or to charge in to correct "wrong" facts. *Hold the phone!* Best to just listen.

- **Do I think of my response or build my defense while the other person is talking?** Concentrating on and planning what you will say next only increases the competition to be heard and understood. Ask that defense attorney in you to please take a seat and chill. That leaves you freer to concentrate on looking for what you DO understand. Starting there will get you *much* further with your sweetie.

- **Am I not ready to listen?** Not every moment is right for you to be a good listener. If you're not able to listen right now, say so and schedule a time when you can be fully present and attentive.

Feelings Matter More Than Facts

Brad and Patty had a misunderstanding about picking up Brad's son, Marcus, from basketball practice. They both were sure they had their facts "right."

"When I agreed to pick up Marcus, you *said* he would be finished with practice by 6:00," Patty fumed. "But he was on the court with the team until 6:30! You *knew* I would have to leave work early to pick him up. Why didn't you give me the right time? I had to sit around for a half an hour waiting in my car."

"Patty, that's not my fault," Brad countered, exasperated. "I told you that the *earliest* he would be done with practice was 6:00 and that you needed to have him text you at work when he was ready to be picked up. What's wrong with you?"

"Nothing is wrong with me!" Patty said angrily. "That was NOT what you said!"

When your facts line up against each other, the argument heats up. Interesting. When we see things so differently, or our intentions are challenged, the amygdala often jumps in with gloves off, ready to fight. No route to connection, problem-solving or resolution here. Patty was ready for a fight. But Brad had been practicing his listening skills. Instead of continuing to escalate the argument, he stopped himself. He took a deep breath and let it out slowly. Then he tried again.

Brad Takes a Breath

"Sweetheart, you are really *mad* at me," he said. "You feel like I gave you bad information and it really impacted the end of your work day."

Patty was still indignant. "You did!"

Brad started to feel defensive, so he took another deep breath. That helped him hang in with his listening. Now he was able to say, "And you feel like I just dropped Marcus on you without thinking it through, and I was inconsiderate about your time and set you up to wait around when you had better things to do."

Hearing her feelings reflected back to her by Brad disarmed Patty. Her anger went down a notch. Now she took a deep breath, too. "Well, ...no," she said. "I know you didn't set me up on purpose. I just thought Marcus would be ready. I rushed to get there on time and when I realized I could have had more time at work I was just so *frustrated*."

Brad nodded thoughtfully. "I hear you. That *is* frustrating, and you've been under so much pressure with that big project." He reached out and took her hand. Patty squeezed his hand back.

Once Brad stopped explaining and instead focused on understanding, he was able to let go of needing to correct Patty—needing to be right. And he was able to start to speak directly to what he understood was upsetting her and hurting her. As Patty felt more understood, she began to soften.

BOTTOM LINE

Seek first to understand. This is your second relationship mantra. Capable listening is a game changer. It is one of the most powerful and effective ways to create the connection you long for with your partner (and with anyone else in your life).

Tool #3: Switch Out of Defensiveness

"*Defensiveness: A war mentality to a non-war issue.*"
—Sharon Ellison, author of *Don't Be So Defensive*

Why It's Important

Defensiveness arises all too easily for many of us—adding mayhem to an already troubled situation. If you had parents who criticized, or blamed and shamed, or who couldn't be present when you emotionally fell apart, it was easy to feel worried down to the core that you were *unlovable;* that you would be *left*. Panic rose up. Sometimes it shut you down. Sometimes became a war cry! These moments were the birthplace of your defensive reactions today—the training ground for your *war mentality*. Happened for all of us.

Think of them as survival strategies. Once programmed, very little upkeep is needed for your war mentality to deploy on the spot. Your most frequently used strategies pop up like *favorites* on your computer screen.

Defensiveness causes us to *act* big, act powerful, act like we don't need anything *except* to be *right*. Or to get small and withdraw to be *safe*. Easy to see how under stress, our most important relationships deserve better. "Make love, not war" can be your new commitment to one another.

How to Do It

To update your personal defensive system, to upgrade your "war mentality" with state-of-the-art diplomacy and peacekeeping skills, you'll have to recognize when your shields have automatically gone up. (Because the bad news is that, in response, your partner's shield will also likely go up!)

When we're defensive, we typically want the *other* person to drop their shields first and be the one who makes things better by giving in, backing down or giving up. All too often this becomes a nasty standoff. If *you* switch out of defensiveness, perhaps your partner will put down their guard, lower their shield and open up to you. (For those with a competitive spirit, see who can switch out of defensiveness first and who can help the other calm down and engage the fastest!) Together, you'll soon be ready to problem solve.

> **Helpful Tips for Switching Out of Defensiveness**
>
> With new insights, you're ready for boot camp where you master the gentle art of self-defense. This means deploying strategies to calm yourself during a fight, calling in backup to be sure you're listening deeply and bringing in interpreters to sharpen understanding. Here are some ideas for how to do it:
>
> - **Bring your best self.** When we're under stress, we often let go of our best self and we let our *not-so-noble* self take over. That leads us to say hurtful things, or do things out of spite, or hold a grudge. That makes a bigger mess. Therefore, consciously decide to bring your best self to your relationship, even (especially!) during stressful times.
>
> - **Identify your own (favorite) defensive reactions.** Ask yourself:
>   - *Is it my adult self or my younger scared self who is protesting, protecting and insisting that it's not my fault, that I'm right and that I'm lovable?*
>   - *Did my young self learn to give up and withdraw? Is this my most solid adult self or my terrified younger me who is so defiantly asserting, 'I'll do it myself!' (and blocking any attempt by my partner to repair or problem solve with me)?*
>   - *Is there a part of me desperately trying to take over the situation and control the people around me? Do I puff up, blow up, drown out or outdebate the other?*

Most of us are very good at identifying another's defensiveness and not so good at seeing our own. Check out the list of common defensive behaviors below. Identify one or two of your preferred reactions. Going forward, try to catch yourself in the act. When you do: Take a breath. Take a break. Calm yourself. Then try it again with more listening and understanding.

Switch Off the Autopilot to Change Your Conversation!

Difficult conversations are considered difficult for a reason. Learning to switch off your own defensive reactions will transform difficult conversations into courageous ones. Below are techniques that will help:

- **Use "I" Statements, Not "You" Statements**

    - *"You never call me . . . you always make plans with your friends . . . you don't care . . ."* Consider these wise words from the website Rise4u: "Any sentence that starts with 'You are' and doesn't end with 'wonderful' will be experienced as name-calling." "You" statements will also be heard as blaming. So they work to put your partner on the defensive, which may seem to let you off the hook. But beware: "You" statements will keep you stuck.

    - **Instead, make it about "I."** *"I'm having a hard time with the long breaks between calls." "I wish we could make some clear plans." "I'd love to find a way to feel more loved by you when I don't see you."* Versus, *"You're not being a responsible partner."* Or *"You clearly don't care about me."* "I" statements open you to being vulnerable. That's why we say that switching off defensiveness transforms *difficult* conversations into *courageous* ones.

- **Tear Up the Scorecard and Take Responsibility**

    - *"You criticize me— I'll criticize you!"* Tit for tat—a very common fighting technique. So is trying to even the score: *"You did X!" "Well, you did it, too!" "Well how about when you..."*

    - **Start with "I hear you."** *"I'm not sure I completely understand but let me think about that."* Or, *"Huh! You're right, I did do that! I apologize."* Or, *"I get it—I was a bit sharp. I'm sorry."*

Versus, "You've got it all wrong." Or, "What about the time when you…"

- **Respond Directly Instead of Deflecting Away**

    o *Stay on topic.* "I see what you're saying. I get that this was important to you." Or, "Yes, I did forget to tell you about that; I apologize." Or, "Honey, I'm feeling attacked so it's hard for me to hear you. Please give me a minute to respond." Versus, "What difference does it make?" Or, "You don't know what you're talking about…"

- **Be Vulnerable; Skip the Contempt**

    o *Find the courage to express vulnerability.* "This is hard for me." Or, "I'm scared you're saying I'm not good enough." Versus, "You disgust me … This whole conversation is ridiculous …" Or, "Why should I listen to someone so stupid?" Contempt is extremely toxic to relationships. If this is your defensive strategy, *pay close attention!* Contempt often masks unbearable feelings of vulnerability. You're so scared that you lash out and try to diminish the other person's value or minimize the importance of the issue.

- **Open Up, Even When the War Room Screams, "Batten Down the Hatches"**

    o *Instead, use your words.* "I need space to think about what you're saying … I'll have to consider all this, but I will get back to you in a few minutes." Use your best calming techniques to get grounded first.

    o If you find yourself repeatedly shutting down when a conversation becomes overwhelming, you're doing something called "stonewalling." Withdrawing verbally, physically or emotionally is extremely disconcerting to people close to you. It leaves the other person feeling terribly stranded. It is so painful that it is often read by the other person as punishment.

- **Step Up Rather Than Collapsing into Helplessness or Despair**

    o *Instead, ask for what you need.* "I just really need you to understand what this was like for me." Or, "I need you to stop

> yelling at me." Or, "I do need us to find some time alone, even if it doesn't work right now because your kids need you." Versus, "I can't believe you did that to me again." Or, "Ohmygod, I'm freaking out! Now I'm getting a migraine!" Collapsing can look like crying hysterically, slumping in the corner or displaying a dramatic physical symptom. These are likely automatic responses that were incubated in early, desperate attempts to reach unavailable, angry or otherwise self-absorbed parents. They can also be your younger self's expression of total helplessness.

This is not an exhaustive list of defensive behaviors. Your hurt young self may have learned lots of other ways to try to get your needs met, or to take care of you when adults didn't or couldn't. Your job is to identify your own preferred strategies so that you can begin to switch out of defensiveness and bring your best self to your relationship.

BOTTOM LINE

Stay on the high road. This is your third relationship mantra. Make this an every-moment-of-your-life choice!

Tool #4: Balance Five Positives for Each Negative

> *"Too often we underestimate the power of a touch, a smile, a kind word, a listening ear, an honest compliment, or the smallest act of caring, all of which have the potential to turn a life around."*
>
> —Leo Buscaglia, author of *Living, Loving and Learning*

Why It's Important

Positive interactions not only improve your health, but they also raise the love quotient in your relationship. When you focus on the big and small ways that your partner offers affection, caring and kindness, it creates ripples of sharing, caring and respect. The opposite of *taking for granted* is appreciating. This is the absolute best nourishment for a relationship!

All couples have negative interactions, so expect that there will be times when someone is hurt or disappointed. (A relationship with no negatives is a relationship where too much is getting swept under the rug.) However, John Gottman, expert researcher on successful long-term relationships, has found that "master couples" maintain an overall balance of *five positive interactions to every one negative interaction.*

Interestingly, couples in danger of splitting tend to notice the negative and miss the positive. In fact, researchers have found that couples in trouble fail to notice *half* of the good things happening between them! When you're coupling with someone and kids are in the picture, adding interruptions, interference and general commotion into the mix, there will be plenty of negatives. All of this makes it that much more critical for you to develop your awareness and appreciation of the positives. This is really important for success—and by "success" we mean your satisfaction and connection with one another.

Thriving couples emphasize the positive in their lives. We know that when couples express their gratitude for even small things, and when they actively appreciate their good moments together, they're less likely to hold on to negative feelings and unpleasant memories. Filling your emotional piggy bank with positive moments gives you much more to draw upon during hard times. This will help you reach toward each other and stay gentle during conflict.

How to Do It

Positive interactions include a direct expression of caring and appreciation (*"Thanks for picking up Marcus from practice today."*). A simple thank you, a warm hello and a welcoming smile are all positives. They also include saying "no" gently (*"I'm so sorry, no, that doesn't work for me."*). And when your sweetie is appreciating you, your job is to stop and take it in! *Ka-Ching!* Another direct deposit into your love savings account.

> ## Helpful Tips for Maintaining the "5-to-1 Ratio" Separately and Together
>
> Happiness is both a relationship skill and an inside job. In order to keep your communication ratio at 5:1, you also need take good care of your own *internal* happiness ratio. Here are some ways to strengthen both:
>
> - **Practice gratitude.** Develop your attitude of gratitude. Openly express your appreciation to your partner and the kids!
>
> - **Savor goodness.** Notice good things as they happen. Swish positive memories and feelings around in your mind, which, in turn, bathes your nervous system in a wash of beneficial chemicals.
>
> - **Care for your body.** It's hard to feel well emotionally when you don't feel well physically.
>
> - **Enjoy something new every day.** Feed your childlike curiosity by trying something new, exploring something different, sampling something foreign or discovering something interesting about something you already know. Invite your partner to join you once in a while.
>
> - **Laugh together.** Laughter shortens the distance between two people.

Because coupling with children inevitably involves so many twists and turns in the road, it's even more important for you and your partner to consciously find your thankfulness for the positive moments between you, to be grateful for each other and to nurture your sense of wonder at the marvels of life.

BOTTOM LINE

Cherish one another. This is your fourth relationship mantra! Cherish is a verb that means three things: 1. To treat with tenderness and affection. 2. To nurture with care; to foster. 3. To hold dear; to indulge; to encourage.

Tool #5: Repair the Hurts
"It hurts because it matters."

—John Green, *Author, Looking for Alaska*

Why It's Important

We all trip up at times and hurt one another. You're going to blow it from time to time . . . we all do. That's why knowing how to repair matters!

How to Do It

When you make mistakes, your first instinct may be to defend and deflect, minimize what you did or criticize the other person. There's actually a better way—a way that demonstrates more respect.

Helpful Tips for Repairing the Hurts

Here is another courageous moment. Go ahead, push aside your own defensiveness, your feelings of vulnerability and your fear, and step forward to *own it, listen, understand and apologize*. If this seems hard, remind yourself: *"No matter what I've done, I can clean this up, face the hurt I've caused, apologize and still be okay."* Let's walk through the steps of a good repair job:

- **Own it. If you mess up, fess up.** Don't wait to be caught; don't make excuses; don't blame someone else. Apologize for it in a simple and clear way. *"I'm so sorry I forgot to tell you that Marcus had practice until 6:00."* No explanations (*"It was because . . ."*). No blame (*"But if you'd just texted, it wouldn't have been a problem."*).

- **Listen. Give your partner a chance to express hurt and upset feelings.** Listening for feeling is a key part of good repair. You can show you accept their feelings (whether you like or agree with their way of seeing it or not) by reflecting back what they say. *"You are really mad at me that I confused the time."* This sends the message *"I get you."* That's healing.

- **Understand.** Ask, *"Is there anything more?"* You may be eager for your partner to stop talking about the things you've done that upset them! However, it is absolutely in your best self-interest and in the best interest of your relationship to hear your partner (or your child, or even your ex or your coworker) as fully as possible. This increases the chances that your repair will feel complete to the other person.

- **Apologize. Do it sincerely.** Not every goof-up requires a full apology. Still, your relationship will benefit if you err on the side of more, not less. A full apology has three essential ingredients:
  - **Description:** I see what I did and I see what happened as a result. "*I forgot to tell you that practice ends sometime after 6:00. And because of that...*"
  - **Impact:** I understand the impact I had on you. "*So you rushed to the school from work. And then you had to wait. That was tough and you felt... I'm so sorry.*"
  - **Commitment:** I say how I'll make every effort to prevent this kind of thing from happening again. "*In the future I'll try to be clearer about the details I have so you can plan accordingly.*"

Often, a misunderstanding leaves both of you feeling hurt, so you may need your partner also to own their part, listen, understand and apologize. In a good relationship, you each take turns stepping up to go first.

Helpful Tips for Asking Your Beloved for Repair

If you're disappointed by or upset with your partner, you may want them to understand why—maybe even to apologize. If you're triggered, start by getting your own head together. Then try the following:

- **Focus on the behavior(s), not the person.** Attack the problem, not the partner. Try to stick to the data, describing what you actually saw and heard. "*We had a date and now it's changed*" as opposed to, "*You are so unreliable.*"

- **Own your assumptions.** "*When that happened I started to imagine that you don't care about our time together*" as opposed to, "*You obviously don't care about our time together.*"

- **Describe your feelings.** "*I am so disappointed and sad.*" Avoid labels and criticism. "*You're always letting me down.*"

- **Acknowledge good intentions.** Most blunders are accidental and happen from a lack of awareness rather than with purposeful intent. You can help the situation by saying, "*I know you wouldn't want to hurt me.*" You can also help the repair work with your empathy. "*I know this is a really difficult situation for you.*"
- **Give credit where credit is due.** Look for ways to give positive feedback. "*I know you've been working on this.*"
- **Make a request.** "*I'd love it if you'd . . .*" "*It would really help me if . . .*"

Prioritizing relationship *repair* over rushing to be *right* is your road to long-term happiness in every relationship, not just your romantic one. Repairing the hurts will help you work, play and sleep easier.

A final word on accepting apologies: When someone has done something we judge as egregious or when our feelings have been deeply hurt, it may be hard to accept an apology at the time it's offered. You can't force yourself to accept an apology before you're ready but try at least to acknowledge the other person's effort.

Then ask yourself whether you're withholding acceptance to punish the other person or because you just need more time for the sting to go away. Or perhaps there is a bit more you need your partner to fully understand. In healthy relationships, partners are able to accept apologies and move forward together with a renewed sense of closeness and understanding.

BOTTOM LINE

Apologize with heartfelt words. This is your fifth relationship mantra. The words "I'm sorry" mean something when you own what you did. The ability to deliver a sincere apology is powerful medicine for a relationship.

Learning to calm yourself in the midst of life's emotional storms is key. ***Take a breath. Take a break.*** Careful listening will help you understand your partner much more fully. ***Seek first to understand, and then to be understood.*** Making a conscious effort to live from your "best self" (instead of getting mired in defensiveness and negativity) brings home your strengths and capacities to the people who really matter: your loved ones. ***Stay on the high road.*** As you practice gratitude and appreciation with one another, you exercise that all important heart muscle, keeping five positives to every negative. ***Cherish one another.*** And finally, you can repair the hurts you've caused and you can ask your partner for repair. ***Apologize from your heart with heartfelt words.***

* * * * * * * * * * *

At times, the road gets rough. No worries. Recite the five relationship mantras and practice, practice, practice! You two can totally do this!

Now, you're wondering if it's time to introduce kids and partners. Yes, you're at that juncture in this journey. You've checked your backpack and restocked supplies and you're ready to move forward. Part II provides the map of the step-by-step process of including children in your relationship.

PART II

GETTING SERIOUS: INCLUDING THE KIDS

> *"One small changed family doesn't calculate into a world that has been spinning for a billion years. But one small change makes the world spin differently in a billion ways for one family."*
>
> —Mary E. Pearson, children's writer best known for *A Room on Lorelei Street*

The early months of dating teach us that life isn't tidy. Partnering with kids (even if the kids are only in the background) often isn't as easy as it would be if you were both footloose. This path is not for the faint of heart, but it's got many ups to balance the downs. Taking your next steps carefully will set the course for a smoother, more even journey through partner-kid (and maybe kid-kid) introductions and this next phase of relationship building.

You are now entering the "in-between" time. Your relationship becomes more serious and more solid, children are introduced and partners increasingly play a part of the day-to-day routine during a parent's residential time. This is a period of a year for some, several years for others. "Bummer!" you may say. *"I'm ready to roll— why don't we just live together!"* But we'll caution: *Not so fast.* One step at a time will make a big difference!

Part II focuses on this "in-between" time. In Chapter 5, you'll get the lay of the land on when and how to introduce children and the best ways to include them in your deepening intimate partnership.

What do kids want parents and partners to know? Chapter 6 offers a view of what these changes are like from their perspective. We'll unpack their typical reactions to a parent's sweetie entering their lives, breaking it down by developmental stages (their ages).

Once a new adult is in a parent's life and is interacting with kids, the co-parent becomes more influential. Chapter 7 explores ways to set the conditions for a respectful relationship with the children's other parent.

Chapter 8 describes the complexities and tender realities stepfamilies face when dealing with the death of a co-parent.

If your new couple relationship began as an affair, Chapter 9 walks you through waves of upset that affairs so often create.

Chapter 5

Introducing Children and a New Partner: A Step at a Time Saves Nine

"Part of being a good parent [and the partner of a parent] is remembering what it was like to be a kid."

—Unknown

Your readiness to move forward in your deepening relationship is exciting. And . . . please realize that your enthusiasm may not be, and probably *isn't,* shared by the kids. They're likely curious, sure. But ready to *share* a parent's time and attention? Maybe, not so much.

One of the toughest, most self-sacrificing steps adults can take is to slow down their own love lives to honor children's needs. Kids need time to adjust to change. We have met very few parents or partners who find slowing down easy or, in some cases, even doable. However, moving slowly and thoughtfully creates better outcomes for kids and ultimately eases adjustment to stepfamily. With that in mind . . .

Slow and steady wins the race!

Introducing kids and partners changes the family flow, activating lots of new dynamics. In this chapter, we'll look at the beginnings of one of those challenges: *Insiders and outsiders* in your couple relationship. We'll give parents some tips on how to share information with your co-parent, which activates another set of dynamics as you anticipate introducing partners to kids. And we'll lay out the nuts and bolts of how, and when, to best introduce kids to new partners (and in some cases their children)—lots of potential dynamics there!

> 🌹 Think about early stepfamily formation as a tree starting to bud. We use the metaphor of buds in part II because buds are early signs of unique stepfamily-related challenges that will begin to appear during this stage of your relationship. Part III will explore each of these challenges in depth as they go into full bloom.

OUTSIDERS AND INSIDERS

As you start to spend a little more time together, the presence of kids in your lives makes a kind of *push-me-pull-me* dance. In a *first-time* family, parenting is usually a joint effort. However, in a *next-time* family, partners must often take an "outsider" position when the parent turns to care for kids. And parents may start to feel pulled into an "insider" position when they turn to care for their kids and notice that their sweetie feels left out. Or when they turn to their sweetie and notice that their kids feel left out.

> 🌹 **Insider/outsider dynamics** are the "first buds" of a core stepfamily challenge. They can be deeply confusing, emotionally jarring and generally unsettling if you're not expecting them. Right now, we want to help you see it, name it and learn how to work with it as you continue down the path.

In this in-between time, partners are likely also becoming more aware of the many kinds of insiderness between a parent and their kids: History, ways of doing things, turns of phrase, right down to the "proper" way to make fried eggs. Parents have the inside scoop on many things new partners are just not familiar with. The little and big ways that you and your partner are building your couple relationship, your own jokes, styles and experiences pale in comparison when the kids enter the picture.

Parents may feel stuck trying to straddle the middle, struggling to keep everyone on both sides happy. Your kids generally come first, but every time you turn toward them and away from your sweetie, you know you're likely causing some upset. And when your children are clamoring for attention, every time you turn away from them to focus on your love, you know it's leaving kids feeling ignored. No fun!

What should you do? Start by reassuring yourself that this is all normal. Here are some other *normal* things you might notice:

- **The outsider position:** If you're dating or getting serious with a parent, you might be starting to notice that kids seem to create a kind of "invasion of the body snatcher": Your partner turns into a *parent!* You knew this before, but you weren't there to witness the transformation firsthand. So, we ask gently, "How does that feel to you?"

- **The insider position:** If you're the parent, you want to be close to your children *and* be close to your partner. You're probably starting to notice they often have opposing needs, and you are torn between the people who love and need you. Oy! This *is* hard!

- **Parents are also insiders with their co-parent (the children's other parent) on issues involving the kids. Partners are outsiders.** For parents, maintaining an engaged, constructive relationship with co-parents is critical for their kids. But sometimes that makes double-trouble with your sweetie.

Note to self: The co-parent, living nearby or far away, alive and well or deceased, a positive or not-so-positive force, is going to be a permanent fellow traveler on this journey. The complexity can be frustrating, so of course you both might want to push them off a cliff from time to time! What you're aiming for is all the adults learning to hike cooperatively in the same direction.

"THIS IS GETTING REALLY REAL!"

At some point, the infatuation stage of a deepening relationship gives way to a more realistic view of each other and the partnership. Rose-colored glasses come off, replaced by a sincere appreciation of partnering with someone you love. Imperfections are part of the deal, and you no longer worry that morning breath will be a relationship ender. The real work of building an enduring day-to-day life together is now underway.

Are You Good Partners?

How do the two of you disagree, argue . . . *fight*? During the falling-in-love phase, small tiffs come and go without any lasting damage. Now that kids are part of the picture, squabbles and outright fights may feel different. You may notice that your "fall-aparts" often arise around *something* related to kids or perhaps requests, even demands, from the co-parent. Buckle up, the ride is just beginning!

Here is where the communication tools in Chapter 4 will be immensely helpful. You need all those great relationship skills to be good partners. You'll have to be able to open up and have courageous conversations about your differences and the disagreements that emerge as the children (and all their expanded family "peeps") become more involved in your partnership.]

Are You Capable of Having Tough Conversations?

The hike will change when kids are introduced into the mix, so this is the time to dig down deep and find the courage to talk about what you want more of and less of from your partner and your relationship. Consider the following questions:

- Are you both feeling safe to voice your wants and needs? Can you acknowledge what each of you yearns for while also talking about what's realistic, given the complexities the two of you face?

- Does your partner respond with curiosity and interest when you ask for what you want and need or are your requests met with defensiveness?

- When asking, can *you* maintain your calm? Can you ask constructively? Do you have a tendency to lose your head and attack with blame and criticism? Or withdraw and go silent?

- Can you talk constructively about your process—the ways you both handle the myriad differences, disappointments and

> misunderstandings that are a normal part of life and intimacy when kids are involved?
>
> - Are you having honest and respectful conversations about your different approaches to parenting (which you're now seeing more up close)?
>
> - What about the personal habits that may be starting to drive you each a tad bit crazy? Can you make direct requests for change? Can you keep your sense of humor? Or are sarcasm and resentment sneaking into your communication?
>
> - If you are the parent, are you able to focus on your kids when you need to? Are you able to comfort and empathize with your partner without ignoring your kids?
>
> - As a partner, are you taking care of yourself when your sweetie turns away from you to focus on kids?
>
> - Are you continuing to have fun together as a couple, and on your own, and with friends and extended family in your child-free time?

CO-PARENTS NEED TO KNOW

Now that you are getting more serious with your new love, the news that Mom or Dad is dating someone *special* will likely reverberate across the two-home family to your co-parent. This news is best heard from *you!*

Why in the world would you want to tell your ex about your love life? You wouldn't! You're not sharing personal information about yourself. You're sharing information, *for the sake of your children,* about an adult who is a potential new partner, a person who might have an impact on the whole family.

> ### You Tell Your Co-parent So Your Kids Don't Have To
>
> Your love life is no one else's business (especially your ex's). We do know that *some* co-parents may overreact to the news and cause drama . . . so why on earth are we coaching you to tell? For a few excellent reasons:

- **Never ask kids to keep secrets from a parent.** Ever. Asking children to keep a secret from their other parent is asking them to hide a part of themselves from Mom or Dad. *If you don't want your ex to know, don't involve your kids.*

- **Don't leave it to children to be the messengers** of information that is potentially difficult for their other parent to hear. Kids don't belong in the middle, and it's certainly not their job to field their other parent's emotional response if they cause a parent to have a "fall-apart" over something the child causally shares.

- **Give co-parents the chance to be the best parent they can be.** Giving them a heads-up allows them to prepare and be able to respond in a friendly, calm way the next time.

IMPORTANT: If a co-parent might be even slightly reactive at this news (and some will be), we suggest that you inform them at the beginning of *your* residential time (when kids are with you). That gives a hurting co-parent some time to process the news and manage their own emotional responses without children present.

Allowing a reasonable amount of time to pass before you introduce someone new gives your co-parent space to come to terms with the fact you've moved on. This can help you both avoid a whole host of complications for your children. Recovery is often *considerably* slower for the person who was left—that's actually very normal. If you rush into bringing someone new into the kids' lives, it will likely exacerbate emotional drama in the family system. Everyone will be unsettled and upset—your co-parent and the kids, and then you and your partner.

"A step at a time saves nine" is an easy way to remember that it pays to be patient.

How to Tell Your Co-parent the Kids Are Meeting Your Partner

A child's ability to accept a new adult will be partly influenced by their *other* parent's attitude. Do your best to set the table for a tolerant, possibly even supportive, co-parenting response. Your work to maintain a respectful relationship with your co-parent pays big dividends during this step and during each step going forward.

There are many ways to share this information, and they largely depend on the quality of the relationship you and your co-parent have with each other.

Zoe and Levon had an agreement to inform each other prior to introducing a new romantic partner to their kids When Zoe was ready to take the next step with her new love, Brian, and introduce him to the kids, she sent Levon an email to give him a heads-up.

Hi Levon,

I'll be picking up the kids this afternoon as usual after school. I hope you and the kids have had a great few days.

I wanted to let you know that I plan to introduce them to the person I've been seeing the last many months. There's a neighborhood gathering on Saturday and he's going to drop by for an hour. His name is Brian. He has three children who live most of the time in California.

Thank you in advance for supporting them when they get back to you Sunday night. I will, of course, do the same for you when the time comes.

Regards, Z

Notice the child-centered focus. Zoe isn't sharing details about her private life. She is co-parenting skillfully and doing her part to maintain agreements. *And* now she can tell the kids, "Of course Dad knows." No secrets. Relieved kids.

FINALLY ... INTRODUCING PARTNERS AND KIDS!

You turn a significant corner when partner and kids meet for real (not just a sneak peek) for the first time. It's a very big deal! There are definite ways to do this well and set everyone up for a positive—OK, at least *neutral*—experience. Some kiddos may have a more difficult time meeting a new partner than others. And that's normal, too.

Asking a child to start a relationship with a new person (or people, if the partner also has children) is *no small request.* Their temperaments and developmental stages will be at play. We describe some predictable stages below, but please do your best to listen to *your child*'s signals for when they are ready to take another step forward and when they need the whole process to slow down or pause.

> ### Helpful Tips as You Begin to Involve Kids
>
> **We strongly recommend you try to wait** to introduce kids until after dating seriously for at *least* 4 to 6 months! The children have probably been curious about your "special someone." They may have wondered aloud, *"When do we get to meet them?"* It's time to s-l-o-w-l-y introduce the kids. How to start?
>
> **A gathering of friends who have children can be an ideal situation** to include a new love without forcing too much too soon. An afternoon at the beach with other familiar adults, an ice-skating outing with family friends, or a backyard barbeque with neighbors would work. If both you and your partner have kids, meet each other's kids without your own kids first. There will be plenty of time to include all the kids later.
>
> **Preparing the kids before the meeting** can be done with a brief explanation. Say something like, *"We're invited to the Ramone's for a picnic this weekend. I'm going to invite Brian, the person I'm dating. That will give you a chance to meet him."* Short and sweet.

What Kids Need During First Meetings

The children need to know that this new interloper *won't take their parent away*. This isn't just true for little ones. Teenagers and adult children often feel a loss of attention when mom or dad falls in love. Parents may long to show their children how they *really* feel about their beloved. Partners may long to be openly embraced, no longer a secret to be kept from the kids. However, being lovey-dovey in front of the kids, especially this early in the children's new relationship with a parent's sweetie, will almost always leave children feeling excluded from something special and leave them uncomfortable.

Pay attention to how each child responds. A child who struggles at the beginning will need a chance to adjust before you increase the amount of time together. Relationships build as trust builds; trust builds through well-designed shared experiences *over time*. We have no way of knowing how long this period of trust building will take for a child. It may in fact be different for each child in a family. Believe it or not, a child who is friendly and open at first may have a harder time as your love relationship grows more serious. Even if kids are excited, *slow and steady.*

If you're the partner meeting the kids for the first time, bring your warm, easygoing self to the meeting (but no acting like a golden retriever puppy, please!). Children need a chance to check you out, come closer on their own terms, even wait to have a conversation until *they're* ready.

As the new partner, you are not only building a relationship with the kids, you are also at the front end of establishing a relationship with the children's other parent vis-à-vis how the kids talk about you. Co-parents appreciate it when a new romantic partner doesn't come on gangbusters and try to win a child's affection. They can certainly get freaked if you do.

BOTTOM LINE

*Bringing a romantic partner (and their children) together will create waves through the whole the family system. The partner's job is to try to enter the system making warm gentle ripples—certainly **not** a tidal wave!*

Helpful Tips for Partners' and Kids' Getting-to-Know-You Time

You want this to go as well as possible! Here is a quick summary of pointers for introducing kids and partners.

- **Tell kids when a new partner is going to be present.** Kids like surprises that involve cake or puppies, but best to give them a heads-up when they are going to meet the new partner.

- **Short and casual at first.** Activities that include familiar friends will help kids get used to a new person without putting a lot of pressure on. After a while it can be just kids, parent and partner hanging out together. Maybe the partner drops by for dinner and then goes home before kids go to bed. Or you all meet at the park and then go your own ways.

- **Parents, spend post-meeting time with children,** "just us," doing something familiar and reassuring. Listen to their thoughts and feelings about the new situation and let them know you understand.

- **Wash, rinse, repeat!** Schedule casual-activity get-togethers, the occasional meal and so forth.

- **Adjust!** If children seem increasingly easy with sharing you and allowing others to join in without interfering distress or acting out later, keep moving forward, a little at a time. If kids are struggling—step back and consider slowing down.

Introducing the Partner's Kids to Your Kids

Two parents; two sets of kids. Double the fun?

Once the cat is out of the bag, their kids might want to meet your kids and vice versa. Or you two may be eager to get this going because it opens up so many exciting vistas of a future together. You glimpse the possibilities of having a more normal family life with each other after months of separating dating and parenting. Yes! *...and keep it slow and steady.*

Helpful Tips for Introducing Kids to Kids

Ages and stages will guide much of what you say. Young children looking forward to a playdate will feel much different about meeting new kids than teens meeting other teens or adult children meeting a parent's new lover's family over cocktails. You'll be able to modify how you message things, but let's start with the tips below:

- **Prepare the kids** with enough information to make them feel like they have some element of control. For example, names, ages, preferred interests and a few details that help them feel interested in the new kids.

- **Be an ally** to your kids. "*You might like each other, but it's okay if you're nervous about it,*" for little ones. Or, "*It might be weird, I get it,*" for teens. Or, "*I appreciate your doing this,*" for adult children.

- **Meet for an activity** that has a start and stop time. A shorter first meeting that goes well will make the prospect of another get-together more likely to be positive. A longer experience may result in exhaustion or meltdowns, leaving bad feelings all around.

- **Parents remain parents** to their own children— no different from any other playdate or social get-together with friends.

- **Spend post-meeting time with your children,** "just us," doing something familiar and reassuring. Listen to their thoughts and feelings. Allow for a full range of expression—even the negative— without judgment or defensiveness.

- **Wash, rinse, repeat!** Schedule casual-activity get-togethers, the occasional meal and so forth.

- **Adjust!** If relationships among the kids seem to be building, keep moving forward, slowly. If children are tense with each other, give them space.

More Time with Kids as Parent *and* Partner (After Dating Seriously for *at Least* 7 to 9 Months)

Pacing is key! As you increase the number of activities and length of engagements with kids and partners, you want the time spent together to feel as comfortable as *possible* for everyone. Notice we're not saying that it *will* be *comfortable* for everyone, because it's a huge transition, especially for kids. (And also possibly for a partner. Being with someone else's kids is intense, let's face it.)

Managing "Togetherness"

Depending on their ages, children may be going on with their lives as usual, relying on Mom or Dad for a ride to the mall or help with a homework project even as a new partner arrives for an evening of dinner and a movie at home. If you're the parent, you can expect your kids to be civil with a new partner, but please don't push them for *family*-like displays of togetherness.

Forcing children to entertain your partner's children is also not a good idea. They may well resent you for foisting children they didn't choose to have in their space, use their stuff, share their treats and more. This rarely goes well. Allowing kids to step at their own pace into relationships with both the new adult and their kids shows them respect and gives them healthy self-determination.

Meanwhile, as a parent, don't be surprised if your six-year-old or your thirteen-year-old suddenly has needs that *only you* can meet. "*You have to come in my room . . .*" "*I need you right now!*" In kid-code language, your child is asking for confirmation that they're still your priority and they're not losing you. We'll help you decode more of the typical ways children express their needs in Chapter 6.

Discrepancies in your ideas about parenting, limit setting and discipline will start to show up now. Partners may find themselves thinking, "*If these were my kids . . .*" Each parent needs to handle limit setting and discipline for their own children. Partners focus on getting to know each other's kids. You can learn about their interests or shoot hoops or play a board game with them. Let go of controlling or correcting them. That almost always backfires.

> **Increasing awareness of differences in your ideas about discipline** *and* keeping parenting and stepparenting roles distinct are "first buds" of a core stepfamily challenge.

You may also be discovering that your two families have different values, rules and styles of play. For now, you can each explain to your own children, "They do it differently than we do." When on each other's turf, you and your kids are good guests. The rules of that home apply.

Any time two different *(in this case family)* cultures come together, there's discovery, confusion and learning. There are misunderstandings and resentments. You and your sweetie will set expectations that everyone deserves respect; that everyone must use their words; that it's important to learn from one another and take turns and so forth. Nothing new here. But because you are bringing two groups of kids together who don't know each other, it's important to make these things very clear.

Introducing Children and a New Partner: A Step at a Time Saves Nine

🌹 **Building a shared culture where differences are respected** describes the "first bud" of another core stepfamily challenge. At first blush, differences can feel like conflicts that have to be fixed by figuring out how to do things *the same way*. Down the road, you'll find ways to honor them. Perhaps you'll gently weave some of them together. For now, focus on just being *curious* about your differences.

Choosing More Time Together Than Apart (Dating Seriously for *At Least* 10 to 12 Months)

You and your partner may spend much of your non-kid time together. And you're still figuring out how much *together* versus *apart* time with the kids makes sense. Partners may now be spending time with the family a night or two a week. You may be talking about moving in together or making a more formal commitment. Or you may have hit the Pause button because, frankly, things are a bit too fraught when everyone (adults and kids) gets together. There's a whole spectrum of *normal* possibilities here.

What About the Kids?

It's possible that the kids were fine about the partner at first. But as time goes on, parents might start to hear complaints. *"They're always here!"* If the partner also has kids, there might be complaints that those other kids are *annoying*. What's happening is that the initial excitement of meeting new people and doing fun things is wearing off. The honeymoon (if you had one) is over.

Kids may swing wildly from acting like best friends to treating one another as archenemies. You may see increasing incidents of sibling rivalry, tattling, fights and mean behavior. Parents, hang in there with your best parenting skills. Partners, keep breathing and take a break if you need to! And you may be picking up signals that the kids need you to slow the pace a bit.

But, why now?

Everyone's feeling the effects of more closeness and the novelty's worn off. For some, it may be too much or too scary. Others may have landed in another round of grief. Or they may simply be tussling with the awareness that sharing time, attention, and things is *hard!* This is a predictable struggle. You may want to slow the pace of your partner's presence around the home for a little while and give the kids more space from one another. "*Looks like you need some 'just us' time. Am I getting that right?*" "*Looks like you and Joey are wearing on each other. What do you think?*" You are taking a step back in order to go forward with more confidence.

Spending longer amounts of time together poses both challenges and opportunities. Over time, with more shared experiences and more trust developing among partners and kids and parents and kids, couples might start planning longer visits, even overnights at home or vacations with everyone.

First Overnights

Parents and partners often wonder when's the right time to start spending the night together when kids are in residence. Like all things *kids*, we look at this through the lens of *is this relationship "kid-worthy"*? Beginning to spend the night together says to kids that a dating partner is now embedded much more deeply into their sense of home and their security with a parent. What may be casual for adults is not casual for kids.

Adult relationships unfold in phases: The first phase we described in part I: that luscious, hormone-driven lust time of wonderful sex (about months one to three)! The second phase often unfolds during approximately months four to eight in which partners begin to find their footing again, reality sets in, the first fights are likely to happen and the capacity to repair is tested. Knowing that you can safely navigate this stage of an adult relationship is an important step toward knowing you've got a long-term, more mature love where it's safe to involve kids' hearts at yet a deeper level.

That's why overnights don't appear until you get to "spending more time together than apart." Get through that rough patch of relationship deepening with each other—wait until you know that you can successfully resolve conflicts and negotiate differences—then you're on better footing to involve the kids in a big change for them.

Introducing Children and a New Partner: A Step at a Time Saves Nine

Overnights-at-Home Debacle

Brian spent most weekend days with Zoe and her children at their house. His children visited from out of state multiple times during school breaks and weekends, and they would switch off houses. The adults were relieved that everyone got along and seemed to be enjoying family time together. Even though Brian was around Zoe's house a lot, he went home every night to give Zoe time with her kids.

After a few months like this, Brian was over late on a Friday night and Zoe suggested he spend the night since they planned on leaving early the next morning to go skiing with her kids. Seemed like such a simple step to take.

Gigi, Zoe's fifteen-year-old daughter, was in the kitchen that morning when Brian came out of her mother's bedroom. She froze. The voice in her head screamed, "WHAT IS HE DOING HERE??" Gigi left her toast burning in the toaster and fled to her room, slamming the door.

It's not that she didn't like Brian. She did. But she hadn't been prepared for him to be in the kitchen, in the morning, when she was in her pajamas with no bra on, no hair combed... it was *embarrassing*! It felt like an invasion of her privacy. No one told her Brian would be there. Gigi was *mad*.

As the adults loaded the car, Gigi sullenly refused to help. She was curt to her mom and downright mean to her younger brother. When Brian tried to joke with her, she gave him a scathing look.

Zoe was surprised and concerned about her daughter's moodiness. She tried to find out what was going on, but Gigi shut down all attempts at communication. Zoe tried to be patient. She figured her daughter would snap out of it on the ski slope. Gigi loved to ski.

But the day was tense and unhappy for everyone because of Gigi's foul temper. At lunch she was disrespectful to her mom and ignored Brian. During the car trip home, she popped in her ear buds with frosty disdain. Brian and Zoe looked at each other in confusion. What on earth had gotten into Gigi?

It's not hard to relate to Gigi because we know what it's like to be taken by surprise, to be at a loss for words—to be upset and not be sure exactly why—and filled with indignant outrage. Her mom

[63]

hadn't given her fair warning that Brian would be spending the night. The encounter unleashed a flood of emotions that were beyond Gigi's ability to name, process and resolve with any maturity.

Later that night, after Brian had gone home, Zoe went into Gigi's room. Resisting the urge to scold her for acting like a brat, she sat on her daughter's bed and said, "So what's going on with you, honey? Why was today so hard for you?" At first, Gigi stayed glum and silent. But Zoe was patient and finally the teen opened up. As Zoe listened and empathized, she finally understood why her daughter was upset. She said she could see why it had been distressing. She apologized for putting Gigi in that situation. Zoe also promised that in the future she would talk with Gigi before inviting Brian to stay over.

Rushing the next stage, whether for the sake of convenience or because you can't bear waiting anymore, can end up setting relationship building back *many steps.*

Preparing Kids for Next Steps

Brian and Zoe skipped the step of preparing the kids for the new situation of Brian staying over. To the couple, staying over seemed like a natural next step. Things between Zoe's children and Brian were going well. The kids knew that Brian spent the night with their Mom when they were with their Dad. So why was it a big deal? Kids need time to prepare for how it might feel to have a new person in *their* home with *their* parent.

When children are prepared, it's easier for them to cross over yet another threshold in relationship development. Sit down and let your kids know (kid-level) when any shift in the normal family routine is going to happen. Listen to their concerns and problem solve together.

Rewind the Tape

Let's rewind and try it again and see how things played out when Zoe didn't skip the important step of preparing the kids for a change in the family routine.

Zoe realized early in the week that it would make sense for Brian to stay over on Friday night so they could leave first thing the next morning for their ski trip. He agreed, so on Tuesday, during dinner alone with her kids, Zoe broached the idea.

"Hey, guys, I've been thinking about our ski trip this weekend. We want to be on the road by 7:00, so I'm thinking that if Brian just stays here Friday night, it will be easier to get packed and on the road. It will give us more time on the slopes. What do you think?"

Her son, Mitch, shrugged. "I don't care. Where would he sleep?"

"Don't be stupid," Gigi said, rolling her eyes at her brother. "He'd sleep with Mom!"

Zoe picked up not only the usual sibling poking, but also Gigi's focus on *sleep with Mom*. "Sweetie, would it bother you? I know he's never stayed over here while you two were home." Zoe slowed and softened her speech to make lots of space for Gigi's response.

After a moment, her daughter said, "I guess it's okay. As long as you keep the door closed."

Zoe nodded. "Of course, Hon. Is there anything else?"

"Yeah. I don't want him in the kitchen before I'm dressed. That would be weird."

"I get that. I'll ask him to stay in my room until you're dressed. Anything else?"

"I guess not. I'm good with it." Gigi sounded calmer.

Zoe turned back to Mitch, "So, buddy, anything you need?"

Stuffing a forkful of pasta in his mouth, he shook his head no. After he swallowed, he said, "Yeah. Tell Brian to bring his extra snowboard."

By giving her kids time to prepare, and by listening to their needs, and by continuing to ask, "Anything else," Zoe was able to move her family to the next phase of relationship building in a respectful, well-paced way.

Travel with Kids and Partners

There's nothing like a road trip with kids to test the adults' patience! If you both have kids, then good luck! As your families are coming together, packing two sets of children into a vehicle for an overnight at the beach may sound like a fabulous idea in the planning stage . . . and then the fights start over who gets to sit by the window and someone announces they won't eat the bagels with cream cheese you packed.

These normal skirmishes among children will inevitably expose the adults' differences about how these things should be handled. Remember, each parent will step in and parent their own kids. However, the differences may remain front-and-center in both your minds.

Our advice?

Start with a few well-spaced overnights at home and see how that goes. Time away "as a group" significantly ups the ante of intensity for children and can trigger a surprising number of kid meltdowns, the need to call the other parent and other similarly unexpected responses.

So, limit vacations, including road trips, to bite-size distances and short-term adventures. This will set everyone up for success.

Sleep apart at this stage. Give thoughtful consideration ahead of time to who will sleep where for that camping weekend or hotel stay. We recommend that parents sleep with younger kids or, for teens, in their own separate rooms so kids have easy access to their parent. Use the nighttime to reconnect and spend some "just us" time with kids and provide reassurance on these first "all together" trips away from home.

Expect that *the temperature will go up,* perhaps even before you start driving to that cabin in Rocky Mountain National Park. Finding ways to lower the heat of too much togetherness will be important. As always, preparing kids for what's going to be different is crucial to making new situations feel safer for them.

"I Want My Daddy..."

Three months later, Zoe and Brian decided to take all their kids to Colorado for spring break. This time, both parents let their kids know that the adults would be sharing a room. They also made plans for each adult to have "just us" time with their own children, as well as for each parent to have a little time alone with the other's kids. Brian invited Mitch to go fly fishing. Zoe arranged to take Gigi and Brian's daughters, Gracie and Ashley, horseback riding. These "breakout" times were meant to give each child ways to ground themselves in what's *familiar* while taking what's new a step at a time.

Ashley, who had just turned seven, was upset that Brian wouldn't stay in the room with her and her sister, as he had in the past. "No!!!" she protested when he explained it to her. "That's not fair! I want to sleep in *your* bed, with you." Ashley's big eyes welled up with tears.

A child's age, stage of development and sense of comfort with the romantic partner will inform their response. Zoe's children, Gigi and Mitch, were older and had spent significantly more time with Brian than Brian's kids had with Zoe. Ashley let Brian know she was *not* ready to share her daddy in the night. Although it was disappointing for the couple, Brian and Zoe agreed that they would have to be patient and give Ashley more time to get used to the idea.

One-on-One with Your Stepkiddo-to-Be

When families are spending more time together, partners can look for opportunities to spend time alone with their stepkids-to-be. Find low-key activities that you both enjoy: Make a child's favorite dessert together, sew a quilt together, or shoot baskets together, or give the stepchild a ride to a friend's house and talk in the car. Participate as a caring adult in your partner's children's lives, helping them out where you can. Focus on being friendly, available and genuinely curious about their interests. These time-limited experiences give children a chance to build familiarity and emotional safety.

Do We Go Forward from Here?

As you might have noticed, this question comes up at every new juncture. You're noticing you need to keep evaluating things, sometimes for years.

> **HAZARD** ◉ Insider/outsider positions for you as a couple often *intensify* as you spend more time together. They can cause big feelings. If you find yourself handling those feelings by saying, "*If you really loved me, then you'd . . .*" or thinking, "*Once we move in together, then it will be . . .*," then it's time to stop and assess. If you keep getting triggered, then being part of a stepfamily *may not work for you*. As sad, frustrating and difficult as this may be, now's the time to listen to your gut.

Courageous Conversations Can Help You Prepare to Become a Stepfamily

Hopefully, you're having open, honest, caring conversations about important topics. There's no avoiding the hard stuff or believing that "love will conquer all." You will face some passages where the climb gets a bit steep. Challenging differences and surprising disappointments lie ahead, as well as, hopefully, nourishing, satisfying new relationships.

There really are some beautiful views around the bend. But first, let's check your supplies. Let's make sure you're able to have the conversations you'll need before you start on the next leg of your journey!

> ### Helpful Tips for Having Really Real Conversations
>
> What's most important is not *agreeing* with each other but *understanding* one another. Do your best to stay caring, kind and curious as you tackle these difficult subjects:
>
> - How is your sexual relationship going? Are you able to talk about what feels good and what doesn't?
>
> - Are you managing the ups and downs so that there is space for intimacy and fun?

- What do you know about each other's finances? What more would you each like to know? Do you have a system of paying for things that feels respectful?

- For parents: Do you feel you can talk openly, and honestly, about your co-parenting relationship? For partners, are you able to express your thoughts without dictating how your love should handle the co-parenting relationship?

- What are each of your ideas and beliefs about religion, rituals and spirituality? Where do you overlap? Where are you different? Where do the kids fit into these practices?

- Where do you agree and where do you differ about parenting? Are you able to talk about your differences without blame or criticism? Are you able to allow the parent to discipline their children?

MAKING THE DECISION TO BECOME A STEPFAMILY

You're now moving toward making a *family commitment*. This is the stage where plans may be in motion to move in together or engagements are announced. You're getting ready to step onto yet another new path on your journey, and you want to be as in-step with each other as possible. That means—you guessed it!—lots more talking.

If you're struggling with doubts, second thoughts and uncertainty, be honest with yourself and each other. Step back. Build your skills. Give yourselves more time to feel this through. *Moving in together will not make doubts, fear, and second thoughts better.* It may only increase their intensity.

Note that the children's other parent will have their own reaction(s) to the news of your decision to live together or marry. Deciding to move in together will require addressing a lot of questions about how you'll coordinate drop-offs and pick-ups, retrieve lost belongings, etc. Co-parents may also have protective reactions to a non-family member adult living with their children. They may worry about being upstaged by a partner, or be concerned about having their values disrupted, or feel undermined by another adult influencing the kids.

All this will now come more front and center to some degree or another. Assuaging a co-parent's fears at this stage—if you can—will help smooth the waters.

> **HAZARD** ⊘ Are you moving toward living together *without the necessary ingredients for a committed relationship*? Consider the stakes. Are you certain enough to ask children to form important emotional bonds that could be broken? Address the things that make you feel uncertain so you don't drag your kids through an experiment you suspect will fail.

Preparing the Kids for *Another* Family Change

It is important to tell kids about changes that are coming down the road, but that's only the first step to preparing them. You have to see it from their point of view and try to speak to their concerns.

"We're going to live together," means a new person in their lives, 24-7.

"We're going to find a new home for all of us." They have to move?! Will they like the new neighborhood?

"And we'll be looking for a home for all of us." Will they have to share a room with stepsiblings? What if they don't want to!

"We're going to wait until school is out. We'll plan to move at the end of June." Does that mean they'll be switching schools? What about their friends!?

That is a lot of change coming at them at once! How can you make it easier?

Helpful Tips for Supporting Kids Coping with (More) Family Change

The points below will sound familiar, perhaps. They will serve you well during any major family change.

- **Continue to carve out regular, reliable parent-child time** without the new partner or their kids.

- **No big surprises.** Let your kids know about each change. Give them time to process each step and mentally rehearse and prepare.

- **Be ready for *lots* of questions.** Set aside time to explore kids' questions. Answer simply what you know and what you don't. Tell children what will and won't change. ("*You will still see Daddy every Friday.*" "*We'll still have breakfast, just us, on Wednesdays.*" "*You and Jenny will be sharing a room. You'll still have your same bed and your dresser.*")

- **When possible, include children in decision-making.** Children do better when they're involved in an age-appropriate way. Be clear about where they have a choice ("*What color would you like your room to be?*") and where they have input but you have final say ("*We've found two possible homes. Would you like to see them and tell us what you think?*")

- **Hold steady with routines and good parenting practices.** Children will adjust to family changes more easily *if you maintain their fundamental routines, familiar objects and comforting ways of caring for them to the extent possible*. Although the adults may be up for all-new everything, the kids may do better if they can bring familiar things into their new relationships.

- **Expect grief, protest and push-back**, particularly during transition times, and at the beginning and end of the day, when children's resources are lowest. Provide extra time and emotional bandwidth at these times to field the sadness and crankiness associated with change.

- **When kids fall apart, help them name their feelings.** "*You're really upset about all these big changes.*" "*You are so scared about how this is gonna be.*" "*You are really mad at me!*" Helping kids feel safe to express their worries and concerns will help soften them. Listen for clues about ways you can meet your kiddo's needs: "*But Mommy, I wanted to be just with you on switch days!*" "*Oh Sweetheart, we can do that for some time before dinner. Would that help?*"

- **Provide both empathy and loving, developmentally appropriate limits.** Kids have every right to be upset. But it's not okay to do mean or dangerous things.

If children are not adjusting, accepting and settling down and nothing seems to help, you very likely need to slow way down. You may possibly need professional help. Please see the appendix for guidance on finding stepfamily-savvy therapists.

Meanwhile, step back, try to unpack what's going on for them, ease any tensions in your relationship with your co-parent if possible, and continue to work on building the child's sense of security with both their parents. With guidance, lots of preparation, skillful parenting and supportive partnering, struggling children may eventually come along, and then you can continue forward again.

And please remember, there are other options for moving toward commitment besides living with your partner.

Living Apart Together (LAT)

In every family, some kids will be more ready than others for a partner's involvement. Children who have experienced more loss and change, or who have another parent who is upset over your relationship, will generally need more parent-child time and less "new family" time. Some children may bring more intense special needs, for instance, anxiety, severe depression and/or neurological differences, such as those associated with the autism spectrum. Or perhaps one of you has a medically fragile child.

If there are kids on board who are extremely vulnerable, an extended period of "living apart together" (LAT) can be a wise choice. LAT couples are in a fully committed relationship (sometimes even married), but they live in separate homes. LAT may last until the most vulnerable child is considerably more stable or until the child's next residential step is completed. (For older children, this may mean adult supported housing.)

．．．．．．．．．．．

A step at a time saves nine. As adults, you're hopeful and ready to fulfill your dream of being together, but kids often have different needs. Somehow you have to manage all these competing forces in ways that care for everyone. It sometimes feels like a slog through mud! Changes piggyback one on top of other changes, and it's a lot for kids, no matter what age. And then there will be times they—and you—start to feel like it's too big a mountain to climb. When you take it slowly, you can make this trek successfully together.

Chapter 6

. . . .

Children's Responses to a Parent Repartnering

*"Grownups never understand anything for themselves.
It is tiresome for children always and forever
to be explaining things to them."*

—Antoine de Saint-Exupéry, author of *The Little Prince*

There are so many things kids wish adults understood about what it's like when a parent brings their new partner into their lives. So, we're going to help the kiddos out and share the kid-perspective with you.

You may have a good hunch about some of these things, but just to be sure you have the full scoop, read on!

Along the way, we're going to give you a developmental framework. Children tend to react to new people coming into their family life in different ways at different ages. Our goal is to help parents, partners and co-parents support kids in this major change in their lives.

IN THE AFTERMATH OF SEPARATION AND DIVORCE

Divorce and separation create enormous emotional and physical upheaval, along with considerable grief. This is true for the kiddos and, usually, for the parents as well. When a family is dismantled, it's like the ground you were standing on suddenly isn't there in the way it always was—the way you expect it to be. For kids, the separation of parents and changes involved in living across two homes can be an upsetting time.

Children have amazing abilities to weather change, build resilience and recover from their parents' separation, especially if parents remain tuned in to their children and keep things between the adults constructive and child-focused. Divorce, in and of itself, does not necessarily cause harm or lasting damage.

HAZARD ⊘ What does leave lasting scars for children is ongoing conflict, fear of losing a parent and feeling caught in the middle with nowhere to turn for comfort during the divorce process and beyond. It's even harder for kids if good parenting starts to slip. If you're dating during the divorce-recovery period, or if you're wrapped up in divorce tensions, it's easy to miss the signs that the kiddos need more support, more calm and more parental connection. Avoid a major pothole!

Children fare best when they have positive, engaged relationships with both parents after separation/divorce. Kids of all ages also want to know that everyone in the family— both of their parents, themselves, their siblings—will eventually be OK. (For more information about this, see Karen's book, *The Co-Parenting Handbook: Raising Well-Adjusted and Resilient Kids from Little Ones to Young Adults through Divorce or Separation.*)

Whether the split for the parents was conflicted, collaborative or in-between, most kids need a year or two to reestablish a secure home base with each of their parents. Even after they've done this, new significant family changes (positive *or* negative) can sometimes trigger memories and unresolved feelings from the separation, especially if parents got lost in their own upset.

But guess what's also happening during the first few postseparation years when kids are just trying to get settled? Parents often start to date again. Even when kids have had a long adjustment period, a parent's romantic interest in another adult can easily spark feelings of insecurity and uncertainty. That's because, while parents are excited and hopeful about having a new sweetie, *kids likely have some apprehension about what it all means.* Their parent's attention has shifted to some new person. From the kiddos' perspective, that makes their mom or a dad *feel* less available. And the newly solidified ground gets shaky again.

The good news is that there are lots of helpful things parents, partners and co-parents can do to make this next change easier for kids. The first thing is for parents to assess whether your kids are ready for this next fork in the road.

> ### Are the Kids Ready?
>
> You can't know *for sure* how children will respond until you make a move and see what happens. But here are a few clues that the timing to introduce your dating partner *may* be right.
>
> - Have you and your kids fallen into a solid rhythm with each other?
> - During parent-kid time, can they rest with you and you with them?
> - Have the kids' daily routines, school responsibilities and friendships mostly returned to normal?
> - Have the kids been generally healthy in the past few months, including eating and sleeping normally?
> - Has the drama (if there was drama surrounding the separation) quieted down? (If not, consider getting coaching on how best to disengage from and reduce conflict with your co-parent so that any new relationship you start doesn't add more fuel to the fire.)
>
> If you can answer *mostly* "yes" to these questions, your kids are likely ready to handle more change—one step at a time.

Recoupling: What Kids Need Adults to Understand

> *"I am your parent,*
> *You are my child,*
> *I am your quiet place,*
> *You are my wild."*
>
> —Maryann K. Cusimano, author of *You Are My I Love You* and other children's books.

It would be so marvelously convenient if there were one cookie-cutter way all children responded to change in the family. But ages and stages of development, temperament and gender make that impossible. And kids change over time. A child who seemed relaxed and friendly with a partner in the early stages of a parent's dating relationship may turn surly or anxious as the relationship gets more serious and time together increases. This can be surprising, frustrating and confusing for all the adults, but trust us: It's completely normal.

Many things go on under the surface for kids that you'll want to consider. For example: They're apprehensive about losing their parent. They may get tangled up in a loyalty bind where they feel it's hard to love both of their parents *and* like a new dating partner. They may worry about their other parent's emotional state. And they have their individual make-up and special challenges to deal with.

Children's responses to change are often expressed in imperfect, frustrating or confusing ways for the adults. But the uneasiness, fear and needs behind their behavior are *important*. When all you see is upsetting behavior, it's easy to judge a child: "*Maddie is an ungrateful brat!*" We hope this chapter will help you to be aware of the complicated jumble of feelings, thoughts and relationships kids are struggling to manage, so you can be more curious and compassionate: "*It's so frustrating that Maddie is acting this way, but I can tell she's just unsettled. I wonder what's going on for her.*" When adults can respond in ways that create connection, you can then coach children to express themselves more skillfully.

BOTTOM LINE

*What children show us on the **outside** is not always what they're experiencing on the **inside**.*

Losses: What Kids Need Adults to Understand

Put yourself in a kid's shoes for a minute. You're living your life—a familiar life; it's *yours*—and something happens *not in your control* and your life is up-ended. Not your fault. But even so, you find yourself facing lots of big and small losses. Things maybe settle for a bit as you start to divide your time between two homes. And then, all of a sudden, there's a new adult in your life. Or maybe two, if both your parents have new partners. More change. More potential upset and, along with the gains, *more loss*. "More loss?" you ask. Yes. Here's why.

Parents turn away to their new love. Kiddos feel left when they sense that a parent's attention is glued to their new sweetie. As things move along, time alone with Mom or Dad has to be shared more and more with this new adult. Not their choice! And frankly, if there was going to be another person, your kiddo kind of wishes it was their other parent . . . not someone new.

The presence of a new partners dashes kids' hope for *reunification*. Some children unconsciously or consciously long for their parents to reunite. That reunification fantasy is doused with cold water when a new partner enters the picture. This can unleash feelings of grief and anger. Some kids may even blame the new partner for preventing their parents from getting back together. All of this may show up in sulking, angry, sad or rejecting behavior.

Listening for Kids' Feelings

Jim's sweetheart of eight months, LeAnn, was spending increasing time on weekends with Jim and his daughter, Janie, age 10. Jim was in love and happy, and he just wanted his little girl to be happy, too. Janie had liked LeAnn in the beginning, but now she was sulky and clingy whenever LeAnn was around.

"I hate LeAnn!" Janie finally erupted one night when Jim came to tuck her in.

Jim took a deep breath and let it out slowly, giving himself a moment to choose his response carefully. The defensive part of himself wanted to say, "But LeAnn is a nice person!" The impatient part of himself bit back the words, "That's out of line! I never want to hear you say that again." He knew it wasn't the right thing to scold her. But what to do? He took another breath.

And he managed to say instead, "Something's really bugging you, huh, honey." Janie looked at the floor. "Daddy, we used to have Saturdays together. Now *she's* here." Jim resisted the urge to say, "But LeAnn's so much fun!" He thought a moment. Suddenly he got it. "It was just us two for a while there, huh. Now LeAnn's around more, and you're not happy about it!" Janie nodded. Jim's heart sank a bit. But he continued, "What's hardest for you, honey?" "I miss you, Daddy," Janie was able to say, sadly.

"You miss having me to yourself sometimes?" Jim added for her.

"*Yes!*" she said, relieved that he understood. Janie relaxed and snuggled next to her daddy. Later, Jim told LeAnn that Janie was struggling a bit with sharing him every weekend. "She let me know that she needs more 'just us' time." LeAnn said, "Maybe I can help."

The next morning, LeAnn greeted Janie with a gentle smile and said, "Janie, I know things are different than they were before your dad and I met. I can understand that you could be missing having your dad for *just you*. How about we make sure you get some time with just Daddy on Saturdays. Deal?"

Janie's eyes teared up and she nodded. Later, when LeAnn was getting ready to leave, Janie gave her a hug.

Loyalty Binds: What Kids Need Adults to Understand

Loyalty binds are really hard for kids. In some part of themselves, many children feel that if they care about a parent's new partner, they will be disloyal to their other parent. This can happen for children whose parents split up, for children who lost a parent, and even for adult children whose elderly parents have a new partner after decades of being solo. These feelings are perfectly normal—maybe even wired into our DNA!

However, when parents, stepparents and/or co-parents complain about one another, compete with one another or insist that children align with them, loyalty binds can tighten unbearably for kids. As a couple, you have control of one side of this dynamic—yours. Use your power for good! Resist all urges to throw stones, to blame, to bad-mouth, to twist the truth to your benefit. Resist the urge to react to a co-parent's attempts to disrupt your new relationship or to interfere with your time with the kids.

Your Dating Impacts My Other Parent: What Kids Need Adults to Understand

Children need you to understand that they are inextricably connected to their other parent, who may have died or who lives down the street, who may be wonderfully loving or completely inadequate. This is not about how much you like, agree with or want a child to be influenced by this other parent. This is about the fact that *they are this child's other parent.*

New partners, in particular, need to respect the role of the child's other parent. Be kind to them in public places. Respect the distance they may need from you. Don't be intrusive or overly demonstrative and affectionate toward their children in front of them. If necessary, help free kids from adult tension by lying low. This will never ever be the time or place to mark your territory as the new or chosen partner.

When a co-parent wants more phone or video access to their children or hopes to have casual contact after a swim meet or a run-in at the grocery store, children need their parents to support them in being open and affectionate with their other parent. Likewise, kids may feel a need to reach out by phone or text to reduce their own anxiety about being with a parent's dating partner. So within reason, and in a socially responsible way, let your kiddos connect without stress and tension.

What kids want you to know is that it's much easier for them if the adults in their lives can be civil and mutually respectful. The kids want to know that *none* of the adults will get upset or tense because they want to talk about or connect with their other parent!

Discipline: What Kids Need Adults to Understand

As a new partner spends more time with kids, it may be very, very tempting to begin asserting authority and correcting, even disciplining, children. Parental discipline often slips during solo parenting. Seeing the problem clearly from the outside makes many partners feel even more compelled to step in (trying to be helpful!) and "put things right." Remember, as Patricia says, to concentrate on **connection, not correction.**

The *Other* Kids: What Kids Need Adults to Understand

When bringing two sets of kids together, the adults of course hope everyone will be delighted to have more kids around to play with or hang with and to have them as stepsiblings someday. Some children may feel that way; others may not.

The adults are doing *all* the choosing. That's the bigger issue here. Can you imagine if your child found a new best friend and then came home and insisted that you spend every weekend and vacation with the new friend's parents? And that you share your room and your favorite stuff with them? And that you like it (or pretend to)?

Just sayin'... bringing children into relationships with a new adult and their children is no small ask. All too often it's not an *ask* at all, but rather an expectation that children will get on board with the plan.

News flash! Forcing children to behave like "we all like each other" when they aren't *feeling it* will not work.

BOTTOM LINE

*Children need the adults to know that just because they're kids doesn't mean they don't have preferences, opinions and friendship needs. And, they need the grown-ups to understand that they only have so much bandwidth to make room for **strangers** (meaning people who may for a very long time remain **nonfamily** members, from their point of view) in their family time and space.*

Helpful Tips for Managing Kids with Other Kids

This is NOT a time to "let the kids work it out." It is the adults' job to keep kids safe. Both adults need to monitor behavior, but, again, *each parent disciplines their own child*. If kids are having repeated difficulties with each other, don't force it. Here are some things to try:

- Find some activities that keep them apart—some kids make cookies while other kids take the dog on a long walk.

- Find something where they'll all lose themselves in—something fun, especially something fun that doesn't require too much cooperation: the trampoline park, skiing, the state fair.

- Shorten the amount of time spent together.

Some kids will act out if they don't feel safe. Others will resist attempts to force them to bond with the new kids by being hard to get along with, misbehaving, acting sullen, teasing or bullying or not sharing. Still others will become quiet and depressed, isolating themselves and hiding in a corner or in their room. Honoring a child's need for space or a break from forced togetherness may be frustrating and disappointing for the adults, but it's good parenting for kids.

BOTTOM LINE

You can't legislate relationships. *Relationships are formed from many positive experiences over time. Overdoing kid-with-kid time is less likely to build familiarity and more likely to build dislike, resentment and discomfort. Remember, for every* **forced** *action, there is often an equal and opposite reaction.*

What to do about rules, then? The best guideline is to let each parent's rules apply to *their* own children. Prior to living together, house rules apply the same way they do for "good guests." If guests take their shoes off at one adult's house, then everyone takes their shoes off at the door. Whether a "no shoes" policy continues when you share a house together is something we will help you figure out, *later.* If my kids get to eat sugar cereal on vacation, then they still get to have Lucky Charms at the beach . . . even if your kids *don't.*

HAZARD ⊘ Making sweeping changes to *the rules* may seem unifying, but it will be one more in a big bunch of unwelcome and upsetting changes for kids. It's likely to make more misery than more togetherness. (This will continue to be true even after you move in together.)

Do We *Like* One Another? What Kids Need Adults to Understand

What if your kids don't like your partner? What if the two sets of kids don't get along? What if it's a disaster when everyone is together?

Whether any of us *likes* another person or not can be *complicated*. There's enormous power in *liking* or *not liking* someone whether you're four years old or fourteen (or forty). For children who need a bit more control over lives that have been disrupted by adults, it could show up *here*.

Children don't stop their limit-testing and emotional outbursts because a parent's fallen in love—or because you want to impress your partner with what great kids you have. Kids want grown-ups to know that they will still have a need to hassle, argue, fight, slam a door or two, only to come back and ask you to throw the football in the backyard as if none of that happened. You have to discern the normal vicissitudes of development (terrible twos or adolescent angst) from behaviors that are reactions to changes in your family. Or both!

If you're the partner, do your best not to assume that all this commotion is bad behavior that should be managed more effectively. Try to look through compassionate eyes as you witness a kiddo and a parent working things out *their way.*

Underneath all kinds of "difficult" behavior, kids truly want everyone to be OK. If their actions persistently defy this—shouting, swearing, defiance, tantrums, silent treatment and so forth—they're telling the adults that "something's really wrong." They're saying, *"I'm stuck." "I can't go forward." "I don't understand my feelings." "I'm overwhelmed." "I feel trapped." I" don't recognize you anymore." "I'm out of control."* Or something very close to this.

Helpful Tips for Dealing with Kids Who Don't Like Your Partner, or Their Kids

We don't like everyone we meet, so we shouldn't assume kids will like someone just because we like them (or because we *really* want them to like our new partner and their kids!). That's just the way it is. But it can sure be uncomfortable to be around people who dislike one another. What can you do?

- **No agenda.** For the moment, try to put your longing for harmony gently but firmly aside. Remind yourself to avoid pushing, cajoling or threatening in any way. Breathing will help!

- **Help kids find words.** If kids withdraw or melt down, help them find words. *"Sounds like you're mad." "Sounds like doing something together is too much right now."* In appendices A and B, you will find handy forms from the National Stepfamily Resource Center that can be used to help children express themselves.

- **Problem solve together.** Ask, *"What might help?"* You might not like the answer! *"Tell LeAnn to leave."* Instead of reacting to that, you can ponder the idea for a moment and then offer, *"Maybe we can*

> ask LeAnn to leave a little earlier so you and I can have some time alone before bed. How does that sound?" Often kids don't have an answer to "what might help?" You can offer some options: "How about more time with just us? Would that feel better right now?"
>
> - **Ease off the pressure.** It won't work if you insist that children like a new partner, or vice versa. But what you can insist on is respectful behavior and basic civility from both adults and kids. *Grown-ups have more responsibility here than kids do to create safety.*
>
> - **Talk as a couple.** Partners: Ask for hugs (in private) from your sweetie if you need them. Rejection is hard for all humans! Parents: Make sure your partner understands any change in course if you need to slow down to allow kiddos to catch up.

New relationships can be turbulent. Sometimes, there's no way out of the bumpy ride except *through*. On the other hand, sometimes you decide it's wiser to turn back or get off this path rather than continue.

Think about this. It's important. If you feel like, *"This is not what I signed up for"* or, *"This is going very badly,"* it might be time to step off the trail.

If you're still in and willing to keep going, there is good news! With good support, going a step at a time, children usually adjust *over time*.

Understanding a little more about how children's development informs their responses to new adults and to change in the family will help you help them cope, adjust and be happy. That's what we're going to do next.

WHAT DOES AGE HAVE TO DO WITH IT?

Let's look at how children of different ages typically respond to a parent's dating and eventual recoupling. There are strengths and hazards with each developmental phase.

Keep in mind that children often enter and exit typical developmental categories with a margin of plus or minus six months, so you may see developmental shifts six months early or their current stage may linger six months longer. Children also mature in different areas of development at different rates: A child may be intellectually advanced but emotionally much younger. All of this can be completely normal. (Of course, if you have concerns, please discuss them with your child's healthcare provider.)

There are six core needs that apply to kids of all ages. If you want a healthy, thriving stepfamily, this is what the children will need:

- **Secure attachment and positive engagement with parents.** This comes from regular warm, loving relationships. Over time, a stepparent may become a treasured adult who plays a part in children feeling loved and valued and known.

- **Opportunity to adequately resolve the impact of previous changes.** When changes piggyback too quickly on one another, children are at risk of all kinds of emotional, mental and physical problems. Children need time to rest and recover from changes.

- **Adults who understand and respect their basic temperament.** An introverted child, for example, may need more alone time, quiet and one-on-one time to process emotions. An extroverted child may need more interaction, activity and connection to feel happy.

- **Experiences that help them build self-confidence.** Children need age-appropriate opportunities to achieve developmental milestones and adults to guide and support them along the way: Learning how to drive at sixteen, or going on camping overnights with Cub Scouts, or being trusted to take care of the family pet.

- **Space to express themselves *and be heard*.** Kids thrive when adults can be patient, good listeners who can empathize and who can sometimes help decode what they are trying to say.

Developmental stages are like a club sandwich. Each stage is a layer that stacks on top of the one before. Sometimes, especially under the stress of family change, kids may slide back to rework a developmental step. For example, teens recycle the tasks of the first five years of life in a more grown-up way. That's why you'll see a twelve-year-old who's suddenly acting like an unusually tall two-year-old, or a fourteen-year-old who's behaving like a four-year-old. Recycling is an opportunity to go back and finish unfinished developmental business prior to the launch into young adulthood. Similarly, parents get a second chance to *do better* in guiding their children through!

We encourage you to *read through all the stages* and read them in order. That way you'll be able to recognize the essential kid-needs that thread through childhood for all kiddos. If you've never been a parent, this information may be eye opening! Being around kids can sometimes feel like you're a tourist in a foreign land and you can't understand what's going on. Whether you're a parent or not, think of these stages of development as your field guide to help you make sense of what you're seeing.

> *Before we go headlong into developmental differences we'd like to touch on a question that comes up regularly:* **"If a babysitter can put your kids to bed, why can't I?"** *Partners, especially in the early stages of forming relationships with kids, are not yet members of the co-parenting team. Especially at this stage when you are just getting serious, many co-parents find it terribly upsetting when an ex's romantic partner "fills in" for them. So... pause. Breathe deep. Slow down.*

"Cooing, Colic and Secure Attachments" (Babyhood: Birth to 3 Years)

For infants and toddlers, adults need to focus on a child's secure attachment to *both of their parents*. Lucky is the child who has a solid handful of loved ones, such as grandparents, aunts and uncles, whom they can rest into and find solace with during feeding, bathing, soothing and playing times. (Note: A dating partner does not have that role in a baby's life—*yet*.)

Separated parents of very young children need to share information consistently, and frequently during transitions. Children this young can't talk. Everything from how a their little one fed and slept to general mood needs to be conveyed by the adults in the hand-off. Ideally, care times are shorter and occur at more frequent intervals in the earliest months to support both parents bonding with the child.

If your partner has an infant, your job is to understand that your beloved and their co-parent both have to be relaxed and calm to help their baby form a secure attachment. Partners take note: The co-parent will likely be around a lot of the time to spend time with the infant. A parent might go to the co-parent's house to bathe and cuddle the baby before they are put to bed for the night.

No doubt, the sheer amount of contact time between parents of an infant can be threatening to a dating partner. Parents pay attention! The right partner for you and potential stepparent for your kiddo honors how you fulfill your parenting duties in a consistent and caring manner. Jealousy or pressure to somehow do things differently at this stage will be a death knell later.

As babies begin to spend overnights in each parent's home, the need for communication between co-parents will remain *high*. A romantic partner may find this challenging, particularly as your intimate partnership evolves and your own relationship with the child unfolds. There can be an impulse to want to box out the other parent.

The need for parents *to parent first and be a partner second* is particularly labor intensive during a child's early months and years. Dating partners will need to understand that *young children especially* almost always come first, and that includes coordinating frequently with the baby's other parent.

It helps in every way when partners are friendly and warm to kids. However, they also need to resist the urge for premature "we-ness." Playing "house" is not a great idea. That can send the message to the co-parent that you and your beloved are attempting to create a "family"—upstaging or replacing the co-parent in the child's life. You'll likely trigger a surge of animosity from the co-parent. Partners, if being very patient about this feels unbearable, this may not be the family form for you.

When can a dating partner begin to share parenting tasks of young children? For the partner who *loves* kids and has lots of experience with young children, there's a normal tendency to jump in and help. Because little ones have lots of needs, this bit of helpfulness can offer a reprieve for parents from the nearly nonstop attentiveness required. Some dads may be especially anxious to pass "mothering" on to a female partner.

Here's what we'd say during the time of "getting more serious" as you're beginning to involve kids in your relationship. (Some of this may need to continue for a while even when you do move in together):

- *Parents* **continue to provide most of the central secure-attachment tasks ("intimate parenting"),** such as bathing, feeding, cuddling, putting down to nap or for the night and meeting a child's nighttime needs.

- *Partners* provide an array of *supportive* functions both with baby and for the parent, such as entertaining a little one as the parent packs the diaper bag or packing the diaper bag while the parent is changing and dressing the baby. (And any new parent will love you forever if you offer to do laundry and pick up around the house!)

- **Before couples move in together,** unless there's acceptance by the co-parent, dating partners should not provide babysitting for an infant/toddler or be the one to deliver or pick up from daycare. This has nothing to do with capacity or safety. It has everything to do with respecting a co-parent by having the conversation first and wanting to share parenting with their co-parent, not with their romantic partner.

BOTTOM LINE

The research tells us that children are physically and emotionally healthier *when they can count on a stable, secure relationship with both of their parents, whether in one home or two. Developing secure attachment with both parents is one of the primary tasks of infancy.*

"Will You Play with Me?" (The Preschool Years, Ages 3 to 5)

The main task for kids at this age is to learn to manage themselves and expand their relationships—form friendships, cooperate, manage emotions and learn how to empathize. The main way they do this is through *play*.

These are the years of imitation and imagination—fairy-tale weddings, evil witches and superheroes; fantasy, make-believe and dress-up. Co-parents shouldn't believe everything a four-year-old says about their other home! Exaggeration is fun for a preschooler. It's a way to play with language. Preschoolers are learning about personal power and self-control. In the process, they will want to control you, your partner, the dog and their "stuffies"!

Consequently, a new romantic partner is likely to be welcomed by most preschoolers if they're a good playmate. Even the shyest child is likely to warm up to an adult who will sit calmly and watch them play or respond gently to their small invitations to join their imaginative world of teddy-bear tea parties, pirate adventures and Jedi warrior battles.

Preschoolers are naturally curious and relational. Most adults find that predictable kindness has very positive results in building a fond adult-child relationship. Because preschoolers like to control their adults, you may find a four-year-old adamantly insisting that YOU (the partner) are supposed to eat, sit or play in a certain way. If you can play along, feel free! If it doesn't feel right, take a deep breath and gently decline their offer.

Similarly, they may quickly and unselfconsciously become openly competitive and demanding if they experience a partner as an interloper on their parent's time and attention. They may display their unabashed need for attention most unpleasantly. Watch for more frequent meltdowns (especially when hungry or tired). A new partner who comfortably excuses themselves to the other room while a parent manages the upset will help the whole scene come to a close sooner rather than later. No judgment needed. Just a preschooler being normal.

Children at this age may ask questions like, *"Do you love Stevie? Are you going to get married?"* Parents need to answer concretely, *"Sweetie, I do really like Stevie. And, no, we are not getting married right now. If that day ever comes, you will be one of the very first to know! For now, we're just going to have fun together."*

BOTTOM LINE

Preschoolers are delightful and a handful. *Their little worlds are still mostly about parents, family, home and* **the familiar.** *Bringing a new adult and possibly new "other children" into the mix will be interesting as long as the secure attachment with their parent is not disrupted, play is involved and their basic needs for food, rest, play and quiet/calm are met.*

"Do You Like Me?" (Early School Age: Ages 6 to 8)

Life expands to the bigger world beyond family once kids start school. Favorite teachers, new learning, best friends and skirmishes on the playground are important topics of conversation. Children in this age group are concerned about fairness and rules—particularly the rules of friendship. For them, this is part of managing the unpredictable aspects of life in a more mature way. This age group cares a lot about the question, *"Do you like me?"*

This is also an age of rapid development in many areas. Most noticeable are the physical changes that unfold. Rapid brain growth brings many new skills, talents, interests and thoughtfulness. This is the age when some children might first contemplate what happens when we die.

Family continues to be the safe base from which they venture out and confidently explore the outside world—school events, sports teams, sleepovers at friends' houses. They rely on family to support them, to notice them and to celebrate them.

In this context, you can see that introducing a new adult and their kiddos into the family can be both interesting (new friends!) and disquieting (more change!). Lucky for most of us, at this age the new *friends* feelings are likely to prevail when adults allow well-paced, positive and activity-based relationships to unfold. Overall, children this age are fairly easily accepting of those who are caring and accepting of them. Because family is still central, they very much want positive relationships with those who are close to or potentially a part of their family.

A partner participates in family activities like a good guest. Relationship-building efforts are most successful when partners move nice and slow. Although this is important with kids of all ages, especially as a child gets older it becomes increasingly important to let the child take the lead on levels of direct engagement—within reason. Helping with tasks that support the parent rather than providing direct caregiving with children is still the better choice for partners. For example, rather than suggesting, "*It's time for lunch*"—hold back. Allow the parent and kids to determine it's time for English muffin pizzas and then feel free to participate alongside, taking your cues from kids and parent.

BOTTOM LINE

During these years of rapid growth, kids can fluctuate between periods of equilibrium and periods of disequilibrium *that can persist for a few months as their inner world adjusts to their growth spurt. Kiddos need gentle guidance and continued support as they navigate their developmental changes.*

"Please Don't Make Me Different" (Middle Childhood: Ages 9 to 10)

Three areas of sensitivity stand out for this age group: The strong desire to be *normal* (which includes having a "normal" family); the need to be accepted by their friends; and the need to feel competent (with school work, athletics, socially and so forth). For these reasons, and perhaps others that we don't fully understand, the entry of a parent's new partner becomes more challenging for children over the age of 9.

This is the age when friendships outside the family become increasingly important, especially same-sex friendships. Children travel in packs of friends and have a strong desire to belong. Peer pressure escalates for these kiddos. Bullying can become pernicious if not monitored appropriately. Anything that calls attention to differences can signal reasons for other kids to have commentary and judgments, which opens the door to self-consciousness, concern and real (or imagined) targeting.

Simultaneously, this is an age where peer support helps protect a child from feeling *alone*. With increased ability to share with one another, increased empathy and increased sense of the importance of relationship, a child's peer group (and their families) can be the very safe harbor for a temporary boost during a period of family stress.

Especially from this age on, support groups led by school counselors that bring together kids with divorced parents or kids in stepfamilies can be very helpful. Children this age are likely to feel particularly defensive when faced with failure, mistakes or incompetence. (They can be very sore losers.) This may make some kids reluctant to have a nonfamily member attend a sporting event or performance at school. For other children, having people come watch is experienced as "the more the merrier." What's important is learning what *this* child needs and how best to support them.

Be sensitive to children's worries and concerns about whether their family differences *feel like* a source of embarrassment or an uncomfortable difference. Having a parent's romantic partner attend events may trigger worries about how the child's other parent will feel or self-consciousness about being the *only kid who* (fill in the blank). Along with being sensitive to the child's concerns, be sure this age kiddo feels like they have a good answer to the inevitable question, "*Who's that person with your dad/mom?*"

Parents, remember: Children in this age group very much want *you* (their parent) to remain involved in their school, sporting events and activities. With their growing autonomy, it can be seductive to think they prefer—or will be fine—with less of you. Not true! If your dating relationship or developing partnership begins to disrupt your time with your child in a meaningful way, please reconsider your pacing. Find ways to stay engaged with your child. Make "just us" time. Have thoughtful conversations about friends, peer pressure, personal goal setting, homework management and success in school and respect for themselves and others. Do things with them.

New partners can bond with kids in this age group by helping them learn something they want to master: How to shoot a three-pointer, make a favorite meal or assemble a model plane. And, as always, new partners can help by leaving room for kids to hold on to their parents. As the relationship strengthens, kiddos at this age may intentionally turn to a more "neutral adult" for advice, to talk through feelings or for input on life experience. That's the "bonus" for partners in thoughtfully building connection.

BOTTOM LINE

Notice that the older children get, *the more they exercise their own autonomy in decision-making with increasing independence from the family. With more age and experience, a child's own perspectives and feelings become more defined. This means successful adults will build relationship in a manner that takes the child's preferences and pace into consideration.*

"I Do Not Want This!" (Tweens and Early Teens: Ages 11 to 14)

Tween and early teens are likely your toughest customers when it comes to a relationship with a new adult (and their children). They're rarely interested in sharing their time or expanding their family membership. With so much going on physically, emotionally, mentally and socially, adding *anything* to their personal drama may tip the balance to "overwhelm!" This can be a challenging age even without divorce and new partners. Self-consciousness about body changes, rapid growth, hormonally induced emotional swings and the increased importance of peers and peer-pressure put kids this age in a developmental pressure cooker.

Girls generally, and particularly in this age group, struggle more with a parent's recoupling than boys. Early teens (not unlike toddlers) can simultaneously be screaming "NO!" at you about something, while insisting you're not paying enough attention to them.

Parenting preteen and early-teen girls under the best of circumstances can be demanding; adding a new partner and their kids is more likely than at younger or older ages to be challenging. Identity for girls at this age is deeply entwined with relationships. A new partner's entrance may strike at the heart of their core sense of being. When a twelve-year-old girl protests, "NOT NOW! NOT *NOW!*" She means it. She will need the empathic, patient help of the adults in her life to manage this transition.

New partners are likely to experience a child's intense possessiveness of the parent. This may show up as wanting to hold the parent's hand, urgently needing to sit beside them or climb onto their lap, much like a younger child. It often shows up as strong rejection of, or withdrawal from, a new partner.

This kiddo may need lots more one-to-one time with Mom or Dad, and a lot less "family time" with the new partner. Loyalty binds can become very intense as well, with girls feeling particularly protective of a vulnerable co-parent.

Boys also present challenges during puberty and early teen years. They are generally less reactive to stepparents. In fact, the presence of a stepdad can sometimes lower conflict with a solo mom. Boys at this age have big feelings, though they may not choose to share them (often big physical feelings). Hygiene may become an issue and working with pre- and early-teen boys on managing their body changes adequately can be frustrating.

Do your best to ride a pubescent child's physical or emotional roller coaster without criticism, hurtful rejection or giving up. Stay steady. Peer pressure coupled with a still-immature prefrontal cortex (the area of the brain responsible for predicting consequences and problem solving) can result in disastrous outcomes if a parent's bumper pads don't remain firmly in place. Parents, keep your expectations clear and express them in a firm and friendly manner; involve the early teen in goal-setting conversations and conflict resolution. Listen, listen, listen . . . and then help them walk forward constructively. Maintain boundaries and supervision and remember: *This too shall pass.*

First forays into sexual exploration show up in this period. Early teens may be especially unnerved and uncomfortable at the thought of your bedroom door closed with some other adult behind it as their own sexual impulses are coming forward. Caution to parents: Try not to upstage your teen's own early dating experiences or overshadow the importance of their discomfort by flaunting a lover. *With this age group, you may want to be especially private and discreet for a much longer time about your sexual relationship.*

For new partners, kiddos need you to walk *very softly* into their family system until they've discerned *on their own* that you're a welcome addition. The more cajoling an adult uses to get early teens to accept a new partner, the deeper the resistance is likely to go. So, no pressure. Let time and a new partner's friendly, unpressured presence do the work. Accept as part of the territory that one day you're cool and another you're unwanted. Cinch up your ego, because you'll be tested by an emotional whipsaw.

Relationship building may often take the form of a "do-me-something." "*Can Liza (new partner) take me to the mall if you can't?*" If this is okay with you, go for it. Use these opportunities to build connection. But please watch your own assumptions that the *child owes you* something because of these favors.

Partners, again, you may be (really) tempted, but…try not to Monday-morning-quarterback your sweetie's parenting style! It's one thing for you to gently and curiously share your concern. It's quite another to push them to lay down the law with a "disruptive or difficult" (struggling) child.

BOTTOM LINE

Central to this developmental stage is moral development,
starting from rather black-and-white, right-or-wrong childhood morality
and evolving into more mature ethical considerations (continued
into the next developmental stage). Both parents and partners may
be subjected to judgment, moralizing and strong opinions (some, or
most, unwelcome!) by children in this developmental stage.

"I Don't Really Care, Just Don't Make Me..." (Middle Teens: Ages 15 to 17)

In the midst of acne, high school dramas and hormone surges, middle teens have to deal with the embarrassment of a parent in love. "Augh! Why me?!"

The ways kids this age respond to the new partner vary depending partly on how they adjusted to the loss of the first-time family. The quality of their relationship with their other parent also makes a big difference. For instance, some middle teens take on the role of the absent spouse with one or both of their parents. A daughter may become mom's best friend or dad's primary support person; a son may become the "man of the house" at mom's or his dad's buddy. Introducing a new adult can exaggerate a teen's need to bring stability to their changing family, or to *right* perceived injustices for a parent who was *left*.

If co-parent strife remains high, middle teens are more likely than their younger siblings to take responsibility for what's happening in the family. If one parent is unable to recover from the split-up (even after years), the now middle-teen child is more likely to feel pulled into becoming the emotional caregiver. In these cases, a new partner's entrance creates an especially painful loyalty bind.

These emotional forces can make it really hard for kids to build a relationship with a parent's new partner. This is when we often see residential schedules fall apart, as when a teen resists transition to a parent's home because a new partner has become part of the equation. Because this age group can vote with their feet more so than younger kids, we often see resistance to transition between homes if the teen's loyalty bind is intense, if parenting in one household is compromised or if a new partner has prematurely stepped into discipline or is responding critically to the teen.

That said, middle teen kids are often curious about an interested adult who is available for nonjudgmental conversation. If you are a new partner, you may be able to engage this age group by expressing interest in what they are thinking and about what moves them (even if it's foreign to you) and participating in some of their interests.

As children grow out of early adolescence and into middle adolescence, the prefrontal cortex (again, the area of the brain responsible for thinking through results and planning for the future) now begins expanding rapidly. There's more self-control. Kids in this middle-teen age range become somewhat less impulsive than younger teens. Their capacity to express their feelings with words improves.

Other pressures may emerge about such things as peer relationships, college acceptance, uncertainties about future and career and increasingly complex sexual and friendship experiences. These more adult-oriented concerns often bring emotional responses that are more internal than the external emotional roller coaster of early teens. If a teen struggles with depression or anxiety, stay close and connected. Professional help may be needed.

BOTTOM LINE

*We have rarely met a middle teen looking for **more** parents! They are in fact doing all they can to accept parenting from, build independence with and come back to the parents they already have.*

"My Feelings Matter, Too" (Young Adults and Adults: College Age and Beyond)

Although the divorce rate has dropped and evened out in the U.S., divorce in midlife and beyond is becoming increasingly common. Older re-couplers often think, "The kids are finally out of the house, they're adults now, the dog's dead, the divorce won't matter…it's finally *my time.*" Well, the divorce *does* matter. Parent-child relationships are still critically important, as is *family identity.* Remember, children's growing-up years are rooted in this particular family. Adult children feel it when their roots are yanked out.

College students need to know that whatever is going on at home, they're still free to pursue their own likes without worrying about their parents and siblings. This is one reason why the idea "we'll split when our kids go to college" is actually very hard on kids. Do not announce a parental split or big changes in the fall when college students are just leaving for school. Rather, try to make major family changes when kids are home with parents and there is ample time for the family to process the changes together.

When children return home at holidays, they need to feel they're walking back into their familiar home. This may often mean no *new* romantic partner at Thanksgiving dinner! Adult children may be surprisingly *inflexible* about including a new partner in favorite rituals. They may be more likely to articulately express their likes and dislikes. They are also even freer than late teens to vote with their feet and stay away in response to a parent's unavailability, a new partner they don't like or who comes on too strong or a strong loyalty bind with their other parent.

"No, you may not…"

Angeline (age 30) said straight up to her dad about his grandson's upcoming third birthday party, "No, you may *not* bring your new girlfriend." She meant it.

Good or bad, adult children have decades of connection to treasured family rituals, habits and many things that really matter.

New partners who can honor this by making room to be absent or recede into the background during important family times are likely to find a way in *eventually*. Both parents and partners will need to accept that parent-child "just us" time is just as important for adult children as for children at every age. Pressing forward too quickly or insisting on inclusion too early may inadvertently create scars that require considerable healing down the road. (Chapter 16 will take an in-depth look at later-in-life re-coupling.)

BOTTOM LINE

Parent-child relationships are lifelong. In many ways, the feelings of young adults about a parent's divorce and re-coupling are surprisingly similar to their younger counterparts. They often need many of the same things from their parents, including taking things a step at a time and providing "just us" time with a parent.

Children Can Adjust and Thrive...
and So Can the Adults

"I am learning every day to allow the space between where I am and where I want to be to inspire me and not terrify me."

—Traci Ellis Ross, actress

Kids of all ages have to find ways to adjust to a slew of changes when their parents separate/divorce. Then they have to adjust to more when parents re-partner. Wouldn't it be great if adjusting were as simple as bringing a bicycle seat up or down to fit the rider? Unfortunately, for the adults it's more like having to learn a wickedly complicated dance with no previous dance experience and no one to demonstrate the steps. There's going to be a lot of tripping over your own feet and crashing into everyone else until it becomes familiar. Parents, smack in the middle of the shuffle, are practicing some fancy footwork—spin to the right to meet their children's needs at every age; spin to the left to support their beloved; spin some more to keep peace with a co-parent. Dizzy!

Partners are trying their best to step back and make space for kids and parents to dance together. Even though partners may often feel like wallflowers waiting on the side to be invited—awkward!—refraining from cutting in and waiting to reach for comfort from their sweeties is their graceful move in this dance when kids are around. Meanwhile, partners are inching their way into relationship with those kiddos.

Children's need for their parents' focus and attention is lifelong. It may be that one day the partner (and their children) will be embraced as a cherished member of the tribe, but it's not a certainty. Right now, the best that can happen is for everyone to try to dance their parts as smoothly as possible. And, try not to tread on too many toes!

* * * * * * * * * * *

Walking toward a family with children already on board is not for the faint of heart. For most budding stepcouples, there are definitely instances when you feel like you're juggling hissing cats. But then there's a family game night and everyone is laughing and getting along, providing a magic-elixir moment that fortifies you for the next leg of the journey. Karen once saw a bumper sticker that read: "ENJOY WILDLIFE: Have kids!" As you move toward including kids more in your lives together, you may at times feel like you're lost or walking in endless circles. When that happens, a sense of humor can really help. In the meantime, ENJOY WILDLIFE with partners and kids and all that love has to offer.

Chapter 7

· · · · · · · · · · ·

Co-Parents as Allies, Not Enemies

*"The best security blanket a child can have
is parents who respect each other."*

—Jane Blaustone, blogger

As your love relationship deepens and gets more serious, it's not just about the two of you. The kids are now part of your dating experience, at least from time to time—and even when they're not, they're texting or calling because they've left their soccer cleats and they need them *now*. Also, you're beginning to comprehend the impact of the children's *other* parent (the co-parent) on you and your relationship as involvment with the kids increases. If you're *both* parents, that could mean you each have a co-parent. Complicated, right? Co-parents will play an increasingly influential role in your lives together, overtly or covertly, through the children. Forever.

We know this can range from supportive to difficult. There are lots of things you can do to ensure the relationship with a co-parent is constructive. If it starts out rocky, you can move it to a better place.

In this chapter, we'll strategize ways to manage the places where partners and co-parents (and their extended kin) may start crossing paths, including the sensitivities to watch for during family events where all the adults are present. Skillfulness now helps lay the groundwork for the co-parent's acceptance of the new partner as a member of the parenting coalition later!

Chapter 8 will turn to the tender and sometimes perplexing issues that come to the fore when a co-parent has died and is no longer physically present, but, of course, remains emotionally part of the family.

🌹 **Co-parent dynamics** are likely making themselves felt ever more intensely now as "first buds" of a core stepfamily challenge.

DIVORCE ENDS THE INTIMATE PARTNERSHIP, *NOT* THE PARENTING RELATIONSHIP

Ex-spouses who share kids remain inextricably connected *until death do they part*. And even after. The co-parents' skill levels and degrees of post-divorce adjustment will determine how it plays out. Will they attempt to occupy front-row seats on each other's lives? Will they glower at each other from opposite corners of the boxing ring and refuse to communicate? Or will they make space for each other to thrive in new relationships while stepping up to their co-parenting responsibilities?

Responses to ending a primary relationship can vary hugely. This can be a relief for some, and it can bring terrible grief for others. It's easy to judge, criticize and feel impatient with your sweetie's co-parent if their devastation makes some emotional messiness, and particularly when it bleeds into *your* primary relationship. But we're here to tell you that an emotionally messy co-parent is *not going away*, as much as you'd like them to. That can be a tough pill to swallow.

Not surprisingly, a new partner can exacerbate tensions with the co-parent. Seeing an ex move on can sometimes unleash some bitterness or stir up unresolved grief. Even if the co-parenting relationship wasn't contentious before, it may be tested now. The new partnership may also stoke an ex's feelings of being replaced, both as a partner and as a *parent*. Co-parents are now exposed to and involved in each other's new lives in a new and uncomfortable way. Children chat about the new partner and the worried co-parent swallows hard.

Co-parents' struggles impact kids! A fraught co-parent can all too often "leak" their upset feelings around the kids, significantly increasing children's sense of feeling torn—caught in the middle—between the people they love.

Worse, a parent who is feeling particularly raw and insecure about the loss of their former intimate partnership or who fears being replaced, may, openly or subtly, influence a child to dislike their co-parent's new romantic partner. This creates loyalty binds for children that make it terribly anxiety provoking—impacting their ability to relax at school, during activities, with friends and at home.

Some children who feel pulled to protect their emotionally distraught parent may go as far as refusing residential time with the parent who has a dating partner. Co-parents begin blaming each other for the child's refusal, and the whole family system is thrown into turmoil.

BOTTOM LINE

*As Karen reminds co-parents, "Children may have two homes, but they have only **one** life—one precious childhood." We do NOT want children to live **in a battleground** of co-parents struggling over who can do what and **with whom** in their own home. These wars are upsetting for adults; they are **devastating** for kids.*

Messy co-parent relationships are rarely a single battle won and done. They are also rarely resolved in court. They are best resolved when co-parents make the extra effort to maintain their agreements, work together and keep children out of the combat zone. If a co-parent can't do their part, you will need to do yours to ease children's pain. Carving out more "just us" parent-child time may help ease loyalty-bind pressure for kids, along with easing back on time for children with a partner (for now).

When Relationship Mis-Steps Disrupt the Entire Family

Todd and Michael adopted their twin boys from Guatemala when the kids were 9 months old. Michael agreed to quit his job and stay home to focus exclusively on helping the boys adjust during this wrenching transition.

Two years later, Michael was in full swing managing the twins' busy schedule of play groups, parent-toddler learning sessions and speech therapy to address their speech delay. Meanwhile, Todd recognized that he and Michael were losing their connection.

Todd spent longer hours at work as he and Michael silently avoided bringing up what was obvious to them both. They were slowly disconnecting.

When Todd finally announced he wanted to move out, Michael wasn't surprised. Still, he was devastated. They both knew how vulnerable the twins were to separations. They worked hard to create a residential schedule that would feel steady and reliable to the boys. Todd came back to the family home to do bedtime routines two evenings a week. Slowly, the boys began spending part of each weekend at his new home.

Michael and Todd collaborated very well as co-parents, and the boys were adjusting remarkably well to the transition.

During this time, Todd began hanging out with Yaval, a new associate at his law firm, who was also burning the midnight oil. Yaval and Todd began spending time together on the weekends with the boys . . . without telling Michael. A few months into this arrangement, one of the boys said to Michael, "I don't like Yaval!" We've all seen this movie before. Michael *knew* what was happening the moment he heard Yaval's name.

Michael was now doubly devastated. He railed at Todd on the phone after the boys were tucked in.

"It's TOO soon! I can't believe you're exposing our kids to a new person who might leave them!"

"You're overreacting!" Todd said, defensively. "You're just angry that I've moved on and you haven't."

Michael hung up, but not before telling Todd he was no longer welcome in his home. Ever.

The boys, of course, heard *every word* of the furious conversation. Even if they didn't understand what it was about, they felt the angry, hateful tone.

Soon after, both boys started wetting the bed again. They refused to get dressed in the mornings and acted up in play group.

BOTTOM LINE

When co-parents fall apart, children often fall apart, too.

You may be wondering how long a co-parent's upset or concerned feelings should delay your plans to move forward together. Our advice is to be reasonable and respectful. Pay close attention to the stress children may be holding or hiding. As we discussed in Chapter 5, parents do need to give their co-parents a heads up when kids are going to meet a new romantic partner. If the situation with a co-parent becomes highly conflictual, seek guidance from a co-parenting coach on how best to respond without giving up or retaliating.

RELATIONSHIPS BETWEEN PARTNERS AND CO-PARENTS

Co-parents are a *fait accompli*. It's a done deal. This can be a bit intimidating—if not outright scary—for a partner under the best of circumstances. If things are rocky with a co-parent, partners may feel like you're an innocent bystander caught in the crossfire of a war you didn't start and didn't bargain on. As the new partner, it might help to know the dos and don'ts of relating to a co-parent.

> ### Helpful Tips for Partners about Letting Your Actions Speak Louder than Words
>
> Kids need the freedom to share all aspects of their lives with each of their parents. A new friend, dating partner or pet may spark lively conversation between kids and parents in each home.
>
> - **Always speak constructively** and respond with respect whenever the child's other parent comes up in conversation. Openly and sincerely acknowledge the co-parent's importance to children.
>
> - **Check all criticism and judgment regarding a co-parent at the door**. Aligning against the co-parent may momentarily feel like a great game of "us against them." You may imagine that you're winning. But we promise this will backfire.
>
> - **Defer all parenting decisions and discipline to the children's parent**. At this juncture, we can't stress too often that it's way too early to try to parent other people's children.

- **Keep gift-giving modest**. It's great that you want to be generous with your sweetie's kids, but make sure these are gifts that are acceptable to both parents. If they have a rule about no video games, don't buy video games! If either parent doesn't want tween girls wearing makeup, don't gift them with a makeup kit!

BOTTOM LINE

*To the co-parent, a new partner is a new, potentially influential adult whom they have **no say** over. Take time to build a good reputation as a responsible and measured person who isn't there to disrupt the co-parent's relationship with their children or to interfere with their parenting. But rather show up as someone who adds to the circle of healthy adults in a child's life.*

Sharing Information about the Partner with the Co-Parent

Any good parent wants to know the basics about people involved with their children. Co-parents are no different. That said, agreements between co-parents about how a new romantic partner will participate with children are all over the map. Some co-parents include guidelines in a parenting plan. More often they're informal understandings. When things go well, both parents maintain them out of mutual respect for each other and interest in the children's safety.

As your romantic relationship deepens, a co-parent's need for information about a partner and their involvement with kids will naturally increase. We advise giving co-parents a heads-up whenever a partner's participation with the children moves to a new level of responsibility—when they provide occasional supervision at home or pinch-hit a swim practice pickup. The goal is to help maintain respect and trust between the co-parents.

For dating partners, it can be intrusive to have your personal information shared with another adult. You might be thinking, "Boundaries!" Fair enough. But keep in mind, this information is *not* for your sweetie's "ex," but rather it's for the kids' other parent. Big difference! It's best to talk openly together about what you feel is appropriate to share and what is no one else's business. Parents also need to be transparent with partners about the established co-parenting agreements so that the partner understands what is expected—what and when information about them is shared and how it will be used.

Helpful Tips for Typical Information-Sharing Agreements

Some co-parents come out of their divorce process with enough trust and good will that they never question their co-parent's judgment. Others want no information at all because it's just too painful. And still others make (hopefully reasonable!) agreements that ease concerns and speak primarily to children's safety. (Note: All these tips assume that there is no threat of violence by either parent. If there is, the parent and new partner will require much more privacy.) Here are some options:

- **First names:** As a parent, when you let your co-parent know you plan on introducing kids to the new partner, you might share your sweetie's first name. If your partner also has kids, you might also share the first names and ages of the children.

- **Relationship information:** How serious the relationship is. Are you just starting to get serious? Are you talking about moving in? Getting engaged? Not the details. Just the headlines.

- **Full names:** As the relationship deepens and activity-time with the kids increases, some parents share the partner's full name and address, especially if you all are spending more time at the partner's home. If there's any chance the partner will be driving the children alone, some agree to share a copy of the partner's driver's license.

- **Basic background check:** Some co-parents agree to share a basic background check (with social security number redacted) before they allow a partner to spend the night while the children are in residence.

Keep in mind that abundant sources of web-based information are a few clicks away. A former partner can pull up all kinds of details about a co-parent's new partner from social media sites. Karen very much supports pulling that process out of the shadows, eliminating the need to go through the backdoor (it's available anyway!). Patricia advises considering whether the information may be unnecessarily triggering for a raw ex-spouse and could be used in inappropriate ways.

No right answers here. We encourage you to make your wisest guess about what is useful and reasonable to share about new partners with co-parents. And what's going to be best for your kids.

When Should a Co-parent and a Dating Partner Meet?

The short answer is: Whenever the three of you believe it would be helpful. Some co-parents have specific agreements in their parenting plans about when they'll meet each other's dating partners. Some parents wait for the child's other parent to express interest in meeting the partner. Others may try to avoid that experience at all costs!

It is nice for children when the adults can have at least a brief, friendly meet-and-greet by the time a romantic partner is a frequent participant in their lives. Again, not all co-parents are open to this. Likewise, some partners aren't eager to meet the kids' other parent.

This journey progresses *at the pace of the slowest hiker*. Insisting on participation before one of your fellow travelers is ready to climb the next part of the trail can create misery. That said, making a connection between co-parent and dating partner can sometimes do a lot to ease a co-parent's fears about an unknown person spending increasing time around their children. A parent often initiates a conversation with their co-parent about meeting the new partner when the time feels right. Or the partner might make the opening with a gentle approach: *"It would so great to meet you; I've sure enjoyed getting to know your children a bit better. They are such lucky kids to have you both!"*

Partners, if you do meet the co-parent, try to make it as easygoing as possible. Maybe grab a coffee or take a walk together. Your goal is just to break the ice so that the children's other parent feels safe and respected. You're saying, *"I just want you to know that I respect that you're the kids' parent and always will be. I hope that I'll be a good support. Since I'm going to be spending some time with your kids, I'd love to meet you. You've done a great job with these kids. They are really wonderful human beings."*

Beginning to Include Partners at Children's Events and in Public Places

Calibrating how much *and* how soon new partners get involved in children's community events deserves thoughtful consideration. In the first year after parents separate, we generally recommend that children's extracurricular activities be reserved for parents only. No dating partners in tow unless everyone has agreed beforehand that it's time. This isn't a hard-and-fast decree, but rather a general rule to help kids and parents adjust after a split-up.

Partners are often confused about their role (and their "rights") in these situations. The motivation to attend may be three-fold: (1) you want to participate and be included in the child's life, and (2) you want to protect your partner from a difficult co-parent or (3) you want to prevent your sweetheart from the loneliness of going solo. We sure understand! Trust that in time, building memories together with the children will proceed more smoothly when everyone is ready.

A potential underbelly: For partners—you may also want to be seen in public as the parent's new love. Perhaps you want to show that you have been *chosen* over the co-parent. For parents—you may want a new sweetie on your arm for this same purpose. Those motivations will lead to some serious wrong turns that land you in some very nasty potholes. Please be mindful and make decisions that won't sow resentment and anger in the co-parent relationship.

Knowing when to assert your rights versus remembering to do *what's right* can get fuzzy. Every single one of us hits that place where we just want to draw the line and say, "I have a right to…and *you* can't stop me."

We ask that you look through the lens of *what will be right for children* when attempting to figure out how to handle kid events. Holding back (as opposed to jumping in) can require serious muscle and considerable restraint from all the adults. If you feel you are on the path to building a thriving stepfamily, do what you can to get off on the right foot. Step lightly.

Helpful Tips When a New Partner Attends a Child's Event

With time, conversation and the buy-in of kids, and possibly also the co-parent, the partner may be welcomed to attend school plays, baseball games and so forth. Here are a few guidelines:

- **Be sensitive to a co-parent's preference** for distance. If your paths cross at public events or during transitions, be reserved in a gentle way.

- **Remain child-centered.** All adult eyes need to stay on the kiddo. You are there to champion their participation. NOT to accomplish ANYTHING else.

- **Keep any signs of romance on the *cool* side.** *No flaunting affection!*

- **Be a friendly adult in greeting the children.** But be aware of how threatening a new partner can be to the other parent. No overly solicitous fawning.

If you're the lucky couple whose co-parent is open and accepting of your relationship, these meetings will be considerably easier. Either way, remember those insider/outsider dynamics we referred to earlier? They will definitely be in play in situations involving kids and parents.

Partners on the Outside with Co-Parents

Partners, doing the *partner* role well by being thoughtful and patient and nonjudgmental and putting your best foot forward won't always protect you from emotional bumps and scrapes. The fact is, the path will get rocky at times, and it may stay rough for long stretches. It's hard sometimes when the insider/outsider dynamic comes to the fore (with you squarely in the outsider position). For instance:

- **You're relegated to the *sidelines*.** A child races over to their parents after a volleyball game or band performance and ignores you completely. *Left out!*

- **You're not needed.** Co-parents often have to function as a "parenting pair" with a child's coach or teacher, leaving partners on the outside looking in. *Lonely!*

- **It's not your turn for attention.** A "family" event may feel strange and hard for you, but your partner cannot comfort you without triggering their ex-spouse. In fact they may even awkwardly distance you to try to create some comfort for their co-parent. *Hard!*

- **You hang back** as an outsider to your sweetie as an outsider when you're around their former established community. Your co-parent's mutual friends, neighbors and extended kin need time to adjust to your presence and sort their loyalties. You might even be shunned by the co-parent's loyalists. *Unfair!*

Try to keep in mind that over time, slowly, these things could change. It might be one step forward, two steps back for a while, but progress is definitely possible. Be sure to ask for comfort from your sweetie and also cultivate other relationships and activities where you feel valued and engaged.

What does success with a co-parent look like? "Success" does not necessarily mean that a new partner will immediately feel comfortable and welcomed by the co-parent. Success means that all the adults come together in agreement that *protecting the kids from strife and celebrating their accomplishments is everyone's top priority.*

LIFECYCLE EVENTS AND OTHER SPECIAL FAMILY EVENTS

Parents may naturally want their partners to be part of family celebrations and other special events that involve children and both parents. Likewise, partners may also wish to participate. Building memories around cherished events begins to weave your lives together in rich ways.

You're getting more serious about your relationship, yes. But to the children's extended family, your partner likely does not count *yet* as "family." This is still the dating stage, which means very different roles at family events. At weddings, funerals, confirmations, christenings, bar mitzvahs and quinceañeras, there might not be a place yet for the partner next to the parent. While the co-parent is front and center with first-time family members, the partner may be watching from the sidelines. We sincerely hope that in time that will change. But for now, *disappointing.*

Even if your relationship is fairly well established, consider the impact on your co-parent when you show up as a couple. If you're determined that their feelings shouldn't influence your decisions, think again. An upset co-parent will likely upset the kids. It is possible (perhaps even likely) that everyone (including the partner) will be happier if they stay home and do something fun with a friend.

Larisa Is Neither Fish Nor Fowl

Jason and his new love, Larisa, had been dating for eight months. The children had met Larisa and all was going well. Although Jason's former wife, Veronica, was not hostile to the children's relationship with Larisa, Jason knew she had been struggling.

Jason and Larisa were invited as a couple to attend the wedding of the children's former babysitter, Ashleigh. Since Ashleigh and her family were longtime family friends, Veronica was also invited, as were the children.

Jason very much wanted Larisa there as his date. He was looking forward to introducing her to his friends. Larisa wanted to be there, too—she liked Ashleigh, and she wanted to meet Jason's longtime friends. But she was nervous about Veronica. How would she act? Would it be uncomfortable? As the date approached, they were still undecided. Should they go together or not?

Jason and Larisa thought long and hard and realized that going as a couple to this wedding would be really hard for Veronica. It was likely to stir up a pot of misery, which they both knew would spill over onto the kids.

This was just not the time . . . not *yet*.

FOR PARTNERS: SOME THINGS TO THINK ABOUT

Being a romantic partner to a person with kids can feel like training for sainthood. Partnering with a parent means living with frequent kid disruptions, potentially unresolved family dynamics, particularly with co-parents, and unfamiliar family history that regularly makes you the less-important newcomer. The whole kit and caboodle can be overwhelming and disheartening. Thank goodness, with love and connection, the journey is worth it.

If you are a partner and you struggle with whether you're "good enough" or truly "chosen" by your sweetheart, an involved co-parent may make those feelings unbearably intense at times. If you find yourself feeling particularly miserable, consider finding a good therapist, preferably somebody who knows something about stepfamilies. (See appendix C for help with this.)

And, again, before you go further, do consider whether this extra relationship dynamic with a co-parent is right for you. No blame and no shame if it isn't. Just a heads up that *a co-parent is forever,* not only for your beloved and their kids, but also for *you* if you stay in this relationship.

WHEN A CO-PARENT IS UNABLE TO ADEQUATELY PARENT

For children, hope (often) springs eternal that a missing parent—*even a totally inadequate one*—will return as a healed, loving parent. They will hope for this even when they've been disappointed over and over again. Often, it is hard for adults to get that most kids will *always* long for a *version* of their other parent—someone who is safe and present, who puts the kids' needs first, who really sees them and is proud of who they are, and who expresses love for them.

If you're the on-duty parent, you may be furious and disappointed with your missing, drug-addicted, or otherwise unreliable co-parent. You might struggle with the pain you see in your children's eyes after each disappointment—another broken residential visit, a parent showing up drunk or high, a parent suddenly moving away to another state to live with a new partner after a month of dating. Learning how to deal with your own outrage and frustrations is key to being able to support the kids with theirs.

Here's why this is so important: Children have complex feelings about a "broken" or missing parent. Children often feel relief and grief when they are separated from a parent due to mental illness, addiction, abusive behavior or incarceration. They also often carry considerable shame (*"My parent is an embarrassment."*) or internalized blame (*"I wasn't loveable enough."*). When other adults communicate disgust or judgment about the missing parent, they only further humiliate the child and deepen their aloneness.

An abandoning or abusive parent leaves children feeling pulled between opposite parts of themselves. Adults often wish kids would just eliminate the part that wants to hold on to wishful thinking or deep attachment. Not possible. In fact, pressure to "give up on" a parent often leaves kids painfully alone with their mixed feelings.

No Room for Judgment

If you're the new partner, it's easy to judge and to feel outraged on behalf of your new love and their kids. Those are moments to bite your tongue! Try to acknowledge the difficulty (*"This is tough."*) without adding to an already fraught situation (*"She's an irresponsible drunk!"*).

You may find yourself feeling you can be a better replacement. You can be a positive, reliable, caring adult in children's lives. However, your more precious contribution may be helping kids to hold *both* their pain *and* their love for an inadequate parent.

> ## A Helpful Tip for Kids Struggling with an Absent Parent: The "Language of Parts"
>
> *It can be a surprise, and an incredible comfort, to kids to realize that more than one thing can be true for them at the same time.* Adults can help a lot with this. For example:
>
> - *"I'm kinda betting part of you is so relieved that you don't have to be scared about Daddy's drinking anymore. And, he's your daddy. I bet maybe another part is missing him a lot. Maybe sometimes it even feels like there's a hole in your heart?"*
>
> - *"It sounds like one part of you wants to run away FAST from Mom when she gets angry. And another part wants to hold on tight because she's your mommy! Those are opposite parts, and both are real. That's a lot for a human to hold. I'll help."*
>
> - *"Is it like there's a part of you that's furious with him, and a part of you just wants him to scoop you up and hug you? And maybe there's another part that just doesn't get why he would do those hurtful things? Both are true. Let's make room for all those feelings. I'll help."*
>
> - *"Does part of you worry that you'll grow up and be just like her? And does another part of you wish you weren't related to her at all and another part feel guilty for thinking that? It's totally normal. I get it."*

In these difficult circumstances, new partners who don't compete with the missing parent can help kids heal. Just understand that it's one step at a time. Honor the sacred place that even a distressed or incompetent parent holds in a child's heart.

When kids are involved, co-parents are part of the package. If you move forward, your stepfamily will include the children's other parent forever, and *for better or for worse*. Even co-parents who were abusive or abandoned the kids emotionally or physically. Children hold both parents in a special place in their hearts for all time. Can you join in with all that love?

Chapter 8

. . . .

When a Child's Parent Has Died

In grieving families, "stepparents are the and, *not the* instead."
—Diane Fromme, author of *Stepparenting the Grieving Child*

What if a child's other parent has died? Both of you may wish that a new adult partner could step in and replace the missing parent. The desire to make what appears to be missing *whole* again makes all the sense in the world. That's not possible.

You might be thinking that your path forward would be easier when a parent's died—no co-parent to coordinate with, no need for kids to move back and forth. Well, likely not easier. Definitely different.

Every story of love and loss is different, and every path to becoming a stepfamily when a co-parent is dead has unexpected twists and turns.

So, what *is* possible, what will be *different*?

Read on: If this is your situation, *holding the memories of their missing parent* with children will be an integral part of your job description.

PARENTS CAN'T BE REPLACED

Every stepfamily journey has its unique challenges. When a parent, and spouse, has died, it leaves a hole in the hearts of both children and the remaining parent.

If you're the widow(er), you know the absence will be felt for the rest of your life, in some way. Hopefully, you've taken things slowly, step by step, and are working through your own acute stages of grief so that now you're open and ready to fall in love again.

Note to self: Your kids may not be *as* ready.

Parent-child relationships are forever. A parent who has died continues to occupy considerable heart space for children. One of the most important tasks of grieving is finding a way to forge a new kind of relationship with the person who is gone. It might be writing them letters or following religious traditions and rituals that remember the dead. It might be through doing activities the parent liked or doing volunteer work for a cause that the parent cared about. Whatever it is, the child's relationship to the deceased parent is lifelong. Adults can do a lot to support this healthy task of grieving, regardless of how long ago the parent died.

The Faces of Grief

Barry had been dating Alva for about six months and was just getting to know her children, Caitlin, age 10, and Kerry, age 8. Alva, a widow, had been raising her children alone since her husband had died two years earlier. During their second dinner with Barry, Caitlin burst into tears, threw her napkin at Barry and dashed upstairs.

"What was that?" Barry asked once he and Alva were alone. "Did I do something?"

Alva said quietly. "No, you haven't done anything wrong. But, I may have. I put your place setting at their dad's chair. I think that may be what's going on. I need to talk with the children about this. I guess I'm trying to figure out how to make a place for you without taking away their Daddy."

"That was the beginning," Barry said later. "I should've gotten it then. I thought I could fix it for them," he said sadly. "I just wanted to make them feel like they had a dad again."

Barry meant well, but as he began spending more time with Alva and her girls, the harder he tried to engage with Caitlin and Kerry, the more sullen they seemed to become.

One night at dinner, the girls were especially rude. Caitlin ignored Barry when he asked her how her math test had gone. Kerry talked back to their mom. Exasperated, Alva sent them up to their room, no video game time.

Later, when she went up to talk to them, Kerry burst into tears. "I miss Daddy," she said between sobs.

GRIEF HAS A HEALTHY COURSE. BUT NO FINISH LINE.

Grief changes over time. In the early acute stages of grief, it may feel to both children and the remaining parent as if they're hiking through a forest that was devastated by fire. Charred trunks stand as monuments to the past, ever present on the path.

There is often a period of living in that charred landscape when the waves of crying come and go, sometimes interspersed with periods of numbness. *"I walked around just stunned for a while,"* Alva said. During this time, parents will need a huge amount of support themselves, and they will need to find the muscle to focus extra attention on their shocked and grieving children.

It is critical during this time that adults continue to be sensitive to how both the internal and external process is unfolding for a child. Giving lots of space to cry, talk, remember and be silent—to *be* with the loss until they find their legs again to walk out.

The next stages of grief may be less clear to delineate. Adults and children begin making sense of the loss, how it occurred, and how to find their way forward. Grief groups for adults and children can be immensely useful after the initial shock and pain of the loss have lifted. Being with others who share this experience can help everyone in the walk back into life.

> **HAZARD** ⊘ We never want children (or adults) to get trapped or stuck in the early acute stages of grief. If you're concerned about your child, please consult a grief counselor who specializes in children losing a parent.

Over time, something unimaginable starts to happen in that burned forest. Those charred remnants of an earlier time start to show signs of new growth. Fresh green sprouts up from the blackened forest floor. Slender grasses and young trees begin to take root. Life goes on. *And* the place the parent held remains clearly marked as children and the remaining parent build a new world model that includes losing a parent (and spouse) before they're ready while simultaneously finding ways to hold precious and alive their sense of their missing parent. Still, the entry of a new partner may trigger another round of grief, as it did with Alva's children.

As the months and sometimes years roll forward for the grieving family, the gripping aspects of grief let go. The young trees and new grasses begin to fill in around the memories. When the loss is held lovingly, children (and the remaining parent) can live fully in a place of no fear of bringing up the past, no worries about shedding a tear when a memory floats in. They don't have to push away their deep longing to be held or to have another conversation with the person who is gone. Healthy adjustment allows for sweet grief to coexist alongside the excitement of all that's yet to come.

He Is Here with Me

Rachel's father died when she was seven. She was now 23, about to get married. As the date of her wedding approached, Rachel found herself thinking about her dad, wishing he could have met her fiancé, Peter, and feeling sad that her Daddy wasn't there to walk her down the aisle.

One night when Peter was over for dinner, Rachel pulled out old family photo albums. She and her mom lovingly looked through them with Peter and Eric, Rachel's stepdad of fourteen years. Pictures from when her dad was alive. Rachel and her mother told stories to Peter and Eric, sometimes laughing, sometimes crying.

"I wish I could have known him," said Peter, pulling Rachel in for a hug.

On their wedding altar, the couple placed a few framed photos of her dad, so he was there with Rachel, witnessing her vows. Her brother wore one of her dad's favorite ties to the reception afterward. The whole family brought her dad to the wedding by talking about him and letting those memories be woven into the present.

"He was there," Rachel said, "standing by me and loving me. And he's here now."

BOTTOM LINE

Grief does not have a finish line—it simply changes over time from painful, gut-wrenching grief, to a period of adjusting grief, to becoming a sweet-grief attached to fond memories, and, often, an ongoing absence mixed with a kind of nourishing presence.

ENTERING A FAMILY AFTER A PARENT HAS DIED

Partners may find themselves walking into a living memorial to the departed parent. It's normal for children to treasure objects that remind them of the dead parent. They want photos prominently displayed around the home of their family when the parent was alive. They cling to some of the comforting patterns from before the death.

It's totally understandable that these things help children feel connected to the missing parent, but it can be really tough on a new partner. Remember that insider/outsider dynamic in Chapter 5? The outsider experience can be hyperintense for partners in families where a parent has died.

Develop comfort as best you can with this *very different way* of loving a partner and embracing their children. You'll also have to come to terms with living with a ghost of sorts—an important *presence* who still lives on in the belongings, rituals and memories of those still here.

> ### Tips for Helping Children Keep Their Missing Parent Near
>
> The stepparent's role is not to replace a missing parent. It's to help them hold their missing parent close as a nourishing, loving presence.
>
> - **Grief needs to be held tenderly, not hidden.** The kids may look "fine." Adults may want them to be "fine." But kids who have lost a parent are changed in very important and fundamental ways. Be curious about what's on their minds and what wrestles around in their hearts as they come to grips with the day-to-day realities of missing a parent who is gone. They're simply growing into the spaces that should have never been left so soon. This is an amazing act of courage and resilience.
>
> - **The goal is not to get kids to "let go."** Children do not need help "moving on" as much as they need help holding on to the love and care and specialness of their missing parent. Walk with them there.
>
> - **Bring the missing parent into your lives.** *"What would your mom be doing if she was here?" "What do you miss most about your dad?"* Look through *family photo albums with children, watch videos, sit with kids and look at family pictu*res on their phones with them.

- **Talk to children about how they want to handle photos and objects of the deceased parent.** "*Where should we make a place for Dad's guitar? Remember how he used to play it with his feet to be silly?*" "*Which are your favorite pictures of you and Mommy together? Let's put those in a scrapbook that you can open it any time and see her smiling at you.*" Both widowed parents and new partners may feel the urge to clear the space of reminders as they make a place for their new life, separate from the past. This will likely be hard on kids. It will not actually smooth the way for the whole family to travel forward together.

- **Pay special attention to special dates on the calendar:** The parent's birthday, the day the parent died, the child's birthday, holidays, Father's Day or Mother's Day, father-daughter or father-son events at school. Anticipate and talk about what it might be like for kids. "*Tomorrow is the day your mom died. Let's think about how we want to mark it.*" "*It's your dad's birthday. Would you like to draw a picture for him?*"

- **Talk about the missing parent during celebrations and other special occasions.** At graduations: "*Somebody is missing, huh. Your daddy would have been so proud of you. I think he's watching. What do you think?*" At a child's wedding: "*How shall we include your mom? Would you like to wear something of hers? Where shall we put a photo of her so she can be here, too?*"

- **Support children's need to connect with their missing parent's extended family and friends.** They maintain precious connections to the kids' missing parents, and they have stories and information about the deceased that kids crave. "*Did you know when your mom was your age she planned on becoming a rock star?*" "*Your dad and I used to sneak out at night and . . .*"

- **Expect unexpected resurgences of grief.** A child opens a drawer and finds a half-written grocery list in their dead mom's handwriting. The loss sweeps over them again, triggering inconsolable tears. A widowed parent comes across an old wool sweater that belonged to their dead spouse and a wave of grief hits hard. Stand near, comfort and help them befriend the grief like a visitor that will return from time to time. They, and you, will become more familiar with the waves, the ebbs and flows. You will all come to identify these visits as a kind of sweetness—never having to worry that their loved one will be lost to them. "*Safely in my heart.*" No deleting.

> - **Assume that, throughout their lives, children will have moments of missing a parent.** Over longer periods of time, sadness may pass, may no longer be on the surface. There's a gentle combination of love-infused memory combined with an ache of the heart for the one who is now gone and a poignant reminder that premature deaths leave us changed. Sweet grief.

Adding To—Not Replacing

A few months after he met Alva's kids, the anniversary of their father's death approached. As Barry said later, "I was finally starting to get it."

Barry, who was Jewish, said to Kerry and Caitlin, "In my religion, tomorrow is what we call your father's *yahrtzeit*: the anniversary of when somebody you love has died. I want to share something with you. It's called a *yahrtzeit candle*. We light it on the evening before the day that somebody died, and we put it in a special place. It burns for 24 hours. Every time we see it we can remember your dad. Would you like to put it here on the table, next to his picture?"

The girls looked at each other. Kerry nodded and Caitlin pelted upstairs. A minute later she walked carefully down the stairs holding a model airplane. She solemnly placed it next to the candle. Barry had seen the airplane in their room but didn't know what it meant to them.

"Our dad made it," Caitlin explained proudly. Barry was aware that it was the first time either of the girls had talked to him about their dad.

"Huh." he said tenderly. "How did he make all those swirly designs on the wings?" he asked.

The girls shyly explained how their dad used a wood burner.

"He was a talented artist," Barry said, sincerely impressed. "I wish I could have known him."

The three were silent together, looking at the airplane. Barry noticed that it was a comfortable silence. He didn't feel pushed away. He felt their tentative trust, at least for a moment. A gift!

They lit the candle together.

"Tell me about some more things your dad made," he said softly.

When Young Children Lose a Parent

In families where the children never had a chance to know the deceased parent because they were too young, stepparents can and do often become more parent-like figures. Even so, kids still have a sacred place in their hearts for their missing parent. And they still do best when the adults understand just how precious that place is.

"But I already have a dad!"

Emanuel's papa died in Iraq while his mother, Rosa, was pregnant with him. Rosa kept framed photos of the boy's dad on the mantel and shared stories about "Papa" as Emanuel, grew up.

When Jorge came into Rosa's life, Emanuel was three years old. The big man scooped up the little boy and showered him with a "dad's" love. He married Rosa and happily stepped into the roles of husband and "daddy." Pictures of "Papa" remained scattered through the house, with new ones of Jorge, Rosa and Emanuel. Rosa continued to tell her son stories about his papa. Over the years, Jorge could recite these stories to the boy, too.

Just before Emanuel turned 16, Rosa and Jorge decided to surprise Emanuel by making Jorge his legal parent. Jorge would adopt Emanuel and they would all share the same last name. No one would ever question again whether they were a *family*.

At a special family dinner, Jorge delivered a heartfelt speech about how important it had been to him to be able to be Emanuel's "Daddy." He ended by saying he would be honored if he could make it official by adopting him.

Emanuel looked bewildered.

After an awkward moment of silence, the teen finally said, "I love you, Daddy, but I *have a dad.*"

WHEN BROKEN PARENTS DIE

When a parent dies and leaves behind unresolved anger, brokenness, upset and ambivalence, the loss becomes much, much more complicated for kids. When we love someone who hurt or disappointed us and they die, we grieve for what's gone *and* we grieve for what we never had. Children simply don't have the emotional bandwidth to hold all the pain of both what they have lost and what they never got. The section in Chapter 7 about using "the language of parts" to help kids name and hold all the complexity may provide some very helpful tips for supporting children in this situation.

LIVING WITH YOUR SWEETIE'S DECEASED LOVED ONE

For many adults, too, honoring a deceased partner remains part of daily life. Many of the tips for making a relationship with grieving children also apply for loving a person who has lost a spouse. The missing partner's birthday, their wedding anniversary, their child's college graduation or wedding will often open a door to more grieving—even decades later. For parents, even looking at their children will stir up wishes that the missing parent could be there to share in the moment. Partners who can bear to help open the door to grieving will likely feel closer to their sweetie. And despite having sorted through clothing and cleaning out personal items before they started to date again, a widow or widower will still want to see reminders of their deceased love through the home, such as an important knickknack on the bedside table.

They're Not Just Cowboy Boots

Gladys had lost William, the love of her life, to cancer. Fifteen years later, she met Clay. She was thrilled to love again. Her children, now adults, were delighted for her. Clay respected that William was still an important family member. The photos and mementos didn't bother him one bit. Not even William's cowboy boots, which Gladys dusted every week and returned to the corner of the bedroom where she could see them every morning. The boots were one part bittersweet reminder of Glady's first husband and one part décor. Clay accepted that loving Gladys meant living with William's enduring footprints on her heart.

BOTTOM LINE

Loving a parent who has lost a spouse to death
*differs in many ways from a parent who is separated/divorced.
You have to ask yourself,* **"Is my heart big enough to hold the
love of my partner for someone who was here before me? Is my
compassion big enough to hold the kids' ongoing loss and grief?"**

WHEN A CO-PARENT DIES AFTER THE NEW COUPLE FORMS

Sometimes a child's other parent dies after a new partner has entered the family; in some cases, long after. All that we've said about co-parents remaining part of your lives forever is still true—with an extra twist. The tips about helping children grieve and honor missing parents also still hold. Children will certainly need the support and presence of their remaining parent *and* all of the other adults in their lives.

If you are the remaining parent, despite having chosen to end your relationship with your children's other parent, *you* may also be grieving. Although you're not officially a widow or widower, and whether that relationship ended well or poorly, you had children and a life together. A partner, perhaps by now a longtime stepparent, may also be grieving, depending on the length of their own relationship with the parent who has died. A loving stepparent can be an immense support to the grieving family.

· · · · · · · · · · ·

The death of a parent temporarily catapults both children and loved ones into another world. Shock and disbelief may mix with heartbreak and sorrow. And, for some, relief that a loved one is now free from pain after a long illness. Partners can play a very special role in helping both children and parents heal. But it is not about becoming a replacement. It is about helping children and partners keep the missing person near as a nurturing, caring force in their lives and honoring those who live on through cherished memories. As poet Thomas Campbell wrote: "To live in hearts we leave behind is not to die."

Chapter 9

. . . .

If Your New Relationship Began with an Affair

"There is no disguise which can hide love for long where it exists or simulate it where it does not."

—François de la Rochefoucauld, 17th century French author

If your new relationship began as an affair, you are likely facing some particularly difficult challenges with ex-spouses and children, not to mention with extended family members and friends. You may be surrounded by judgment. It can be terribly awkward and uncomfortable.

If you are the parent, joy and relief that your new relationship is finally out in the open may sit right up against guilt and enormous tension throughout your family. If you're the partner, the delight of finally being together openly may be tempered by storms of blame, fury and adamant rejection by many people in your lover's life—including their kids.

If you're both parents—well, you get it. Not easy!

Here's the situation in a nutshell: Parent, former partner and new partner are, and will be, bound together through the children. Affairs include all the dynamics we have been talking about, and those we'll describe in Part III if you move in together, but they will likely be intensified. This chapter offers perspective and pointers to help you carefully choose your footing across the difficult terrain that an affair often creates.

PUTTING AFFAIRS IN CONTEXT

An affair may have started as an innocent connection and then progressed to full-blown attachment of the heart. And that changed everything for the entire family. No excuse. No justification. But *lots* of complexity.

Judgments about affairs abound. Americans, particularly, have a knee-jerk tendency to condemn the person who stepped out on a committed relationship—the *cheater*—and new partner—the *home wrecker*. Many believe there's little room for compassion when someone falls in love in this way. There's generally even less forgiveness for the deceptions that typically accompany an affair. Keep in mind that a purely emotional affair—no sexual relationship but all the other intimacies of the heart—still counts as an *affair* from the point of view of the person left behind. No easy way through here.

Nonetheless, conditions for an affair are often co-created from a long series of disconnections and dissatisfactions in which *both* partners contribute to widening gaps that erode closeness. Still, the death of a marriage at the hands of an affair makes the ending considerably messier than deciding to divorce without another person waiting in the wings. Neither children nor the person who was left may be ready to accept the new relationship for a *very* long time.

SHOULD WE TELL?

Our advice is to be discreet about affairs through the time that you remain married and through your separation/divorce process. We co-authors differ on the meaning of "discreet."

Karen advocates for transparency when it is asked for because deception can profoundly aggravate a person's sense of betrayal and pain. A spouse who intuits that something is amiss can end up floundering in a crazy-making soup of self-doubt and mistrust. Coming to grips with the fact of the affair sooner is likely to prevent worse backlash later, when the truth comes out.

Patricia acknowledges that this is true. *And*, she suggests that because knowledge of an affair can be so provocative for a spouse, kids end up getting terribly hurt. If affair partners do their best to keep their intimacy a secret through the ending of the marriage and for enough time after separation and divorce, the ex-spouse's and the children's emotional distress will have time to settle.

That said, we are in *full agreement* that an affair may greatly intensify the level of hurt, betrayal and outrage for the person who was left. And we fully agree that a relationship that began with an affair requires a much longer waiting period before introducing children to a new partner.

So, what do you do to repair the damage and get on a good track as a couple? Your readiness to move forward and your confidence in your new relationship are likely not good indicators of just how slowly you will need to move. It also doesn't lessen the repair work you'll both have to do.

Helpful Tips for Repairing Damage from an Affair

Take the time to clean up (as best you can) the mess affairs make. Give "repair work" your fullest attention and effort, even when you'd rather hide your head or run away. Let's break it down as best we can:

For parents:

- It will go better for all if you treat your soon-to-be-former spouse/partner with dignity and respect.

- If your affair was discovered, your ex may demand that you answer direct questions and expose deceptions. Even if this is uncomfortable, it's now best to try to be honest, though at the same time gentle, with direct answers.

- As a parent, your main focus needs to be on stabilizing your children's two-home family life.

- It's best for kids, for ex, for new relationship and for you, if you do your part to complete your divorce process as respectfully as possible.

For partners:

- You'll need a big (really big) helping of patience. This is going to be a long journey. If you're pushing hard to move forward now, you may need to reconsider whether this can work for you.

- Your kindness will help! Your sweetie's ex-partner may be at their worst and acting terribly toward you and your sweetie. Remember that being in a lot of pain makes it awfully hard to behave well. Your kindness and compassion, even if it's rejected, will go a long way to keeping the situation from deteriorating, and it might quietly help in ways you can't even see.

For both of you:
- Better to be especially discreet about sharing your good news about being in love. Appearing in local restaurants together or splashing your pictures across social media sites will precipitate unnecessary drama, pain and confusion.

- Likewise for moving in together. Even when it may seem "the time" for the two of you, please take it slow to give everyone around you a chance to adjust.

- Can we say this enough? When it comes to involving children, take things very, VERY slow. You can expect that a parent will need at least a year or more to reestablish solid relationships with kids after an affair.

- Prepare for the long haul as a couple. Find lots of ways to comfort each other and hold each other. You chose this new relationship for a reason, but it's going to be a rocky journey with some tough climbs. Carve out lots of places where you can feel each other's tenderness and care.

KIDS AND AFFAIRS

An affair does *not* fall into the "kids need to know" category. Younger children have little context for adult relationship issues and may be confused about affairs. Even young adult and older adult children don't have the emotional understanding or adult road time to truly appreciate how a long-term committed partnership might come to such a difficult end. Consequently, we strongly discourage disclosing unnecessary details. Unfortunately, especially disastrous for everyone, the partner who was left may use the affair as a weapon of blame.

It's up to both parents to protect kids from *provocative adult information about a parent*. It doesn't matter if the information is true, it's bad for kids to be burdened with it. Children will come through much better if *both* parents can stay focused on the underlying reason for the divorce, such as, "*We couldn't love each other the way we needed to.*" Not, "*Dad was a horrible person so I had to leave him.*"

And definitely not, "*Mom is leaving us for another person.*" No! The parent isn't leaving the children; the adults are ending the marriage. Big, big difference.

Children's Fears, Emotional Upsets, Tightened Loyalty Binds

If, despite your efforts, the kids learn about the affair, their healing process will become infinitely more complex. This is particularly so if the discovery is coupled with blaming, judgment and adult fall-aparts. Sometimes kids overhear conversations about or pick up signs of an affair, which leads them to feel confused and afraid that something *bad* has happened. Much worse, their other parent may disclose the news in a fit of despair, and, so tough for kids, continue leaking their pain. This typically drives a destructive wedge between kids and the new couple.

Loyalty binds after an affair can be impossibly tight for kids. Start with the fact that children often side with the parent they see as more vulnerable. Then consider that kids will likely perceive the parent who had the affair as the one who "broke the rules," wasn't honest or *did this* to the family. Children may go so far as to refuse to spend time with the offending parent. That cutoff can last for years.

> ### Helpful Tips for Responding to Cutoffs
>
> Don't despair. This may be a long (long) road, but we have seen many, many families come through. Here's our advice to parents:
>
> - **Continue to send birthday cards, holiday greetings, congratulations** on an accomplishment (soccer team wins the division title; child graduates from high school). No long messages. Just, "*I know you're hurting. And I'm still your dad/mom and I'm proud of you.*" Do not expect a response. So hard, we know.

- **One on one** may be the only way that children will spend time with a parent who had an affair. If they are willing to see you at all, children are often not the least bit ready to be with a new partner. Start with the most available kiddo. Engage each child one by one. Over time, one kiddo may become willing to include the new partner. This, in turn, may open the door for a more reluctant one to join in.

- **The same holds with extended family and friends.** Start rebuilding relationships one at a time with the most available, and slowly expand. Friends and family may also be unwilling to meet an affair partner, sometimes for a long while. Being forced to leave your new partner in order to repair damaged important relationships can be painful for both of you.

Responding with Age-Appropriate Information, Not Explanations or Excuses

Because children are often deeply upset by what they see as one parent "cheating" on the other, parents can become very defensive and feel compelled to respond in ways that are not useful to kids. It helps if you watch your impulse to:

- Give kids long, complicated explanations
- Retaliate by openly blaming the other parent for a multitude of wrongs, hoping the kids will better understand or at least spread the blame
- Pressure children to get on board with the parent's new relationship
- Give up entirely and pull away because it's too complicated, or you feel too guilty
- Or some combination of all the above

It is natural for you to *so* wish your children could see that you're still the same loving parent you've always been. We've watched parents desperately try to minimize or dismiss a child's distress by saying, "*But, honey, we would have been getting divorced anyway!*" or "*Can't you see how happy I am?*" Doesn't help. Doesn't work.

Helpful Tips for Both Parents in the Face of an Affair

When possible, both parents pull together to assist upset children. When a co-parent feels bereft and betrayed, working together on behalf of the children requires significant effort. Here are some considerations:

- **A co-parenting coach or skilled therapist can be invaluable.**

- **Ideally, both parents sit down together** and determine what's best for their children to know and what details are best kept *between the adults.*

- **The only explanation kids (*of any age*) may be ready for** is something very simple like, *"Relationships are complicated. Sometime, maybe in a lot of years, I hope this might make more sense. I totally get that it doesn't right now. I'm sorry for all the hurt."*

- **For older children who know (or will find out) about the affair**, the very best option is if both parents can disclose the affair together and can acknowledge that the affair was not the *cause*, but rather an outcome, of a distant or distressed marriage. This kind of skillful joint disclosure requires considerable strength from the partner who feels left. However, it ends the need to keep secrets, eliminates the fear that the children will find out from a third party and will be left alone with painful information. And sets the stage for supporting kids well.

Helpful Tips for Parents Talking with Upset Kids

What kids who know about the affair need most is empathy. *"I get it— this is so painful." "This is so hard to understand." "Tell me more about what this is like for you." "You are SO mad at me."*

- Kids need you to be present with them, openhearted and ready to hold their pain.

- They need you to slow down and allow them to catch up.

- You do *not* need to relinquish the love of your life or your hopes and dreams—you *do* need to give everyone a chance to find their balance after the earthquake.

- You may need to apologize. Fully. Apologizing is *not* saying, *"I'm a bad person."* It's saying, *"I'm aware that my actions have caused you hurt. Lots of hurt. And I care."*

AN AFFAIR IS A CHALLENGING STARTING POINT FOR BUILDING A STEPFAMILY

Recovering from betrayal can be prolonged and brutal. It will likely take some time for the co-parent to find their footing. The unsettled co-parenting relationship can make it especially difficult for kids to adjust to two-home family life.

You are caught in a whirlwind of family drama. Prior to disclosure, you were shielded from the family's outrage. Once the affair is exposed, the tension and anger bombarding you can be overwhelming. For some, the tumult is a rude awakening. If you had weeks, months or even years of undistracted time with each other, it can now seem intruded on by others who have an opinion, a judgment, a feeling. They're all trying to recover from the shock and disappointment and uncertainty that now reverberate through the family. But this can be the furthest thing from what you imagined it would be like.

Affairs leave you more isolated as a new couple. Right, wrong or indifferent, relationships that begin as affairs often start with a severe deficit of goodwill and support from extended family and friends. Some formerly close family members and friends may refuse to meet the new partner (sometimes ever). The "offending" parent may suddenly become unwelcome at family's and friend's events.

Once the affair is discovered, there's no putting the genie back in the bottle. It's really hard to build a relationship under all the scrutiny and pressure.

Affairs often make insider/outsider positions *much* more intense. One-on-one time for parents and their children (no partner present) may need to continue for years. Also, while the parent may gradually be included again in their kids' extended family and community life (invited to attend a brother-in-law's funeral or a child's graduation), the partner may not be welcome. It just depends on the people and the situation. What the couple can do is manage their expectations.

- **All of this leaves new partners as outsiders even longer.** You can prepare for this reality by purposefully building a support system outside your lover's world. It's an opportunity to lean on your own friends and family and to focus on your own favorite activities during the months, and maybe years, ahead. You may feel frustrated and impatient. You may wish the everyone would get over it and get on board with the new reality of your relationship. Not gonna happen.

- **Meanwhile, parents are stuck insiders.** If you're the parent who had the affair, you're going to be juggling a lot: Staying present for the raging feelings of your kids, attending to your co-parent's ongoing upset, managing the judgment and blame of your extended family and maybe even your friends. Repairing these relationships usually must be done alone, without your partner, leaving them feeling that much more hurt and left out. Meanwhile, you're trying to stay nurturing and connected to your partner (who may be increasingly impatient) a*nd* managing your own jumbled feelings of guilt, regret, relief, worry and hope—plus your own pent-up pressure to finally move on!

In the midst of this harrowing journey, remember that you turned toward each other for good reasons. Take regular intentional breaks from the intensity of other people's reactions to be together. Parents: Open your arms to your partner's feelings of rejection and invisibility and outsider-ness. Partners: Hold your sweetie's painful insider-ness and the need to show up for so much hurt and confusion. *Keep reaching for each other!*

RESOLVING AND MOVING FORWARD

The repair process is likely to be long and slow. Skipping over it will only increase the pushback—more conflict with co-parents, more withdrawal and hostility from kids and more rejection from friends and family.

> ### One More Very Helpful Tip about the Power of Apologizing
>
> Please do not underestimate the importance of apologizing for the hurt you have caused. For parents (and sometimes for new partners), making amends to co-parents and children can be a powerful salve that lessens the drama and softens judgment.
>
> - **Be humble.** This is not about groveling or humiliating yourself. It's about seeing with clear eyes and open heart that something you very much needed to do for yourself has hurt other people and disrupted a family. Let them know you care about that... about them. *"I see the pain I have caused. I am so sorry."*

> - **Make amends.** This may include returning any money from joint funds that you spent on an affair. This includes showing up reliably to children's events after using the excuse of working late to meet your lover. And this includes listening with compassion to children's howls of pain. Hard!
>
> - **Stay present.** This will require strength to stay present while those who are hurting work through their feelings. There is often a very strong pull to want everyone to get *over* it and move on. But investing the time to heal the broken hearts with children, a co-parent and extended family will make future stepfamily possible, so do your best to stay in there, or keep coming back, even when you want to flee.

Recovery Is Possible

And it will take time. *Lots and lots of time.* Relationships with children and extended family often heal one or two at a time. If you're lucky, and you proceed thoughtfully, several years down the road some former partners are even able to say, *"It was for the best."*

∙ ∙ ∙ ∙ ∙ ∙ ∙ ∙ ∙ ∙ ∙

"The heart wants what it wants. It doesn't seek other people's opinions; sometimes not even your own," writes Steve Maraboli, a motivational speaker. Following your hearts into a satisfying relationship that began as an affair can be a gifted twist of fate—both treasured gifts and some very hard hiking. Along with love comes unintended effects that can turn the connection of a lifetime into a nightmare of judgment and upset. If you can proceed slowly, with sensitivity and awareness for what kids and co-parents are going through, you can repair, rebuild and move toward the healthy stepfamily you desire.

PART III
BECOMING A STEPFAMILY

> *"A journey of a thousand miles begins with a single step."*
> —Lao Tzu, Chinese philosopher

You and your love and the kids are now about to take a major turn in the road. You're about to move in together—step on to the path of becoming a stepfamily. While you catch your breath from the climb you just made through parts I and II, please take a moment to congratulate yourselves on getting to the place where you feel ready to take this big step. It took relationship muscle, yogic flexibility, Olympic-level teamwork . . . and love.

Now you may be trying to imagine what this next part of the journey will feel like—the feelings of gratitude and delight in your couple relationship and your shared pleasure in the thriving and healthy kids. You even maybe picture an easy relationship with co-parents or an opportunity to build one that works.

Can't we just BE there already?!

There's more climbing ahead—you can't skip any of the necessary steps without risking injury. The good news is that we lead stepfamilies up this trail all the time. We won't get you lost!

Part III is your trusty guide at this new altitude. We will show you how to traverse the scary places and find the right pace up the steep parts and help you remember to pause and catch your breath when the going gets particularly tough.

Let's take a quick look at the map and describe the landscape we're about to encounter. Chapter 10 orients you to the major differences between first-time families and stepfamilies. Although stepfamilies come in many shapes and sizes, they all share the same distinctive architecture. You need to know this so you'll understand the origins of the *five stepfamily challenges.*

We'll be covering each of those five challenges in Chapters 11 through 15. We've already pointed out when they budded during the "in between" time of getting serious. When you move in together, the buds burst into full bloom. We'll provide research-informed guidance about how to meet each challenge. And we'll help you get unstuck if you get mired in the emotional mud.

What are the five stepfamily challenges? The first is helping children with losses, loyalty binds and *too much* change. Adults are often thrilled to be moving in together and may have no clue what kids are going through. Unfortunately, there is misguided advice out there that urges couples to concentrate on their couple relationship and assures them that the kids will "come along." No! That path leads to a lot of wrong turns and suffering. Your stepfamily will work best when you focus *equally* on your intimate partnership *and* the kids. Chapter 11 will basically remind you to make sure *both* these shoes are firmly laced to prevent trip-ups.

The second challenge is managing the insider/outsider dynamic that comes with living in stepfamily territory. One person in the couple is going to be pulled to the inside while the other is going to be pushed to the outside. It can feel impossible to be together the way you both want and need. Chapter 12 reveals that it's *definitely* possible! Keeping your survival kit of communication skills with you at all times is the key.

The third challenge is all about not wandering off the path that's designated specifically for your role as the parent or as the stepparent in the stepfamily. Who's in charge of kids? Who's responsible for setting limits and following through? There's a steep learning curve on this part of the trail, and Chapter 13 helps you step carefully and deliberately so you don't step over the line.

The fourth challenge is about working with co-parents and taking the steps to build a parenting coalition. Co-parents are an inevitable, often changeable and sometimes volatile atmospheric reality of stepfamily living. Chapter 14 offers ideas for how to put yourselves in the best position to maintain sunny weather between the children's two homes and gives you strategies to avoid being caught in any extreme temperatures or violent storms.

The fifth challenge is about building a shared stepfamily culture. Chapter 15 teaches you how to think about making space for everyone's different and sometimes conflicting habits, routines, traditions, rituals, beliefs and sense of home.

Rest assured, these are *normal* challenges for stepfamilies! Tackling these five stepfamily challenges begs three basic questions:

1. Do you have the flexibility to form a family around not only your relatives and your partner's relatives but also the children's relatives?

2. Can you relinquish your first-family dream in exchange for a next-time-family reality?

3. Can you tolerate a decision-making structure for children that has one primary member outside of your relationship, your home?

Chapter 16 will address the ways the five stepfamily challenges unfold in couples who come together when they are over age 50. If you're on this path, you'll come across some surprising scenery. For older recouplers the usual complexity of a stepfamily now includes multiple generations.

Sadly, even after lots of hiking, not every stepfamily decides to stay together. If you need to let go of your stepfamily dream, Chapter 17 will help you end well. Even if you feel disappointed as you head to separate homes, we'll help you see new paths that make it possible to restructure and honor relationships in a skillful way.

The truth is that stepfamily is not the destination; it's the journey. We conclude *The Stepfamily Handbook* with a helpful description of the life-cycle of a stepfamily. You'll be able to look ahead and draw your own map with a panoramic view of *your* stepfamily over time. It will help you for years to come.

Falling in love . . . easy! Staying in love . . . *challenging*. Hopefully, along with dry socks and a flashlight, you also packed your sense of humor. Keep it handy, next to the nuggets of wisdom you've been collecting during the climb through parts I and II. It will help turn this trip into a grand adventure of a lifetime!

Chapter 10

How Stepfamilies Differ from First-Time Families

"Things should be made as simple as possible, but no simpler."
—Albert Einstein, physicist and Nobel Laureate

THE EARLY YEARS OF STEPFAMILY ARE NOT FOR THE FAINT OF HEART

Making the decision to live together, perhaps to marry, is often the natural next step for a couple in love *when there are no children on board*. Deciding to live together *as a stepfamily* may more like taking a flying leap! That's because it is a much more complex story.

No two stepfamilies are exactly alike, of course, yet it's helpful to hear about the lessons other couples have learned on their journeys to becoming a stepfamily. We'll use Ben and Fran to illustrate what two people in love face when they step across the threshold with kids on board.

Fantasy Meets Reality: Ben and Fran Move In Together

Ben and Fran fell head over heels in love when they were in their mid-thirties. Fran was child-free and had never been married. Ben was divorced and had two children: Annie, age 11, and Luke, age 7.

Like any in-love couple, they were eager to take their relationship to the next level, but they tried to be diligent and took it slowly. Over the course of two years of dating, they took baby steps and gradually integrated the kids into their relationship. On the second anniversary of their first date, they announced their engagement. Shortly afterward, they found the right house. They moved in together, hopeful and excited to create a happy next-time family with each other and the kids.

Fast forward to seven months later. Things at home were not nearly as rosy as they both had imagined it would be. Instead of new-family bliss, Ben and Fran were disagreeing all the time about how to handle Ben's kids. The lightning rod was Annie. The thirteen-year-old had become sullen and withdrawn during her residential time with her dad and Fran. Fran took offense at Annie's rude behaviors. Ben, who had always been close to his daughter, sensed that Annie was struggling and believed she just needed time to adjust to all the changes in their family. But he was also painfully aware of how hard it was for Fran to have a grumpy teenager in the house. Ben's going easy on Annie upset Fran, who let Ben know that she wanted more of a say—at least a vote!—in how Annie was being parented. She had lots of advice about it for Ben (and she wished she could tell Annie's mom, Rebecca, a thing or two as well).

Since Ben and Fran had moved in together, Rebecca had become crankier with Ben and more critical—challenging him on small things like letting Luke go too long between haircuts. Ben tried to be patient, but he felt caught in the middle among his kids, his fiancé and his co-parent. He felt torn about Fran's pressure to be a firm parent and her insistence that he take a stand which he knew would aggravate Rebecca (and it did!). He couldn't see a clear way through all these competing needs.

This is a very typical scenario for couples living together with kids on board. The expectation that your stepfamily can become a "blended family" reflects more *hope* than reality. Wading into family life with kids, especially in the early years, is not a smooth blend at all. It's more like a tossed salad—emphasis on the uncomfortable emotional tossing!

Couples who were diligent in preparing themselves and the kids for the journey, and who have good communication skills, and who genuinely love each other, often expect that they've got this; their "blended family" won't have problems.

Hmm.

THE ROUTE TO "FAMILYHOOD" IN FIRST-TIME FAMILIES

Stepcouples in love are rarely aware of what *might be different* for their stepfamily. They often expect that relationships, rituals and routines will not be much different from any other "family."

The differences are *big* and important.

First-Time Family Development: One Plus One

The beginning is different for the couple in a first-time family. Unencumbered by the demands of parenthood, first-time couples have some uninterrupted intimate time to build trust and develop their own language of words, gestures and actions that express their love, desire, tenderness and vulnerability. They can become accustomed to each other's ways of expressing frustration, anger, disapproval and disappointment. Hopefully, they begin learning that they can turn toward each other with their joys and their hurts—how to be a team in life.

Over time, these couples build *middle ground*. Middle ground is a foundation of established patterns, habits and rhythms of doing things together. Middle ground provides easy pathways to connection, comfort and identity.

First-time families share a single history of becoming family. All couples bring their respective expectations about family across the threshold. First-time-family couples typically have that early period of intimate togetherness, just the two of them—no kids in the picture—to begin integrating their individual histories, family cultures and personal styles.

Ben and his first wife, Rebecca, had time to sort out "my family" versus "your family" and decide "how *we'll* do things" before Annie was born. Will they wash the pots and pans while they cook, or wait until after the meal? When will they decorate the Christmas tree? On the day after Thanksgiving, or wait until Christmas Eve? How to load the dishwasher, whether or not to get a cat, how much time to spend as a couple together at home or out with family and friends. In first-family beginnings, couples are, hopefully, *equals* in the process. A little at a time, before kids arrive, they begin resolving some of their differences, accepting that others are here to stay, finding their own middle ground and creating a foundation on which to build their family.

Children in a first-time family enter hardwired for attachment to *both* parents, *and* vice versa. They arrive into an already-established couple. That's how it was when Annie was born. Her parents already had routines and ways of being at home and together that she absorbed from infancy. When Luke arrived four years later, those routines and norms now included his parents' evolving roles as parents in their growing family. Over time, like most first-time families, many of the family's shared understandings—both little details of daily living and larger core values—no longer needed to be talked about or negotiated. It was just the way their family did things. Easy.

Stepfamily Development: One Plus One Plus Kids Plus Co-Parent

A first-time family's genesis story is very different from a stepfamily's origin story. The stepcouple never has the luxury of just the two of them. The shared middle ground and strongest connections in stepfamily are between parents and children. The couple often feels pulled apart moment by moment. That's the reality.

You have to check your compass again and again to get your bearings, reset your expectations and work on *building* your stepfamily step by step rather than trying to leap there.

New Ground for Ben, Fran and the Kids

Before the divorce, in Ben and Rebecca's home, parents and kids looked at cellphones during meals. They texted one another from room to room. The kids often had ear buds in, listening to music or watching YouTube. When Ben first started seeing Fran, he learned right away that she resented when his attention was on his screen. After several increasingly pointed nudges, he put his phone away around Fran.

Now that they were living together, that sweet starter plot of middle ground the couple had developed together while they were dating was trampled when Annie and Luke were with them. The kids, of course, assumed they could do what they'd always done: use their phones at the table. Ben silenced phone when Fran was around but often joined the kids, surfing his social media, as soon as she left the table. Ben straddled two middle grounds, and it was not comfortable. One foot was planted in the established middle ground with the kids, and the other stood on the new middle ground he shared with Fran. Witnessing this, Fran was also deeply uncomfortable. Would her beloved tip toward the kids or toward her?

Fran wanted the phones off during dinner. But she was outnumbered and outvoted on this and many other issues, including kids tidying up shared living spaces of their shoes, books, papers and games before bed (that was how she was raised). "Mom never makes us do that," grumbled Annie. Adding Rebecca's influence on the kids into the mix, Fran was often outvoted four to one. She was miserable.

Now what?

If you're thinking this is easier for couples if both bring kids to the relationship, you would be wrong. That's just complicated squared—two first-family teams divided and upset over "the way we've always done things." Oh dear.

WHAT'S LOVE GOT TO DO WITH IT?

Children in a first-time family enter hardwired for attachment to both their parents, and vice versa. Not so for stepchildren and stepparents. When Luke needed comfort or Annie had something exciting to share, where did they turn? To their dad or to their mom. Not to Fran. A stepchild might tolerate or even like and accept a stepparent, but it's not the same as how they feel about their parents.

> *"Parents love their own children better than other people do. Children love their parents better than other adults."*
> —Larry Ganong and Marilyn Coleman, stepfamily researchers

When Ben's kids were with them, Fran often felt like *a stranger in a strange land* in her own home. This is very typical for partners in stepfamilies. As she told a friend, *"It's gotten to the point where I dread being home when the kids are there."* Ben's experience of feeling like he's the rope in a tug of war is very typical for parents in a stepfamily. As he told his buddy, *"This balancing act is a lot tougher than I ever imagined."*

NORMAL CHAOS

And as if *all of this* weren't enough, there's yet another layer of stepfamily complexity at play. There's a lot more commotion in two-home family life than in first-time family life, with kids coming and going, negotiations with a co-parent for everything from orthodontist appointments to getting kids to friends' houses to coordinating when the unexpected happens—someone comes down with the flu or gets into a fight at school.

By the time Ben and Fran moved in together, Ben and the children's mother, Rebecca, had been making decisions together as parents for years—first as a committed couple and then as divorced co-parents. So when Rebecca asked Ben to take the kids for an extra night, he automatically said yes, forgetting to ask Fran (again).

Fran understood that Ben wanted to be with his kids, and that he also wanted to foster a good relationship with his co-parent by being flexible. She just wasn't used to how *often* schedules had to be changed for the kids. She wasn't used to the fact that managing their busy lives was Ben's top priority when the kids were with him. She wasn't used to the huge number of people involved in Annie and Luke's lives, who were now overwhelming her life: Kids' friends, parents of friends, teammates, coaches, tutors, teachers, extended family, healthcare professionals and more. A formerly single partner's well-ordered existence goes out the door when the normal chaos of stepfamily life comes in.

Stepfamilies Usually Follow Disruption and Loss

The ending of a first-time family rips the fabric of comfortable middle ground for children. Daily life is often cluttered with reminders of this. At the pool with their mom, dad's energetic water play was missed. Swimming without him wasn't the same. When playing Scrabble Junior with their dad, the kids missed their mom's silly made-up words. Now the favorite game seemed boring and a little sad.

When parents split, kids have to handle a lot of change, and so do co-parents. Solo parenting can be exhausting for adults. Tired parents may let limit-setting slip a bit. After they separated, Ben and Rebecca both asked more of Annie and Luke. Sometimes when the kids bickered, Ben just ignored it rather than stepping in and mediating. When Annie talked back to her, Rebecca, she often let it go—just ignored.

Some changes are easier for kids to accept and even enjoy, as when decisions that were once made primarily by two adults are now negotiated between the solo parent and the kids. When parents do this age-appropriately, children like having more of a say. Ben collaborated with the kids about where to bike ride each weekend, teaching them how to assess the difficulty of the route and the amount of time they needed to get there and back. Rebecca solicited the kids for their ideas on where to spend the holidays, and together they researched fun things to do.

During the separation/post-divorce phase, kids get used to counting on regular time alone with each parent. This solo parent-child connection can be comforting and stabilizing and can be a different kind of bonding experience. A parent who was less available to kids during the marriage now has opportunities to interact with kids in new ways—to learn their food likes and dislikes, or to hear more about their social dramas, or to share feelings and ideas together. For kids (and parents), this can be surprisingly awesome. And then in walks the new partner.

A parent moving in with a new partner represents more loss for kids. Even if that person is introduced to kids in a slow and gradual way, their presence encroaches on solo-parenting time. Kids have to share their parent. Moving in together can feel like the end of the time they shared with "just their dad." It can feel like they're competing with the new adult for their parent's time and attention (and they often are!). They have to get used to a stepparent always being around. All of this can set off a fresh round of grief, resentment and distress.

Grief is often a theme in the stepfamily's genesis story. Even when divorce goes as well and a firm foundation stretches across both homes, even when it seems that kids are adjusting. Grief often runs like a river beneath the surface. Grief about losing their family, grief about losing what's familiar and comforting, grief about sometimes missing one parent *even when all is going well!* For the adults, it may be grief about lives disrupted, or unfulfilled dreams, or missing their kids when they're with the other parent. At moments, it's grief about not being able to share a kid experience that only the other parent would understand in the same way they do. Or it's grief about not having time alone for the couple to share a sacred or passionate moment privately.

Stepfamily: A Very Different Architecture

"BLENDED FAMILY: woven together by choice, strengthened by love, tested by everything..."

—Anonymous

A stepfamily is made up of individuals who aren't all inherently connected through DNA, or shared history, or even shared affection (at first). It can feel like a patchwork quilt unevenly sewn together out of a hodgepodge of squares of clashing colors and designs. It often doesn't harmonize—at least not right away. Time is the master tailor in this process. Time can stitch shared experiences into stronger relationships.

Swimming Upstream

Have you ever watched salmon leap their way upstream? It takes them try after try to progress to the next level, and then they have to leap again. Exhausting. Exasperating! Sometimes that's what their stepfamily felt like to Fran and Ben. It started to seem like everything was a sore point—even the times that were supposed to be fun. For instance, Ben and his kids were Scrabble Junior fanatics. The kids loved word games and would play them day and night if they could. So would Ben. Fran hated board games! She had dyslexia, so Scrabble was her least favorite. She was a terrible speller—always a source of shame—so Scrabble nights embarrassed her. When the kids begged to play after dinner and Fran suggested Jenga (a game of stacking blocks), they rolled their eyes. "That's boring!"

Fran loved to cook healthy meals. Fresh vegetables and fruits and whole grains were all part of her cuisine. Those mac-and-cheese dinners were dreadful for her. And the kids turned their noses up at her kale salads and yogurt smoothies.

It Will Be a Process

You might have started your new family fervently, hoping to "blend." Now you're confronted with quite a different reality. What can help is a more realistic map of the relationships that you will need to build over time:

- **For partners: As much as you love your sweetie, loving their child(ren) isn't always easy.** You may often have to dig down deep to remain warm, friendly and interested through all the pushback as the kids take the time they need to be emotionally ready to welcome you and engage meaningfully with you. Some kids in the family may be more open to you than others.

- **Relationships with stepkids don't necessarily become close bonds.** Over years, not months, and with enough opportunities to return to each other through thick and thin, you, a new partner, *may* find that one or more of the kids comes to occupy a special place in your heart, and you in theirs. But it's not guaranteed to happen. Some very functional stepparent-stepchild relationships, especially with older kids, remain somewhat distant.

- **Kids may not *like*—much less *love*—their parent's new partner.** The child's age and gender, their different personalities, and the circumstances of the end of the first-time family might play a part. It's hard to predict, and it's best not to pressure kids. Civil behavior can be required, but not affection.

- **Stepcouples need time and space alone together to nourish their intimacy.** With a good map, the best intentions, good energy and practice with communication skills, you can build a strong relationship.

- **Children need time alone with their parent.** Balance couple-alone time and parent-child time.

- **Co-parents are part of the stepfamily.** If they are supportive of the stepcouple (even if it's just for the sake of the kids) things will go much easier. The situation, though, can be like having in-laws who were never happy with your marriage in the first place. Co-parents may

> exert a kind of undermining influence. Demonstrating respect for the other parent's role can pave the way for this to change over the years. For now, do your part to right the ship by staying considerate and cooperative.
>
> - **Stepsibling relationships add intensity and complexity to stepfamilies.** More people means more relationships to negotiate and more awareness of different family styles, parenting styles and more.

When a stepfamily begins finding its pulse—a rhythm that works, that holds and that nourishes all the members—it's hard earned and enormously satisfying!

BOTTOM LINE

*Stepfamilies look and feel different from other kinds of families because they **are** different! They are not like other families—not in how they start, not in how they grow over time, and not in how they are experienced by the people in them. **And**, over time, with a good map to guide you, you can develop a sense of "we-ness" in your stepfamily.*

Stepfamilies Are Not Cookie-Cutter

Stepfamilies don't all look the same; they don't all fit neatly into the same box. Yours might include two parents with kids, or one parent and one partner. Kids might live in one home or both of their parents' homes or be out of the house and have kids of their own. Your stepfamily may or may not include kids you and your new partner had, or adopted, or foster together. You and/or your partner may be LGBTQ. You may be married. Or not. What makes all these families fit into that "stepfamily architecture" we keep talking about is that all stepfamilies include *at least one parent-child relationship that started before the couple relationship.*

Culture and ethnicity shape a stepfamily, and so do the laws and customs where you live regarding marriage, divorce and remarriage, sexual orientation, discrimination and gender equality. Poverty and geography affect your stepfamily. In the end, this means that the territory of your stepfamily has its own hills and dales and its own emotional landmarks. As you read the following chapters you'll learn about the five challenges for stepfamilies. You can follow the trails we've marked for you and hopefully choose your steps wisely, no matter the ground you must travel.

* * * * * * * * * * *

The unique architecture of stepfamilies can create a maze of challenges for couples, kids and co-parents. It also creates amazing opportunities to build the family you long for. Like a patchwork quilt, there's not one *right* way to put all the different pieces together. Making something new—and potentially amazing!—means stitching your pasts, your present, your hopes and intentions and your love and respect into the fabric of your stepfamily. Some of those individual squares will never stitch together, and others will create gorgeous patterns. New pieces will be added, and, over time, the threads of connection will stitch your quilt into its own unique whole. Slowly, with hard work and love and patience, your stepfamily can become a source of comfort and warmth for all of you.

Chapter 11

First Stepfamily Challenge: Children Struggle With Losses, Loyalty Binds And Change

"Sometimes sad is very big. It's everywhere. All over me ... And there's nothing I can do about it."

—Michael Rosen, author of *Sad Book* for children

Moving in together is a very big step! You've crossed an important bridge and now you're adjusting to a new ecosystem—the vegetation is different here, sometimes a bit drier than you expected, sometimes overwhelmingly lush and full. And the paths can be unexpectedly rocky and slippery in some places!

You're becoming more expert naturalists. You recognized each of the five budding stepfamily challenges as they appeared in the dating stage. This first one—the one about losses, loyalty binds and change for kids— may have you a bit nervous. You're just hoping that as it blooms, the kids will still be able to adjust.

The good news is that you can team up to help kids, even as stepfamily situations intensify. But please—no hiking in the dark! You'll need to see clearly where you're going. Read on.

> ## Clues from the Research
>
> Although every child and every family are unique, social science research gives us a few general ideas about what's going on for children in stepfamilies. Before we go deeper into the forest, let's find out what the experts have to say about what lies ahead:
>
> - **Children under 9 adjust to being in a stepfamily more easily than older children.**
>
> - **Early adolescents have a particularly hard time when parents recouple,** especially girls in their early teens.
>
> - **Boys generally have an easier time with parents' remarriage than girls**. But boys have a harder time living in single-mom families than girls do.
>
> - **Younger kids who did well when you started on the stepfamily journey may have a bump of difficulty in adolescence.**
>
> - **Step relationships change significantly over time**. The first years are hardest for both children and adults. With patience and thoughtful adult support, children's difficulties may ease and disappear over time. This is true regardless of gender.
>
> - **Family *processes* matter more than family *structure*.** It is not family *structure* (for instance, whether a child lives in a first-time family, single-parent family or stepfamily) that's most important in determining how the child adjusts. It is family *processes*, like the quality of parent-child and stepparent-stepchild relationships, the level of conflict in the family and the amount of change that children experience.

UNDERSTANDING THE CHALLENGES FOR CHILDREN: A TRAIL GUIDE FOR THE ADULTS

One of the unexpected things about forming a stepfamily is that adults and children are often on fundamentally different wavelengths! Your emotional world spins in one direction. Theirs is likely to be spinning in the opposite.

What to do about this? *Understand and empathize with them.* Kids can make it across unfamiliar, even scary, terrain if you're there to walk right next to them. How to do that if your path looks so different from theirs? We're here to help. Here's your trail guide to the kids' experience of losses, loyalty binds and change.

Understanding Children's Losses

Any time several paths merge into one, everyone on the journey has to make accommodations—just as your stepfamily group will face many adjustments as you move in together. This particular fork in the road can stir up some unexpected losses for kids. Why? Well, two main reasons. First, children now have to face the fact that their parents won't reunite. If kids held this secret hope, new feelings of grief and loss may well up when their parent moves in with a new partner. Second, kids have to adjust to sharing the parent with a new partner and perhaps stepsiblings.

Even when parents and partners managed all the demands for time and attention well during their dating phase, merging into one household can make time boundaries between the adult relationship and parenting time considerably fuzzier. Kids often don't have words for these things. Some may seem to get a little sad, others may become a bit more obstreperous. Still others may roll along fairly happily. You'll never be quite sure how it will be for your kiddos until you're settling into your new home life.

The more you can understand their point of view, the better you'll connect with kids. For Ben and Fran, there was a steep learning curve.

What Kids Want Us Grownups to Know

- For kids, a person who used to be around once in a while (maybe even a lot!) is now in their space *all the time*. That's really (really) different.

- Kids feel their parent's attention directed toward the partner, getting settled, their own adjustments. That can leave them feeling lonely. No blame. Just a fact.

- Kids can feel frustrated and confused when parents insist they spend lots of time with a partner "as a family" when kids aren't comfortable in their new home yet and *they* don't feel like "family."

- Kids often have mixed feelings about seeing their parent in love with another adult who is "not my mom" or "not my dad." Depending on the child's age, it can be embarrassing. And it can stir up sadness that their parents aren't connected that way anymore.

- Adults who are distracted by their excitement about (and stress of!) finally living together under one roof may not realize how lost the kids may be feeling.

> - The daily demands of becoming a stepfamily sometimes interrupt good (and familiar) parenting.

The adults can help each other *and* kids by practicing an extra dose of patience. Keep slowing things down to *one step at a time*. Keep letting kids know what will be different and what will be the same as you turn each corner. Keeping these normal, underlying concerns in mind, you'll be better able to give kids the right kinds of support.

"Wait One Minute . . . This is Our Friday Night!"

Ever since their parents separated, Annie and Luke had spent Friday nights with their dad. Over time, they had developed a comforting routine. Their mom dropped them off at Dad's house early Friday evening. Ben helped his kids unpack their backpacks and they all changed into comfy sweats, ate pizza and talked about their week. After dinner, the kids snuggled up with Ben on the couch and they watched a kid movie. Luke often fell asleep leaning against his dad. Ben would carry him to bed and then he and Annie had special time to talk until it was her bedtime. For all three of them, these Fridays had become a special time together.

Now Fran entered the picture. She ate her quinoa salad while the three of them ate their pizza. When the movie started, the kids had to make room for her on the couch. Sometimes Fran claimed the seat next to their dad. Luke started sitting on the floor so his back was to them. Annie tried to ignore them, but seeing the two of them sitting close, sometimes holding hands, gave her a sinking feeling.

On the second Friday night with Fran in the picture, after Luke fell asleep and Ben had carried him off to bed, Fran suggested it was Annie's bedtime, too. When Ben agreed, Annie sulked. She had come to love that special time when she had her dad to herself. When Ben came to tuck her in, she turned away from him.

On the third Friday night together, Annie was the last one to finish changing into sweats. By the time she got to the living room, Ben was flanked on the couch by Luke and Fran. Annie scowled and then plopped down on her dad's lap, sprawling onto Fran so that she had

First Stepfamily Challenge: Children Struggle With Losses, Loyalty Binds And Change

to make room. Fran glared at Ben. Wasn't he going to say something about his daughter's rude behavior? Ben sighed.

"Honey, please give Fran some space on the couch, too, okay?" he said a bit weakly.

Annie scowled and sat on the floor, feeling steamed. Why did Fran have to ruin everything? A few minutes into the movie, Annie said angrily, "This is a dumb movie." She went to her room and slammed the door.

"What's wrong with Annie?" asked Fran.

"She probably just needs some space," said Ben.

Annie waited in her room for Ben to come find her and ask what was wrong. She wanted to tell him it was hard to have Fran here. She waited and rehearsed what she would say, but her dad didn't come talk to her until after he put Luke to bed. By that time she was furious and didn't want to talk to him at all.

"I'm fine," was all she said when he finally asked her what was wrong.

Annie was trying to let Ben and Fran know it was all too much, too fast. Some families might have gotten stuck here, straining to "blend"—trying to create *family time*. It took Ben and Fran a few weeks to figure it out, but together they stumbled upon exactly what stepfamilies often need: some "just us" time for Ben and his kids.

Huh, really? Shouldn't they practice being a family? Actually, no. Not yet. What will really help this family move forward is for Ben and the kids to keep their special Friday nights while Fran finds something fun to do on her own.

Ben and Fran Take a Step Back to Go Forward

A couple months later, Fran found herself blurting to Ben as they were going to sleep, "I *hate* Friday nights." Ben, who had been feeling so relieved to finally be living with all the people he loved, was confused and distressed.

This was the beginning of several difficult conversations about Fridays. Fran expressed her pain. Ben responded with befuddled defensiveness.

Finally, Fran said, "You know what I think? I think your kids need to be alone with you on Friday nights." Ben objected at first: "But I want us all to be *together.*"

"For a few hours, let the kids have you to themselves," she said. She called old friends and made a regular Friday-night plan to be with them.

Weeks later, Ben acknowledged to Fran, "I have to admit, I miss you. But you were right. The kids did need me to themselves. Thank you for seeing that."

It might seem kind of paradoxical, but teaming up to give kids that all-important parent-kiddo time while stepparents take some time away (or spend time with their own kids) is one of the best ways to help your family move forward.

Helpful Tips to Ease Children's Losses

Kids in stepfamilies often struggle with the loss of attention from their parent. There are lots of ways for new stepcouples to make the transition easier for kids.

- **Schedule regular "just us" time with kids.** Multitasking time doesn't count. "Just us" times are time together to feel that precious parent-child connection.

- **Find and treasure small moments to feel close with kids.** Take a few minutes before breakfast, or during a car ride to chess club, or at bedtime, or walking to school and be fully present. You can snuggle, listen, share ideas, laugh.

- **Be conscious of your tone.** Adults are often in a hurry and hassled, so it's easy to use a sharper tone and critical or cranky words if a child is struggling. Do your best to soften and slow down your communication. Your family will do best with a ratio of five positive moments to one negative. It helps to count!

Understanding Children's Loyalty Binds

When kids start living with their parent's new partner, opportunities for closeness with a new stepparent increase. This can leave many children feeling torn on some level. *"If I like them, will my other parent feel bad?"* These loyalty binds, introduced in Chapter 6, can be confusing for young kids and over adult kids. Can they love both their parents *and* like a stepparent? Even children of cordial divorces often report feeling guilty or disloyal about forming a relationship with a stepparent.

And, as we've seen, moving in together can sometimes unearth another round of upset for some co-parents, intensifying concerns about being replaced by a new partner. Frightened co-parents may tug harder on their kids, tightening the knots of kids' loyalty binds.

Fran's Best Intentions Tighten Annie's Loyalty Bind

Annie's birthday was coming up, and Fran wanted to do something special for her new stepdaughter. She took an afternoon off from work and made Annie's favorite chocolate cake. She wrote "Happy Birthday, Annie!" across the top in pink icing and hid the cake on top of the refrigerator.

After the birthday dinner ended, Ben said, "Fran has a surprise for you!"

Fran proudly brought the cake into the dining room, candles lit, and they all sang to Annie.

"Make a wish!" said her dad. Annie blew out the candles and Ben served the cake. Fran watched Annie carefully, eager to see if she liked her creation. But Annie sat a bit slumped, moving crumbs around on her plate. Then, saying she felt sick, Annie left the table without a word.

Fran was devastated. More "icing on the cake" of *rejection*. Annie didn't even say thank you! The next day, Fran vented to her best friend: "Annie can be such a spoiled brat!" Wisely, Fran didn't say these things to Ben, but Fran's feelings for Annie cooled for a while after the birthday cake incident. She never tried to bake her stepdaughter another birthday cake.

Here's what Fran discovered years later, during a late-night conversation with her stepdaughter. As they both sat watching the flames in the fireplace, Annie said, a bit shyly, "Remember when you made me that birthday cake? Well, I still feel bad about not eating it. It was so nice of you, but it just felt wrong." After a bit of silence, "Like, if I ate your cake I was being mean to my mom."

Fran was touched. She thought for a moment. Then she said, "I remember! That was a tough one, huh. I wish I had known more back then about what it was like for you to have a stepmom. Instead of getting upset with you, I wish I would have known to say, *"Oops! I guess I stepped on you mom's territory.'* Would that have helped?"

"I think so," said Annie. "Yeah. Definitely."

"I think what you were feeling is called a 'loyalty bind'," said Fran. "It's when any choice you make will hurt someone you care about."

"That's *exactly* what it was," said Annie, surprised and relieved. "That helps a *lot*."

BOTTOM LINE:

The child's other parent may cancel plans and be chronically late, or struggle with addiction or mental illness, or fall down on the job in many ways as a parent. Even so, they are still the other child's parent. Some part of a child will always be loyal to both their parents, no matter what. Adults help kids by making sure that children never have to choose among the adults in their lives.

Children rarely have language to describe their loyalty binds. Adults can help by staying alert to the possibility that distancing and rejecting a stepparent may be a child's attempt to manage these painful binds. Put those clues to work by doing whatever you can to loosen these binds.

Helpful Tips for Loosening Loyalty Binds

Normally, mild loyalty binds diminish over time with cooperation and support by all the adults. However, when adults put children in the middle, these binds become like a straight-jacket that severely limits their emotional development. Although the power to fix the situation is not *all* in your hands, here's what you *can* do:

- **Remain vigilant that *you* are not verbally, or nonverbally, leaking negative judgments** about *any* members of a child's two-home family.

- **Support children in maintaining family photos and other personal items** that remind them of *all* their loved ones. This includes grandparents, aunts, uncles and cousins from their other home.

- **Encourage children to talk about their other home.** Reacting negatively or silencing children (*"Don't talk about them in my home."*) sows confusion and increases internal conflict for kids.

- **Remember that two-home life is not a competition.** You may have visions of doing things *better* for kids, doing things *right*. But your judgments hurt kids; they don't help them. For kids' sake, *don't* complain about the co-parent's life choices or parenting style. Kids need both parents, however imperfect they may be.

- **Help loosen children's loyalty binds.** For example, any loving adult could say:

"Having a stepmom can be kind of confusing for some kids. I want you to know that a stepmom isn't a replacement mom. **Your Mom's place in your heart is permanent***. It will be there always."*

"I hope you can come to care about your stepmom, but I don't expect you to love her the way you love Mommy. Your stepmom doesn't expect that, either."

A stepdad could say, *"If you start to feel disloyal to me or your dad, I get it. It's got to be hard for you to feel like you're in the middle of all the grown-ups being upset with each other. When adults handle a divorce well, kids don't have to choose. Sometimes we adults are making a mess of this. That makes it harder for you."* (Notice how it's *"We adults are making mistakes,"* not *"Your mom is being horrible."*)

Understanding Children's Responses to *More Change*

By definition, change shifts the status quo. Kids might be doing fine, and then a partner moves in with a parent, perhaps bringing stepsiblings along, and suddenly they're acting up or shutting down. It's more change than they can handle.

Wouldn't it be great if adults could prevent this from happening? Some of this is in your control. And some of it isn't. Read on.

Adults Bring the Skills—Kids Keep Growing Up

Lilly was 9 when her mom and dad divorced. Right before she turned 12, her mom introduced Lilly and her siblings to Cash. By then, Tanzi and Cash had been dating for six months. Cash had an eight-year-old son, Brandon. After many months of slowly introducing their kids, Tanzi and Cash sat down with the kids and shared the news of their engagement.

Over the next few weeks, Lilly's behavior changed noticeably. When her mom wanted to talk about wedding plans, Lilly stormed off to her room and slammed the door. She was angry and rude to everyone, especially Cash and Brandon.

"This behavior is unacceptable!" her mom said. "Cash and Brandon are part of the family now. This is their home, too. You have to be civil."

"You're ruining my life!" Lilly declared hotly. "If you cared about me *at all*, you would never marry him."

"I just don't understand why you're acting this way," said her mom. "You said you liked Cash!"

"I hate him, and I hate you!" Lilly shouted. "I don't want them living here. This is my house! It's not fair!"

Every child has a different capacity to adapt to change. Some kids—Lilly's brother, Rob, and younger sister, Ellie, for example, weren't fazed much. Then there are kids like Lilly, who feel gut-punched with anxiety, stress, fear when confronted with changes.

First-Round Changes: The Divorce

All three kids had been devastated by their parents' divorce, but Rob and Ellie had bounced back from it more quickly than Lilly. Especially hard for Lilly, her dad was extremely unreliable, often cancelling their time with him, or just plain failing to show up. Rob and Ellie were annoyed by this, but Lilly was deeply hurt.

Lilly's mom had always juggled a lot. But after the separation, Tanzi became "super woman," singlehandedly caring for three kids, their family home and her demanding job. Lilly often felt completely lost in the whirlwind of efficiency.

To top it off, just after the divorce Lilly changed schools. *And* she got her period for the first time. So, starting well before Cash showed up in her life, for Lilly, the changes (and losses) were piling up.

Second-Round Changes: Mom's Dating. And Stepfamily

Lilly had been polite when her mom first introduced her to Cash, but each subsequent step the adults took toward stepfamily notched up her anxiety. All the changes were *just too much*. She felt scared, lonely and lost, but, like many children, Lilly didn't have words for her experience, until much later. So she expressed herself in ways that were incredibly disruptive and left her *more* alone.

BOTTOM LINE

Even when you proceed thoughtfully, kids may not be able to manage what is, for them, a rushing river of change. They can end up slipping into troubled waters and find themselves in over their heads. They need adults to reach out a hand and pull them back onto the river bank.

Sometimes it simply takes a village to help us with our children. If possible, try to find a guidance counselor or therapist who knows how to help kids under stress and who knows something about stepfamilies. (Or ask them to read this book or Patricia's.) It's best if therapists are comfortable working with both parents and kids. (See appendix C for important guidelines about choosing a therapist for kids in a stepfamily, or for your whole family.)

Good Guidance from the Village

Tanzi met privately with Lilly's middle school guidance counselor, Mrs. Garcia, and asked for help. Mrs. Garcia invited Lilly to assist her with a program for in-coming sixth graders, which provided an excuse to meet with her a few times a week. As they spent time together, Lilly began opening up about what was going on for her at home. Mrs. Garcia listened supportively and helped Lilly identify her feelings. "Boy, sounds like the divorce was a big surprise." And, "Boy, I bet it really hurts when your dad doesn't show up."

Feeling understood calmed Lilly. As she felt connected and cared about, she began sharing more. "I know my mom and dad love me, but everything is always about them and their lives, and I'm supposed to just go along with all these changes. I wish we could go back to the way things were."

If you're the parent or stepparent, it might be hard to understand the level of confusion and grief that may be underneath kids' outbursts. There are things you can do to make it better. First, you can **slow down requests** that the child participate in stepfamily activities. The parent can schedule **more familiar and comforting one-on-one time**: baking cookies together, going to the park or whatever activities will engage your child. You can also reinstate some of the **soothing rituals** from childhood, including tucking kids in at night—even early teens. A thirteen-year-old under stress may have some of the very same needs that a three-year-old would have.

The hardest thing for a parent is to **meet outbursts with empathy, not exasperation**. Instead of *"Get yourself under control!"* try *"You're SO mad! This is all WAY too much, huh."* And the parent can hold **steady, loving boundaries** when kids lose it. *"You have every right to be angry. But screaming insults at me is NOT okay."* Little by little, a defiant child's brazen attitude may begin to melt and they might start to let you help hold the grief and fear they've been carrying alone.

A Partner's Role in the Stepchild's Adjustment to Changes

Stepparents are not parents. Parenting is the job of the parent. That being said, there are many things partners can do to support parents and kids. You can read the lack of eye contact, dismissive grunts and withdrawal during mealtimes as the child's *code* for *"I'm not ready* yet." You can *try* not to take rudeness personally. And you can support the parent to have more time alone with their child.

Tanzi and Cash did all these things with Lilly. The wedding went forward and the children all attended. Even Lilly. Three years later—not without more bumps and meltdowns—Lilly was adjusting! She was also maturing. She and her mom now had a warm, playful relationship. Lilly's relationship with Cash and his son was generally civil, with flashes of warmth and humor.

Skillful parenting, a supportive partner and good outside support for the whole family helped Lilly pull through. So did her expanding prefrontal cortex—there's very little that growing out of those early midteens won't help!

> *The prefrontal cortex is an area in the very front of the brain that's the seat of thinking, planning and being able to calm down and step back. It's the last part of the brain to develop. It doesn't grow in fully until age 25, but around age 15, it makes a big leap. Especially if the adults have stayed steady and connected, a stepchild's behavior and emotional steadiness often start to improve at this age.*

Let's Talk Specifically about Teens

We have given a lot of focus to Lilly, and to Annie (whose dad, Ben, had brought Fran into their family), because girls, and especially girls in their early teen years, often struggle the most with becoming part of a stepfamily. We want to underscore the complexity for our girls in this developmental stage.

Teen girls need their parents to move especially slowly toward stepfamily. They need adults to look at their difficult behavior as distress signals—a daunting task! They crave consistent, warm, present parenting at a time when they are often inadvertently alienating all the adults in their lives. They may require more one-on-one parent-kid time and much less "family" time—sometimes for quite a while.

More Siblings—More Change—Maybe More *Stress*

Children have a variety of responses to stepsiblings and half-siblings. "The more the merrier" may be the adults' wishful thinking, but it's not always the kids' reality.

Stepsiblings don't choose each other! They are forced to share a home, sometimes a room, often a bathroom, and too many dinners, weekends and vacations together (from their point of view). Some stepsiblings have a lot in common; others have very little. Whether we're referring to whole-, half- or stepsiblings, children in a family can function as friends or foes or indifferent roommates. Not unlike any group of kids, many factors contribute to how kids get along.

> ### Helpful Tips for Handling Stepsibling Conflict
>
> Give kids space to create their own relationships without pressure or expectation. There are of course non-negotiables—respect and safety—but beyond civility, demanding much more will likely start you down a slippery slope of misbehavior. This is true for both young kids and adult children. Close relationships will happen or they won't. Here are a few guidelines:
>
> - **Empathize.** You can never go wrong with empathy! *"Sharing is tough, I get it. We teach you to do it and it's important. But I'll bet it's still hard! Let's figure out what might help."*
>
> - **No second-class citizens.** Think through how to respect both the full-time children's need to maintain some continuity in their home and the needs of kids who mostly live with their other parent or who are away at college and are home on holidays. Everyone needs to have *a place* and *a say*.
>
> - **Give children space they don't have to share.** It can help for each child to have some physical space that is theirs—a particular dresser drawer, one wall of a bedroom, a specific area of the bathroom. Some children will need more privacy than others.

- **Help stepsiblings to connect and/or disconnect.** Some stepsibling relationships do become nourishing and close. Find fun activities for kids to do together, *but only if they are willing*. When they rub each other the wrong way, help them keep a respectful distance to minimize conflict and to help each child to feel safe and comfortable in the home.

Helpful Tips for Making Sure Kids Are Physically and Emotionally Safe

Everyone needs to feel safe and respected. No name calling, threatening or bullying is acceptable. Just like in the classroom, basic civility is key!

- **As a couple, you determine and monitor** just a few basics of what's "in-bounds" and what's "out-of-bounds." *Leaving kids to work it out* on their own is not fair. Share your basic expectations for safe behavior in clear, behavioral terms. Both adults monitor (i.e., share information with each other about how things are going). *Each parent enforces consequences with their own children.*

- **Children have different ideas of "share."** For some, that may mean "What's yours is mine." Tor others, it means "You may only use with permission." The adults' job is to help kids understand and respect one another's needs.

- **If family time is tense, keep it short.** Concentrate on supporting all relationships in the family with one-on-one time while slowly infusing group time and building relationships.

> ### Helpful Tips for Healthy Sexual Boundaries in Stepfamilies
>
> Good boundaries around privacy and modesty and sexuality are really important to making sure people of all ages are safe and comfortable in the home. This is true regardless of your personal values about nudity, sexuality and so forth. Here are some good guidelines:
>
> - **Keep romantic affection between adults private.** New stepcouples are often affectionate and physically expressive. Many adults believe that this sets a positive example for children. Of course, you're longing to model for your children a healthy, loving relationship. Do enjoy each other in private. *But*, even in moderation, public displays of affection or sexuality in the home can actually intensify losses, tighten loyalty binds and alienate kids. When kids are freaked out, they're not learning a thing!
>
> - **Require bathrobes!** A new stepmom (or mom) running to the bathroom in her bra and panties means something much more sexual to her adolescent stepson, or to her own daughter who is now much more aware of Mom's sexual relationship with Stepdad. Except for infants and toddlers, everyone in the family should practice modesty.
>
> - **Keep it G-rated.** It can be upsetting and confusing to be exposed to adult sexuality too soon. Keep your sensual and sexual relationship private. Keep bedroom doors closed and be mindful of sounds that kids can hear through walls. Enjoy each other *and* keep it away from kids.

New Babies: A New Square Changes the Stepfamily Quilt

News that the stepcouple is having or adopting a baby together requires thoughtful planning and preparation for the other children. Research shows that new babies do provide a sense of "glue" for about *half* of all stepcouples. For the other half, new babies may intensify the challenges for everyone. Likewise, some kids are delighted to have a new younger sibling. While for others, sharing mom or dad with a new baby is compounded by watching their stepparent fall in love with a new biological child. Many have *some* of each of these feelings.

As natural, loving and wonderful as the birth of a baby can be, the process of adding this new piece to your stepfamily quilt without causing overwhelming disruption to some of the other parts of the quilt will require very intentional planning and special stitching to be sure.

> **Helpful Tips for Helping Kids Adjust to a New Baby**
>
> All children have a variety of responses to a new baby in their family. Just know that a new little one in a stepfamily creates some extra dynamics. Children who spend time in another home may feel threatened that you're up to all kinds of special things when they're not there that they are now excluded from. They often worry that stepparents, especially, will love the baby more than them. (Since loving your own is so different from trying to love a stepchild, they may.) Kids will need time to see, feel and trust that there's plenty of love for everyone.
>
> - Help kids talk about their feelings, their hopes and their concerns. Your curiosity about how they feel will be helpful. As with all forms of sibling rivalry, it helps a lot to meet hostility or depression with, *"That makes sense. Lots of kids feel that way."* (And, *"You can use your words to tell me about it. But you can't hit him. Or me."*)
>
> - Whenever possible, try to increase parent-child (and also for some kids, stepparent-stepchild) alone time and connection without the new baby. Most kiddos get pretty tired of "the baby, the baby, the baby." Remember, especially in a stepfamily, each child still needs their own unimpeded play and cuddle time.

Special Needs Children in Stepfamilies

The flood of changes that comes with stepfamily can be really hard for kids who bring special needs to the journey. If your kids have significant mental health issues, or a history of abuse or abandonment, or major learning disabilities, or if they're on the autism spectrum, or if they're dealing with the emotional fallout from lots of transitions and losses (including immigration, foster homes, adoption), then you may all be in for a particularly strenuous climb. Extra precautions are warranted.

> ### Helpful Tips for Supporting Special Needs Children in Stepfamilies
>
> With kiddos needing special support, you may have to be very creative. You already know that a coordinated effort across their two homes will be particularly critical to their adjustment.
>
> - It may be best to move especially slowly. Each step forward may need to be especially small. For instance, some kids may need many months, and sometimes longer, of a partner showing up for just an hour or two, with full warning regarding when he or she will arrive and leave.
>
> - Be as consistent, warm and empathic as possible.
>
> - Maintain good boundaries and firm (but not harsh) parenting—routine is often a balm for special needs kids.
>
> - Reach out to helping professionals who are already part of your kids' care team. Tutors, guidance counselors, doctors and therapists can be resources for understanding children's needs.
>
> - Consider the advantages afforded by Living Apart Together (LAT), which we discussed in Chapter 5. It might be the wisest path for all of you.

"WHAT DO WE CALL YOU?"

The kids may ask you what to call a new partner. We strongly recommend that you *let children decide*. Children have no control over becoming part of a stepfamily. Naming a stepparent gives them a little bit of voice to define a relationship they didn't choose.

Who's Your Daddy?

George picked up his six-year-old son, Eddie, from his mom's house.

"Hi, Dad!" he said, giving his father a hug. "Daddy Dan and I played basketball today," he announced. Dan was Eddie's mom's live-in boyfriend.

"Gee, where did that name come from?" George asked his son, trying to keep his cool. He felt angry and hurt that another man was being called "Daddy" by his boy.

"Me!" declared Eddie proudly.

Later, George vented to his friend. "*I'm* Eddie's dad! He shouldn't be calling his mother's boyfriend 'Daddy' anything!"

His friend calmed him down. "Listen, your son knows you're his dad. He doesn't call *you* 'Daddy George.' Relax! It's what helps Eddie feel comfortable that's most important."

Parents need to remember that the names used for stepparents are a reflection of what the child wants and needs—it's a way a child tries to make sense of their changing world. Remember back at the very beginning of the book when we talked about the sacred relationship between parent and child? Well, don't you worry. You'll always be the "one of two" *only* parents. Children are only confused and stressed when the adults become reactive over what they call a stepparent.

A stepparent may be caught off guard when asked by a child if they can call them Mommy or Daddy. Underneath this emotionally loaded question, the child may be saying:

- I want to feel important to you.

- I want to feel you will protect me.

- I want to be like the other kids in the family who call you Mom (or Dad).

- I want to know you will stay in my life.

- I am longing to be a *real* family when I'm here.

When responding, it *is* important for stepparents to be sensitive to stepping on a co-parent's toes. On the other hand, responding too quickly with, "*Oh, honey, you have a mom/dad!*" protects the child's other parent but may leave the child alone with deep emotional longings that they may not have words for yet. Do your best to speak to what's "underneath" the question. *"Oh, love-bug, are you wondering just how much I love you inside and out?" "Are you wondering if I'll help you with important things like homework, or when you get sick? Are you hoping that when Dad's at work I'll take care of you just like Madeline?"*

BOTTOM LINE

Naming a stepparent is best left to kids, not adults. In the event that a young child wants to call a stepparent "momma" or "papa" and that throws a co-parent into-next-week, the key is to work together to find an acceptable alternative that allows the child to make the relationship their own without on-going conflict or escalating loyalty binds.

HAZARD ⊘ Insisting that children call a stepparent "Mom" or "Dad" does *not* increase the sense of family. In fact, it is usually extremely destructive for kids. It asks children to *replace* their absent parent with the new stepparent, and it rushes a relationship that requires time to develop. It also deprives children of one of the few things they have control over: How they experience and *name* the relationship.

ADULTS WHO "GET IT" CAN HELP A LOT

What struggling children need *first* from adults is what psychiatrist Dan Siegel calls *"feeling felt"*: adults who can resonate with the *child's* feelings, and who can tell the story from the *child's* point of view. Sometimes what kids need most is help finding words for their confusion and overwhelm.

Practice Telling the Story from the Kiddo's Point of View

As children respond to moving in together, supporting them through their unease may now become more of a 24-7 job. An important skill is the ability to tell the story *from the child's point of view*. For example, a parent who rushed forward in a relationship, too fast for a kiddo, may now have to back up and tell the story from the child's point of view: *"I was pushing way too fast, huh . . . I'm guessing that was really tough. I bet I scared you. You weren't ready."*

> ## Stepfamily Challenges May Unearth
> ## Old Childhood Wounds for Adults
>
> Children will do best if you can move *toward* their pain, rather than dismissing it, or minimizing it, or even trying to fix it. This gets complicated if you start to experience pain from your past. Sorting out your feelings (is it from past hurts?) can be really helpful. Here are two places to watch for:
>
> - **If you were poorly parented yourself**, or if you were shamed or left alone to manage overwhelming feelings, you may find yourself avoiding, or getting lost in, the child's pain. Be alert if you feel stuck, numb, shut down or anxious to fix the child's situation. This is likely your younger self arriving on the scene needing a bit of help.
>
> - **If you were rejected** as a child, or not protected from physical or emotional abuse, or if your basic need for connection was unmet, you may find a child or stepchild's rejection or their need for their parent especially unbearable.
>
> - **Be alert to persistent feelings** of anxiety and upset and low tolerance for sharp words and unsettling behavior from kids. This could be kicking up a harsh, old parenting voice that lives in the recesses of your childhood history.
>
> (If you decide to look for a therapist, see the guidelines in appendix C.)

WHEN KIDS STRUGGLE AND WHEN KIDS THRIVE

Parents often wonder if they should put their "difficult" kiddo in counseling. They wonder *"what's wrong?"* And often hope someone else can fix them. In our experience, it's actually rare that a child has an "individual" problem requiring therapy. Rather, the family *system* has a problem. An "unruly" or depressed child is like the *canary in the coal mine* alerting everyone that there are family dynamics that need addressing.

> **HAZARD** ⊘ If your child is showing **alarming signs** in mood change or behavior that persist, if they aren't sleeping or eating patterns are changing drastically, if school performance precipitously drops or if their peer

relationships take a noticeable change, please consult your child's healthcare provider about health concerns. *Then*, get good help from an expert in stepfamily! See appendixes C and D for key tips for vetting a good one.

Walk closely beside children as you take this stepfamily journey together. When they struggle, reach out to them. Answer their SOS with curiosity and kindness. Find out what their experience of the hike is like—a hike they maybe didn't want to go on in the first place. Find out how heavy are the burdens they're carrying and how much of those can you take from them or help them to carry with less stress. With that kind of support, patience and love, most kiddos eventually thrive!

· · · · · · · · · · ·

You're on this path because you're in love, and that will go a long way toward putting a spring in your step. But kids are more likely to be ambivalent about this trip. They drag their feet, complain, resist, want to quit and go back to the way things were. That's perfectly natural. Just know that what will give them a second wind is feeling respected and heard by you. What will give them stamina is being seen, appreciated and loved. The more you can balance your desire to start a new life together with your sweetie with children's needs for security and connection, the more everyone will be able to make the climb to stepfamily—and flourish.

Chapter 12

Second Stepfamily Challenge: Insider/Outsider Positions

"The opposite of anger is not calmness, it's empathy."
—Mehmet Oz, cardiac surgeon and author

Very few experiences are more painful for humans than to be *ignored*—or to be *left behind*. A partner, from their place at the campfire, all too often experiences a parent jumping up and running off with the kids. Partners may find themselves trying to make just enough noise in hopes their loved ones will return to them—sometimes it feels like gentle calls will do. Other times it's the fierce cries of a stuck outsider filled with accumulated hurt.

Similarly, if the adults run off to skinny-dip and the kids feel their absence, kids often telegraph, *"What about us!?!"*

Parents find themselves in an equally painful place best described by the saying "caught between a rock and a hard place." Turn towards their partner, kids beat their drums. Turn toward the kids, even a supportive partner may let you know they're wearing thin over time. If you've ever wondered what it's like to feel like you're "never enough," jump into stepfamily as a parent!

New stepcouples find themselves having to befriend both these positions as they learn to hold on to the safety ropes of *stepcoupleship*. Are there things you and your sweetie can do to secure your safety ropes between you more comfortably? Yes! Read on.

UNDERSTANDING THE CHALLENGE

While you were dating and getting serious, maybe you were waiting for "someday" when parents wouldn't have to turn away from partners to focus on kids, and partners wouldn't feel left. *"When we live together, this will be easier."* Ah, sweet fantasy.

By now you are learning that this insider/outsider situation is part and parcel of being in a stepfamily. Hopefully it will soften over time, but for now, daily life together may actually intensify these dynamics.

First, let's look at how to gently untie the binds that hurt, and then give you the tools to safely *tie the knot* of connection.

Stuck "Insider" and Stuck "Outsider"

Back in Chapter 11, Fran moved in with Ben and his two kiddos, Annie and Luke. Here they are, six months later, doing the insider/outsider dance.

Wednesday Nights

It was Ben's regular midweek time with his kids. Fran met Ben and the kids at the door with a smile. Luke, age 8, walked in and gave Fran a fairly friendly "Hey!" Annie, age 12, ignored her and continued chatting away with her dad about a school project. Fran, eyebrows raised, tried to catch Ben's eye, but he was engaged with Annie and didn't notice.

The kids dropped their backpacks on the living room couch and kicked their shoes off by the TV. Luke wandered into the kitchen and stared into the refrigerator.

"I'm hungry!" he announced.

"Bears in the woods!" Ben called back, and both kids shrieked with laughter. Fran didn't get the joke.

"Want me to start dinner?" Fran asked.

"I got it," said Ben.

"I'll help you, Dad!" Annie leaned against Ben and he put his arm around her.

"Great!" he said.

Fran stood in the doorway and watched Ben and his kids make their traditional Wednesday night macaroni-and-cheese dinner.

"Does anyone want salad with that?" she asked faintly.

"Vegetables? Yuck!" said Luke.

"I hate salad," said Annie.

"None for me, thanks," said Ben.

Fran was appalled by her new family's eating habits. "*Seriously,*" she thought to herself, "*Who feeds their kids mac and cheese once a week? And not a single vegetable in sight!*" But she bit her tongue and fixed herself a salad to bring to the table.

Over dinner, Annie and Luke chattered to their dad. The conversation slid into stories of past camping trips with Ben's family.

"Remember how Aunt Jenna always burns her marshmallows?" Luke said with his mouth full.

"And she'd always say, '*This* time, I'm *not* going to set it on fire'!" Annie giggled. Annie and Luke cried together, "And she *always* did!"

Ben laughed with them. "She's been like that since she was a kid."

Fran, who met Jenna exactly once, just listened. She felt depressed. As usual, no one looked at her or made an attempt to include her. All her tries to enter the conversation were ignored, or met with hostility by Annie.

Fran was fed up. She'd been a good sport for the past six months during this weekly Wednesday night ordeal, but she was tired of feeling so miserable.

Ben wasn't totally oblivious to her discomfort, but he had no idea how to fix it. His kids had to come first. Fran said she understood, but then she acted so wounded and unhappy when they were around. He secretly thought Annie and Luke might warm up to her faster if she tried a little harder—or tried something different? He wasn't sure. He just knew he felt dread in the pit of his stomach. He and Fran had already had a number of semi-disastrous spats about other issues since they had moved in together. Her silence felt ominous.

After the kids went back to their mom's, Fran and Ben tried to talk about it.

"I just feel so left out when you and the kids are together," she said. "I was in the room, but I wasn't part of the conversation. Annie ignored me. Luke tolerated me. And what was hard for me was that you didn't seem to notice. I get it—" she said quickly, before he protested. "When they're over, you're on dad duty. I'm not blaming you. I just need you to understand what this is like for me. It's really hard!"

Ben didn't *want* it to be hard. It made him anxious to hear Fran state it so blatantly. Not knowing how to fix the situation, he didn't know what to say. Fran interpreted his silence as disinterest in her, even anger that she'd criticized him. They slept on opposite sides of the bed that night, each feeling stuck and lonely.

Parents and Stepparents Experience "Family" in Fundamentally Different Ways

You probably wish you and your love could enjoy the easy closeness and connection that couples have when they see and experience things the same way. Especially if you came into your family hoping for "blending," you might be feeling disappointed that you and your sweetie are so often out of alignment.

Shared values, comforting routines and deeply rooted heart connections are just a few of the many invisible threads that connect parent and kids. These threads were woven into the fabric of their *first* family. So a*t the very moment* parents feel fully engaged with kids, outsider feelings can pop up for partners. That's the tough thing here. The partner's experiences of family are just different.

By the way, some of this can happen in first-time families, too. At certain developmental points, children may cling to one parent and reject the other. However, in first-time families, *both* parents can draw on a comforting history of sweet secure connection with their children. If things are going well enough, left-out partners in first-time couples draw on their already-established relationship with each other for comfort.

In contrast, stepcouples have no long-term, solid history of connection to help them when kids choose their parent over their stepparent. *Partners have no history of being the "chosen one" with kids, and no easy, shared activities with their parent-partner or with their stepkids to soften the experience of feeling shut out or ignored.* It is often hard for a parent to imagine what it is like to feel so constantly disconnected and left out. Likewise, it is often difficult for partners to really get how a parent feels when they are constantly pulled by meeting their kids' needs, tending to their partner's upset, and maintaining a cooperative-enough relationship with the children's other parent. Ouch. Hurt all around.

Second Stepfamily Challenge: Insider/Outsider Positions

Ben and Fran Get Stuck in a Pothole

As time went on, Ben and Fran ended up pushing each other further and further away. At first it was chilly distance, and then it was hot arguments.

"Why can't you ever put me first?" Fran said angrily the day after another dreadful (for her) Wednesday-night homecoming with his kids. "When your kids are here, it's like I don't even exist!"

"You knew I would have responsibilities to my kids! We discussed it before you moved in," Ben shouted back. "*Don't make me choose*! They're only here part-time, and you and I have plenty of time together when they're at their mom's."

Fran's protests turned increasingly bitter, "How is it that you can't see how rude they are? Why do you never stand up for me?"

Ben's responses became more dismissive and defensive, "Oh, come on. You're overreacting. They're just being kids!"

Fran and Ben's hopes of a new "blended family" were fraying. Badly.

Fran was sending the distress call of a stuck outsider stepparent. The kids' repeated rejections (some small and some that just felt out-and-out rude) were chipping away at her faith that this would ever feel like family for her. Ben was lodging the plea of a stuck insider parent. His partner's unhappiness filled him with an overwhelming sense of fear that he was failing at being the parent and the partner he wanted to be. What to do?

> ### Helpful Tips for Connecting Across the Insider/Outsider Divide
>
> Whether your experience in your stepfamily is more like Ben's or more like Fran's (or sometimes some of each), please remember that it's nobody's fault. It's just the lay of the land in stepfamilies. Here's how you can help each other:
>
> - **Reach for each other.** Saying, "*This is hard. I need you to understand,*" has a higher chance of forging connection than, "*How could you do this to me!*"

- **Stretch your empathy muscles.** Compassion releases hormones that soothe pain and shift us from "fear mode" into "well-being" mode. It's so much easier to feel close then.

- **Build your capacity to do what we call *both holding both*.** As a stepcouple, you can't be a team by feeling the same way. But you *can* become a team by "*both holding both*." Both parent and partner can hold *both* the insider's feelings of juggling so many needs and the outsider's experience of feeling invisible.

- **Find someone outside the family who "gets it."** Maybe it's a dear friend, another person in your position (outsider partner or insider parent) or a counselor who knows something about stepfamilies. This will help reset your optimism and enable you to return to your family feeling more grounded.

BOTTOM LINE

Sweeping insider/outsider feelings under the rug won't make them go away. Fighting over them frays your safety rope. Naming them for one another with gentleness and understanding can help.

Mastering the skill of both holding both is a bit like learning how to work a Chinese finger trap! The risk comes when each person attempts to pull hard from their own place in the picture, while the other attempts to tug just as hard from theirs. That's what happened to Fran and Ben. Kind of like getting your two opposing index fingers stuck in a Chinese finger trap—the harder you each yank on each other, the more stuck and upset you both feel.

What's the way out? Like the Chinese finger trap, when you can both move *toward* each other, toward holding both perspectives, you can, together, gently release the stuck place.

Let's look at how Vita and Sheryl find their way to caring and tenderness rather than painful stuckness.

"Both Holding Both" Prevents Getting Painfully Stuck

Vita's son, Jonas, age 9, was having a really tough time with the transition to living with Sheryl, his mom's new partner. When Jonas dissolved in tears, Vita had learned to gather him in her arms, let him howl, and just hold him until he calmed. After the tear storms, Jonas would often spend the rest of the day as his twinkly self. During Jonas's meltdowns, Sheryl tried to fade back. She'd step away to read a book, go for a walk or talk to a friend.

Sometimes, though, fading was tough. After one of those days, as they snuggled in bed, Sheryl said to Vita, "Sweetie, I'm having a tough time."

Vita turned toward her. "What's up, honey?"

Sheryl sighed. "I know you need to take care of Jonas. You're doing such a good job. I can see the difference it's making. But sometimes when Jonas is here, I just feel sort of, well, . . . kinda invisible."

Sheryl had said this softly and tenderly, holding Vita's hands in the dark. Vita felt a wave of uneasiness. But she could also feel Sheryl reaching for her. Vita took a breath and wrapped her arms around Sheryl.

"Say some more." And, after hearing a bit more, "Gee. . .That sounds hard. I get it."

They went to sleep in each other's arms.

A few weeks later, Vita put her head on Sheryl's shoulder and sighed. "It's like everyone needs a slice of me! I feel like I'm always disappointing somebody!"

Now it was Sheryl's turn to feel uneasy. And take a breath. She was quiet for a moment, until she could feel her caring for Vita. "I guess I can see why you would feel that way!" she said thoughtfully. They held each other for several moments.

Sheryl and Vita had many more of these conversations. Each time they talked (well, almost each time), they gained a bit more understanding of the other's difficult position. As Sheryl said at their second-year anniversary, "We've learned to both hold both."

You might be interested to hear that successful stepcouples and struggling stepcouples face the same challenges. It's just that successful ones use better interpersonal skills.

> ### Helpful Tips for Living with Insider/Outsider Positions
>
> In successful stepcouples, insider parents grow their compassion for the outsider stepparents. Outsider stepparents develop understanding for the parent's insider position. Here are some more strategies:
>
> - **Choose family activities wisely.** Try to find activities that are both fun *and* that level the playing field for all family members. You can all learn a new thing together or do something everyone already loves. You can also take turns choosing.
>
> - **Look for activities that shift outsiders in and insiders out.** If Dad is a terrible ice skater, but his kids and partner are experts, then ice skating will be a wonderful family activity that brings the partner in as an insider and shifts Dad to the outside for a while.
>
> - **Give stepparents a break.** The outsider position can be draining. Think about creating a sanctuary at home where a stepparent can retreat. You might invest in soundproofing a room or even a good pair of headphones to give stepparents some respite!
>
> - **Refresh your energy.** As a stepparent, you'll need your own friendships and activities outside the family where you're a solid insider. If stepping away to do these things feels *unfamily*-like, you may want to look at it this way: You're preventing your own burnout *and* making space for parent-child time.

Cultural Forces Can Intensify Insider/Outsider Divides

Sheryl and Vita's insider/outsider divide is compounded by their very different levels of being "out" as a same-sex couple, and by a culture that remains quite unsafe for LGBTQ people in some communities.

Sheryl Is Double "Stuck"

Vita, now in her early thirties, had been out as a lesbian since her late teens. After the initial surprise, her brothers and parents were now completely on board. They all loved Sheryl and warmly welcomed her into the family. Vita worked in a gay-owned accounting firm, played on a lesbian softball team and was actively involved in the lesbian community in their town.

Sheryl had been out for only a year when she and Vita started to date. As the principal of a Catholic school, disclosing her personal life would have cost Sheryl her job. When she came out to her large Irish Catholic family, all but one niece received the news with chilly disapproval. They refused to acknowledge Jonas's or Vita's importance in her life. All except her niece refused to meet them. When Sheryl did attend family events, she went alone, leaving her loved ones at home.

When Jonas was staying with his other mom, Vita enjoyed lots of close connections with friends, family and community, and of course she had Sheryl. It was very different for Sheryl. When Jonas was with them, and Vita was focused on parenting, Sheryl had no place outside their home to turn to. She often felt intensely lonely. You can see that these forces added yet another layer of complexity to the couple's insider/outsider divide, making their capacity to *both hold both* all the more impressive.

Insider/Outsider Challenges Often Come Early and Stay Late

The good news is that over time, the insider/outsider challenge does soften, especially for couples who learn to "hold hands" across the divide. Still . . . the tinge of insider/outsider dynamics may hang in the background of your relationship, even in very successful stepfamilies. Major transitions—a wedding or birth of a grandchild—or a crisis sometimes provide new opportunities for knitting insiders and outsiders (including co-parents) together. Sometimes though, under stress, that old challenge can come to a rolling boil again. The latter was the case for this stepcouple in their fifties.

Insiderness and Outsiderness Reappears for Lucien and Sabina

Lucien and Sabina had been together for fourteen years when Lucien's son, Steven, now 24, was in a serious car accident. Between them, Lucien and Sabina had four boys. Sabina's two, now ages 23 and 25, had lived with the couple almost full-time. Lucien's boys, now ages 24 and 27, had lived primarily with their mom, Vicky, and had spent every other weekend with their dad and stepmom. The early years of their stepfamily had been rocky as Sabina and Lucien navigated their ever-changing insider/outsider positions. Most of the time, Lucien was the outsider to Sabina and her boys. However, when Lucien's boys arrived, they absorbed his full attention, giving Sabina a taste of what it's like to be the outsider.

The last handful of years had been a lot more peaceful and stable for the whole family. Lucien's co-parent, Vicky, had remained problematic, though, continuing to snidely badmouth Lucien and Sabina to their sons. Despite these attempts to undermine her, Sabina had slowly, patiently built a solid relationship with her stepsons.

Now the car accident. Steven's injuries were life threatening. For the first time since the divorce, Vicky reached out to Lucien for help with their son. Lucien dropped everything to be there for Steven, staying with him in the hospital and collaborating with Vicky to make complex medical decisions on his behalf. For Lucien, who had felt peripheral to his sons' lives in so many ways since the divorce, this was finally the opportunity to fully parent his son, cooperatively with his son's mother—a small bit of silver lining in an otherwise dark and frightening cloud.

In the intensity, Lucien overlooked Sabina, sometimes even forgetting to let her know when, or if, he was coming home. For the first few days, fully understanding the urgency, she stayed steady while Lucien came and went. But after a week, she felt *deleted*, both by her husband's failure to include her and by feeling excluded from her hard-won relationship with her stepson. Lucien's absence, combined with her own worry for Steven, left Sabina *sideways* with upset.

The urgency of his son's crisis had tapped into Lucien's grief over his lost parenting time with his boys, creating a powerful mix with his longstanding distress over the chronic discord with their mom. Lucien later realized he had assumed Sabina would *just know*, would understand, would even be *proud* of him for stepping up so fully.

Enraged and distraught at being marginalized, Sabina's best self bit the dust. She found herself screaming an old refrain at Lucien, "What about me?!" Which of course only deepened Lucien's distress. Reeling with the pain of their suddenly re-intensified insider/outsider positions, Sabina and Lucien found themselves drop-kicked into couples counseling to find their way back to each other.

DOUBLE FAMILIES AREN'T EQUAL

What if both you and your partner have kids? Even though it *sounds* easier, it doesn't actually turn out that way most of the time. (So much for popular TV sitcoms!) In reality, when both adults bring children, a variety of factors may pull one adult into the more stuck outsider position and the other adult into a more stuck insider position. Here are just a few ways this can happen:

- **One set of children may come into the family for weekends** while the other set lives with the stepcouple more full-time. For most of the time, the full-time parent is the insider. However, when a part-time parent's child(ren) comes into the household, the part-time parent and their child(ren) often need more intense one-on-one time together, suddenly reversing the couple's positions. This was the situation for Lucien and Sabina when their kids were young.

- **One set of kids may simply be temperamentally** more energetic and outgoing, and the other set more quiet and introverted. Outgoing kids find it easier to be more welcoming of a new adult in their lives, softening the stepparent's outsider position. Quieter kids may need more distance from a nonparent adult, intensifying their stepparent's sense of outsiderness.

- **One set may be carrying a heavier burden of vulnerability**. Kids with tighter loyalty binds, more losses or particularly intense special needs will be less available, and those entering their teen years may be less available than younger children (under age 9).

EASY "WRONG TURNS" FOR STEPCOUPLES

The urge to fix the insider/outsider dilemma can easily lead a couple to take a few wrong turns. No worries! If you stay alert, you can avoid unhelpful detours and save yourself the scraped knees and bloody noses of having to backtrack.

- **Choosing the Kiddo Over the Couple:** Kids' needs are intense and important. We've certainly made the case for maintaining solid parent-child relationships. However, some parents put kids so far in front that they don't pay enough attention to the couple relationship. (That's where Lucien took a wrong turn after his son's accident.)

- **Choosing the Couple Over the Kiddo:** The internet is full of advice to put the couple first. As we saw in Chapter 11, that leaves kids alone and adrift.

BOTTOM LINE

*Again, stepcouples practice **both/and** not **either/or**. You want to carve out some regular "just us" time for **both** the parent-child relationship **and** for the couple.*

Making "Just Us" Time a Part of the Equation

Making time for your couple relationship while still attending to parent-child relationships can be tough in a busy family. The good news is that *even tiny moments can make a difference.* Look for them and use them! For instance, you can **establish daily routines for intimate couple connection**. That could look like giving each other a moment of loving connection before going to sleep and before leaving bed in the morning, or sending sweet texts, or checking in for a quick call during the day. Marriage researcher John Gottman suggests that a *20-second hug* or a *6-second kiss* can make all the difference for couple happiness. During family activities, you can make loving eye contact. (Stepparents may need a signal to remind parents to do this.) Or you can sit near enough to play footsie (privately) under the table. These tiny moments can be immensely soothing for outsider stepparents and stressed parents.

Another good idea is to **separate couple intimacy and "play time" from problem-solving time**. Yes, stepcouples do need time to talk about challenges. But nothing throws cold water on a potentially intimate moment than having a tangle over kids. Setting aside a regular time to talk about important stepfamily concerns can help you protect your play time.

You may also want to **limit devices** when you're together. The distraction of screens can cut into your intimacy. Look into each other's eyes instead of at your phone or tablet.

> **Helpful Tips to Meet the Needs of All the Relationships in Your Family**
>
> Find things to do that are fun for everyone. We completely understand the old adage "practice makes better." But remember, pressuring everyone to "blend" will get you taking too many steps forward to *all be together* only to find yourselves taking steps back to recover from the fallout.
>
> - **Stepfamilies *do* need to spend time together to build their new family.** Just keep in mind that challenges can often be *most* intense when the whole family is together. Solution? If things are tense, keep it short! If things are going well, go for it!
>
> - **Adult-only time is crucial.** Both of you need to rest in the insider position with each other without competing with powerful parent-child bonds.
>
> - **Parent-child time provides the reliable secure base that is so key to** children's well-being and, therefore, for stepfamily success. Parent-child alone time also gives parents space to attend to their kids without worrying about their partners.
>
> - **Stepparents and their stepchildren** also need time alone together to build their own new relationship. When parents are present, the stronger, pre-existing parent-child bonds dominate, pushing stepparent-stepchild relationships to the side.
>
> - **Stepsiblings** may need time—through play or shared projects—to build their "pack." Do continue to monitor for respect and safety. Keep in mind that stepsiblings, even of the same age, may or may not want a lot to do with each other. If that's the case, try to give them space from each other.

Falling into "Compassion Traps"

Some kinds of "support" can actually fan the flames of stuckness. You decide to seek the help of a therapist or to share your heart with a close friend or family member. All good. And—if the listener doesn't get the complicated architecture of your stepfamily—they may empathize with your point of view and end up aligning with your upset, accidentally closing your heart to the other people in your stepfamily. That's what happened to Sabina and Lucien.

Sabina's Therapist Meant to Be Supportive, But...

Sabina complained to her therapist that Lucien was completely ignoring her, not communicating with her, not including her while his son was in the hospital. "He's talking every day to his ex-wife and he's barely speaking to me. He doesn't even tell me when he's coming home at night!"

Her therapist, intending to be supportive, responded, "I can't believe he's doing that to you! After all the help you provided him with his sons."

Sabina teared up. "I can't believe it either! I'm *so* mad at him!?"

Sabina's therapist had meant to be helpful. But let's think about this. Will the therapist's response leave Sabina more kind and compassionate the next time she wants to say something to Lucien? Not likely! A better-informed therapist could have helped open the door by supporting them both: *"It must be so painful to feel your husband turning away. I bet you're worried sick for your stepson. These situations are so hard on everyone."*

Lucien's Buddies Meant to Be Supportive, But...

Lucien took a break from hospital duty and met his three best friends for a beer. When they asked how things were going, he complained, "Sabina is off her rocker! I can finally help my son and all she can do is nag me about when I'll be home."

"She needs to get a grip," said one of the guys.

Second Stepfamily Challenge: Insider/Outsider Positions

"Definitely," said another. "This isn't the time to nag!"

"That's right," agreed the third. "It's totally unreasonable to demand anything from you right now, when your son is lying in the hospital with broken bones and a concussion!"

Would these responses help Lucien approach Sabina in a calm and caring way, and ask for space to be with his son? Not likely. More helpful might have been: *"Boy. That sounds hard all around. Have you been telling her how much you love her?"*

* * * * * * * * * * *

Sometimes when you're hiking, one person gets tired, or feels a bit wobbly, or is questioning whether this climb is worth it. If you reach back and extend a hand, and if they take it, the whole trip gets easier for everyone. That's what we're talking about here. Check the safety ropes regularly. Reach for each other.

Chapter 13

. . . .

The Third Stepfamily Challenge: Divided Over Discipline

"Let's not forget it's you and me vs. the problem . . . NOT you vs. me."

—Steve Maraboli, motivational speaker

Discipline can be a thorny issue in many stepfamilies. Who makes the rules and who's in charge of whom? Who will listen to whom? And what do we do when they *don't* listen?

Here's a fun fact: Stepcouples and first-time couples have about the same amount of relationship conflict (believe it or not!), and they both typically fight about money and kids. But first-time couples fight more about money. *Stepcouples fight more about kids.* And they often fight in a very particular way.

> Turns out that stepparents everywhere seem to want more limits and structure with their stepchildren. Parents everywhere seem to want more love and understanding for their children.

Let's wrestle with these seemingly opposite pulls, find out what puts them there and look at what you can do to bridge the divides over discipline that tend to bloom more now that you're *in it* 24-7.

Your first supply stop for this challenge is understanding parenting styles and their impact on children. You're likely to be banging up against your different needs and ideas about parenting as the new normal becomes a daily reality. This stuff can drive you crazy and pull the kids right along with you. At the next comfort station, you'll become acquainted with the differences between parenting and *step*parenting, especially when it comes to discipline. You'll find an easy-to-read placard on interesting research—insights into what works and what doesn't!

By the end of this chapter, you'll have some solid ideas for how to create a strong coalition—you and your partner caring for kids—that honors your different roles.

Ready? Let's do this.

UNDERSTANDING PARENTING STYLES

Children need two things from parents: warmth *and* structure. The chart on the next page shows you that parenting styles can range from warm to cold in one direction, and they can go from permissive to firm in the other. Decades of research combine these into four parenting styles: **authoritative** (warm and firm), **authoritarian** (cold and firm), **permissive** (warm and permissive), and **disengaged** (cold and permissive). And there's a fifth style: **unpredictable**.

Your Primer on Parenting Styles

The nub of this challenge is that stepfamily seems to create a tug-of-war effect between parents and stepparents when it comes to parenting styles. Stepparents try to pull for more firmness and limits. Parents often respond by becoming more loving and lenient. Stepparents are left thinking, *"That's the last thing that kiddo needs!"* And you guessed it, the stepparent goes for *more* limits. This is the making of a vicious circle. If kids catch wind of it, they're caught in the middle between parent and stepparent.

It's no fun to be caught in this kind of struggle with your beloved. Let's take a look at each of these styles, how they impact kids and how they show up in stepfamily.

PARENTING STYLES

	WARM TO COLD	
AUTHORITATIVE	Warm and Firm	Cold and Firm	**AUTHORITARIAN**
PERMISSIVE	Permissive and Warm	Permissive and Cold	**DISENGAGED**

(Vertical axis: FIRM TO PERMISSIVE)

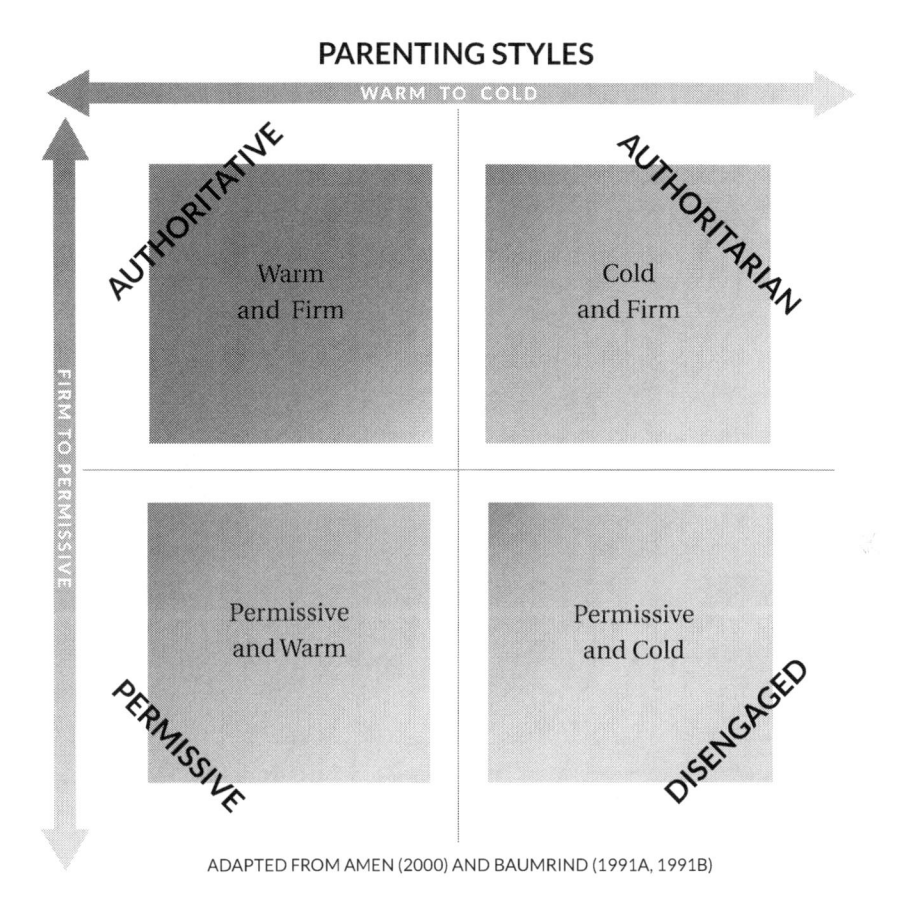

ADAPTED FROM AMEN (2000) AND BAUMRIND (1991A, 1991B)

***Authoritative* parenting is both warm *and* firm.** *Authoritative* parents are loving, empathic and caring. They *also* set moderately firm limits for their children, and they give them adequate supervision and follow-through. This parenting style respects kids. Parents encourage children to express their ideas and feelings and give kids options to choose, within reason.

> **Bottom Line:** *Authoritative* parenting leads to the most positive outcomes for children on every measure imaginable. Kids with authoritative parents do better in school, have better social skills and have higher self-esteem and confidence. They also have lower rates of drug and alcohol use, behavior problems, depression and anxiety. Warm and firm is the winning combination!

***Authoritarian* parenting is firm *but* cold.** *Authoritarian* parents set clear expectations and consequences, but they don't give kids the affection, empathy and warmth that all children need. Authoritarian parenting values *obedience* over *connection*. As a result, this parenting style is often rigid, coercive (*"If you don't obey, I will not love you or will turn away from you"*) and dictatorial (*"I'm right. You're wrong"*). The adult's need for control becomes more important than understanding and addressing the reasons a child may be struggling. Adult expectations may be unrealistic and delivered with too much force. Sure, you might see obedient behavior from kids. This gives the *illusion* that authoritarian parenting is effective, but it actually can cause a lot of problems for kids.

> **Bottom Line: *Authoritarian*** *parenting is more likely to foster anxiety and insecurity. Higher levels of stress hormones make kids more excitable and emotionally unstable, which makes it harder for them to control themselves. They struggle more academically. (As you'll see, stepfamily unfortunately pulls stepparents into authoritarian parenting. This often feels "right" to stepparents—as if it will correct unhealthy behavior or habits. But, unfortunately, it's not good for kids or, it turns out, for stepfamily well-being.)*

***Permissive* parenting is warm and caring, but not firm enough.** Although permissive parenting is often very loving, permissive parents don't ask enough of children and they often don't provide sufficient supervision, monitoring and follow-through. Permissive parenting makes *too few* developmentally appropriate demands for healthy responsibility and appropriate maturity.

> **Bottom Line:** *Children raised with permissive parents are less likely to stick with difficult tasks and are less likely to take responsibility. Stressed solo-parents sometimes find themselves defaulting to somewhat more permissive parenting after separation/divorce and other stressful times in life because they just want to make life easier for children or to avoid exhausting battles.*

***Disengaged* parenting is *neither* warm *nor* firm.** A disengaged parent leaves children way too alone with all their emotions and thoughts—and without either warmth or discipline. A parent may be physically present, but they're emotionally absent. This style of parenting has extremely serious negative consequences for kids, leading to major trauma, difficulties with relationships, worse school performance, lower self-esteem and self-confidence and more.

> **Bottom Line:** *When children find themselves adrift, isolated with their feelings and thoughts and without adults to help them hold it all, they are left with few options other than to shut down or become overwhelmed, or swing wildly between both. Disengaged parents don't support kids to learn to say what they want and need in constructive ways, and they don't help them learn other important life skills, such as how to organize tasks, manage their time and get homework done.*

Unpredictable parenting can whip back and forth from permissive on Tuesday to authoritarian on Saturday. We often see unpredictable parenting when a parent suffers from addictions and/or mental health issues. Children end up feeling deeply anxious, insecure, lost and chronically frightened. Some children become hypervigilant—anxiously watching for the next switch. Others withdraw, numb out or collapse.

> **Bottom Line:** *Unpredictable parenting can crop up in stepfamilies when parents swing between permissiveness to protect kids and then jump into strictness under pressure from stepparents who want lots more limits. Sometimes stepparents who have been biting their tongues finally can't bear it another second and explode.*

Most adults move along the spectrum of these five parenting styles. Parents usually change styles depending on stress level, skill level, a child's temperament, particular circumstances and the way the parent was raised. Generally, though, most adults have a certain preferred style—a parenting-style comfort zone.

When Parents and Stepparents Get Caught in the Tug-of-War

Again, stepparents typically pull for more limits for their stepchildren, while parents typically want more kindness and care for their kids. When this goes badly, it can become a relentless tussle—stepparents tugging so hard that they tip over into authoritarian parenting, and parents pulling just as hard so that they end up dropping into permissive parenting. What kids need is *neither* of these! And they certainly don't need to feel there's a tug-of-war about them between the adults.

In ordinary, everyday stepfamily life, this parenting seesaw looks like . . .

- Stepparents hear "back talk"; parents hear "a lively conversation."

- Stepparents sees "disrespectful ignoring"; parents see "shy and overwhelmed."

- Stepparents call out "laziness"; parents describe "difficulties with attention" or "not a big deal."

- Stepparents say parents are "giving in" or "being oblivious"; parents say they're "being flexible and responsive" or "choosing my battles."

When stepparents feel frustrated at what they see as a lack of structure and limit-setting, they may take parenting matters into their own hands and step into the disciplinarian role. And, sometimes, tired parents are relieved to have stepparents "take over."

Red alert! Red alert! This will not end well!

Kids are just not ready for stepparents' attempts at discipline. All too often, the result is that their behavior actually gets *worse*! Parents step up their protectiveness, which frustrates stepparents, who become more desperate and more demanding. In turn, parents try to soften the impact of dictatorial stepparenting by making runs around the partner (*"Never mind what she said. I'll give you the cell phone back before school tomorrow."*). Stepparents cry foul at the broken agreements.

Patricia calls this the *Polarization Polka*. It isn't pretty. And it isn't good for kids.

The Third Stepfamily Challenge: Divided Over Discipline

The Polarization Polka is One Dance You Want to Miss!

Warren and Lizabeth each brought a daughter to their stepfamily. Briana, age 12, and Mitsy, age 7. Both girls lived half the time with Warren and Lizabeth and half the time with their other parent. Briana was an introvert, easily distracted and overwhelmed. She struggled in school. Mitsy was an outgoing, charming and well-behaved second grader who excelled in school.

Because Warren's income easily supported the household, the couple decided that Lizabeth would stay home with both girls. Lizabeth could already see lots of areas where she could assist Briana with more consistent structure than Warren had been providing. For instance, Lizabeth wanted both girls to have assigned chores in the house. Warren agreed that Briana could use a little more guidance, so Lizabeth waded right in. When Briana forgot to clean her room or left her homework undone, Lizabeth responded by taking away her tablet. When Briana objected, Lizabeth sent her to her room for being "disrespectful." (Lizabeth certainly didn't want Mitsy emulating *that* sort of rudeness.)

Briana's behavior did change, but not in the direction Lizabeth was aiming for. The girl withdrew and began refusing to talk to her stepmom or dad. She stopped doing her homework, left her room even messier than before and made faces and gagging noises at meals to insult Lizabeth's cooking. Lizabeth saw these behaviors as further evidence of Briana's "insolence" and declared that Warren and Briana's mother had spoiled the girl for far too long.

At first, Warren appreciated Lizabeth's firmer hand with his daughter. But Lizabeth's increasingly harsh tone and Briana's deepening depression began worrying him. He started to feel protective of his daughter. After yet another run-in between Lizabeth and Briana, Warren went up to Briana's room to comfort her. He told her, "Don't worry. I'll give you your tablet after we leave the house."

Lizabeth was outraged that Warren wasn't backing her up.

"We had a deal and you went behind my back and gave her the tablet. You undermined my authority!" she shouted.

"You're too hard on her." Warren objected. "She's just a kid. Cut her some slack!"

"She's rude and disobedient." Lizabeth declared.

Warren was offended. "That's *my* daughter you're talking about. She's a normal teenager."

"Look at my daughter. You *never* see Mitsy act that way."

"Of course Mitsy behaves," Warren retorted, "She's terrified of you!"

Lizabeth shot back, "Maybe if Briana was a little more scared of you, she'd behave better!"

Warren slammed out of the house. Unfortunately, both girls had heard the fight. Briana went to her room and texted her mom. Mitsy, feeling extremely anxious, ran to set the table, hoping to ease her mother's stress.

Oh dear. This was *not* what Warren and Lizabeth had been looking forward to when they became a stepfamily! And, it turns out, it is also not what either of their children needed.

There are better ways to do this! Stepparents can support parents to become firmer parents, and parents can help stepparents become warmer and more understanding with kids. But first, let's understand a bit more about what drives these differences between parents and stepparents.

Why Do Parents and Stepparents Feel So Differently About Kids?

Parents start out in love. Psychologists call it "attachment." It's the kind of bond that comes from that absolutely in-love feeling that parents feel holding their babies—love big enough and strong enough to ride them through late-night feedings and nights with no sleep, toddler tantrums, runny noses and teen meltdowns. Stepparents don't have this kind of bond with their stepchildren. Even in very good stepparent-stepchild relationships, the stepparent-stepchild bond often has a very different, more hard-earned, flavor.

Even when their children act in ways that upset them, parents can draw on their strong foundation of attachment to help them reset their own emotional temperature—cool off, warm up or whatever adjustment is called for. Stepparents just don't have that foundation with their stepkids. That means parents can more easily simply *ignore* a whole list of behaviors that stepparents find impossible to ignore. ("*Oh, she just gets distracted easily.*" "*He's just never been good at wiping up the crumbs around the toaster.*" "*She's just not the kind of kid who says hello when she comes into the house.*")

Parents and children have a million and one shared understandings. Parents and kids both know what they mean by acceptable table manners, or keeping the noise down, or how much is too much to pay for a pair of sneakers. And even when they don't agree, they speak the same language.

Parents also know their own child's vulnerabilities and strengths, and they know the historical context behind "difficult," provocative or irritating behavior. When kids are under stress, parents may care more about providing emotional comfort than correcting their lapses into "bad" behavior.

Stepparents often carry significant support functions for the family, without the benefits. Stepparents may cook the kids' meals, do their laundry, mow the lawn, chauffeur kids around, *and* pay half the bills. Struggling kids often don't give much affection or appreciation in return. This can leave stepparents in serious emotional *deficit spending*—which makes kids' ordinary levels of messiness, noise and impulsivity that much *more* irritating for a stepparent.

Unfortunately, even when parents do start asking more of their children, stepparents may remain irritated at what they see as a lack of progress or a much-too-*slow* pace of change. Stepparents can find themselves thinking, "*You never listen to me—you just don't care!*" Parents may end up thinking, "*I'm listening and doing my best, and it's never enough for you.*" Sigh.

What We Know About What Works in Stepfamilies

You're in luck, because there's a huge amount of research that can help you figure out how to best manage these discipline divides. Some of these findings may surprise you!

- **Children in all families do best with *authoritative* (warm and firm) parenting.** The need only gets greater during a major transition such as becoming a stepfamily.

- **Parents need to hold on to the role of disciplinarian.** Even *authoritative* discipline from a stepparent, when it comes too early, can backfire with stepkids. It really is best if stepparents can leave discipline to parents until or unless the time is right. (More below!)

- **Successful stepparents focus on connection, not correction.** Relationship building is your primary goal right now (and sometimes for a long time), not trying to control or correct your stepkids

- *Authoritarian* **(strict and cold) parenting by stepparents is toxic** to stepparent-stepchild relationships. Sadly, it's exactly the parenting style that "feels right" to many stepparents.

- **Once children feel they have a trusting, caring relationship with stepparents,** stepparents can move *slowly* into *authoritative* parenting. It's easier to take on this role with children younger than 8, and harder with older kids.

- **In many mature, thriving stepfamilies, stepparents do not ever step into a disciplinary role.** They form strong, loving relationships (or at least civil and friendly ones) with their stepchildren and parents hold on to the limit setting.

In fact, it turns out that the word *discipline* has its roots in a Latin word that means *disciple*, as in someone who learns from you. Not someone you *punish* or *control*. As a stepparent, your evolving role as mentor, guide and trusted adult can be a warm and positive lifelong, caring connection with your stepkids that you'll both treasure.

EMBRACE THE STEPPARENT ROLE AS A DIFFERENT ROLE FROM THE PARENT ROLE

"Being a stepparent has been one of the great joys as well as one of the big learning edges of my life....It requires a large amount of love and a small amount of self-importance," writes Christopher Mills, psychotherapist, author.

Stepparenting is (*very*) different from parenting

Unless children are young when the stepcouple begins living together, building a close stepparent-stepchild bond can take lots of and lots of patience and, sometimes, warmth without immediate return. For older children, or children with a strong loyalty bind, psych yourself up to build this relationship over many years. Here are a few things to think about:

- **Every stepparenting relationship is going to be different.** With some kids, it's a long, slow grind toward acceptance. With others, maybe you inch forward, leap ahead and then slide back. And, especially if kids are young, it can also be a fairly smooth ride—nice!

- **Stepparenting is a long-term investment.** If you're a stepparent and you're finding it hard, *you may not be doing anything wrong.* Try to remember that you're in it for the long haul—the return on your investment may go up and down, but ultimately it will pay off.

- **You might be wondering and worrying if you can really** *do this.* Unlike becoming a parent, becoming a stepparent is a choice that *can be* undone. When a stepparent throws their whole heart and soul into creating their stepfamily, the waves of complexity and disappointment may be overwhelming at times. Aligning expectations with reality may sometimes feel heartbreaking. Give yourself room to grieve.

- **Enjoying your stepkids may be hard on your kids.** Speaking of conundrums. Your four-year-old stepdaughter flies full-body into your arms the moment you walk in the door. Your eight-year-old daughter, who has just arrived from her other parent's home, looks on in horror.

- **Giving up control as a stepparent can be tough.** Successful stepparents defer to parents when it comes to setting limits with children. It's for the best, but that doesn't mean it sometimes isn't frustrating and disheartening to let go of control over what does and doesn't get done, how it gets done, when it gets done in your own home.

- **Staying on the sidelines of someone else's parenting is tough!** Parents often joke that the "perfect parents" are the ones without children. Watching someone else parent from the sidelines can be maddening, especially if you don't get right away how it's a 24-7 job that gets under your skin and on your nerves, fills your heart and sometimes breaks it.

Stepparent-Stepchild Relationships Are Built Over Time

Close stepparent-stepchild bonds *can* grow from persistently friendly interactions and respectful timing. Stepparenting is different from parenting. But it doesn't have to be second-best. In fact, it can become an enduring connection that sustains both children and stepparents throughout their lives. Exciting! Even the most distant stepparent-stepchild relationships, with *enough* time and careful tending, can grow and flourish.

We promise that *your* stepfamily has these seeds. Here's a story of how this happens, even when things look awfully dire for a while!

We described Cash and his stepdaughter, Lilly, in Chapter 11, when Lilly was becoming more and more openly defiant with every step forward of her new stepfamily. When we last saw them, Cash had learned to "fade" so that Lilly's mom, Tanzi, could reconnect with her daughter. Lilly was inching slowly out of her early-teen rebelliousness.

Lilly Discovers Her Stepdad's a Good Guy

Four years after Tanzi and Cash's wedding, Lilly had slowly warmed up to her stepdad. As she approached her sixteenth birthday and her driver's test, she begged her mom for more driving practice. However, every test drive was becoming a battle over what Lilly saw as her Mom's overly anxious corrections.

After conferring with Tanzi, Cash casually offered to take Lilly to the school parking lot on a Sunday to give her some practice with parallel parking. They had rarely been in the car alone together. Cash felt a bit apprehensive about how this would fly with his still sometimes-obstreperous stepdaughter. It flew just fine. Lilly grabbed the keys!

Cash's first move: "Choose a good radio station!"

"Sure," Lilly said. He thought her saw her relax a tiny bit.

As Lilly's stepparent, Cash wasn't burdened by the cloud of anxiety parents of a new driver often feel. In fact, he was able to see that Lilly was rather a careful driver. He commented on her good habits of checking the mirrors and turning her head to make sure no one was behind them before she put the car into reverse.

By the *third* trip out, Lilly suggested, "Hey, want to stop at Starbucks and get a Frappuccino before we go back?"

Cash smiled to himself and said, "*Sure.*"

They spent an hour together talking about boys, school and upcoming cheer tryouts.

"It was worth the wait!" Cash told Tanzi later that night. "She's growing into a lovely young woman."

> ### Helpful Tips for *Care-Filled* Stepparenting
>
> As Patricia says, strong stepparent-stepchild relationships are not a given. *But they can be gotten.* These guidelines will help:
>
> - **Stepparents function best as sounding boards, not as saviors.** Your beloved may *want* you to back up their limit-setting. RESIST.
>
> - **When a parent is absent, the stepparent enforces "the rules of the home."** Much of the way an adult babysitter or relative would, a stepparent communicates the parent's expectations to the parent's kids. *Parents* set the framework. A parent might say, "*Steve is in charge while I am gone. You know the rules. No social media before homework is done.*" Stepparents report infractions to parents, but it's up to *parents* to enforce consequences.
>
> - **When a child says, "*You're not my parent!*" take a breath.** If your emotional temperature is still up there, take another one. When you've got your cool back, there are lots of things you can say: "*Yep! You're right. You already have a dad. Meanwhile, though, I am the adult in charge tonight. We both know that your mom's rule is no TV until your homework is done. I'd like to be able to tell her that's exactly what you did. Your choice!*"

Positive Stepparent-Stepchild Relationships Matter

In fact, stepparent-stepchild relationships matter a *lot*. Research tells us when these relationships are warm and caring, it makes a big difference in kids' adjustment to being part of a stepfamily. And the impact spreads throughout the family: When stepparents and stepkids have good relationships, it makes for happier couple relationships and better adjustment for the whole stepfamily. This is true across racially and economically diverse stepfamilies.

Helpful Tips for Building an "Intimate Outsider" Role with Stepkids

In the best of all possible worlds, stepkids come to realize that their stepparent is . . . actually kind of cool! Over time, stepparents can often become what Patricia calls an *intimate outsider*, a person that a child—particularly a teen—can turn to for advice and mentoring when parents are too emotionally involved. We've talked about "connection before correction." Here are a few more tips for moving forward:

- **"Relationships before rules."** Get interested in your stepchild. Lead with your genuine curiosity about what interests them and what perplexes them.

- **Look for positive feedback.** Stepparent-stepchild communication can easily turn tense and negative. Once it starts downhill, it's easy to keep sliding. Actively look for specific things you can appreciate. *"I hear you did well on that math test you studied for. Good going." "I noticed you took the garbage out. I know that's a stinky job. You rock."*

- **Calm, factual Public Service Announcements** can be very useful, especially if they can be delivered with a twinkle. Engaging a child in a two-way dialogue (especially a distant adolescent stepchild) can be extremely frustrating. A PSA is often best delivered to the window or to the kid's left elbow—not directly to their face. *"Just so you know, I know this stepfamily business has been tough. We'll both hang in. I think it will be OK. But right now, I know it's hard." "Just so you know, I think we could both be a bit more civil. I'll work hard on my part. I'd love to see you work on yours!"*

- **Tolerate some back talk.** Back talk is generally much harder for stepparents to bear, or even to witness, than it is for parents. Giving children some freedom to disagree and to protest is actually essential in building healthy, hardy adults.

Parenthood in a Next-Time Family

*"I'll love you forever,
I'll like you for always.
As long as I'm living,
My baby you'll be."*

—Robert Munsch, American-Canadian author

Parents face some tough challenges, too. As the parent in your stepfamily, you may feel a jumble of different things. For one, relief and delight to have another adult share home life and help with kid chores. *And*, tired, because you're the rubber band that keeps getting stretched in multiple directions—it's hard work not snapping back at anyone or breaking altogether. At times, you're likely feeling, surprisingly, *really alone*.

- **Parents love their kids like no one else loves their kids.** A common fantasy parents have when they get serious with a new partner sounds like this: "I love you. You love *me*. So of course you'll love my kids!" Hmmm. Not necessarily. Chances are, you will *always* be more excited and moved by your kids than your partner will ever be.

- **Parents often continue to be stuck insiders.** When a child in a first-time family needs something, both adults usually feel fine about either parent attending to the child. In a stepfamily, when a child needs something, your sweetie may be not so glad, even sometimes hurt.

- **You are still the sole disciplinarian**. For now, and for some kids, for the long haul, you're it when your kids need someone to set firm limits. You are also the advocate for warmth and caring when your partner wants harder discipline than you feel is right for your kids.

- **Grief goes with the territory.** In those moments when it becomes starkly evident that a partner just doesn't love your kids the way you do, it can be an emotional stab in your heart and a slap in the face of your hopes and dreams about your new relationship. *"I'm so sad. I'm getting, finally, that my husband just doesn't feel the same way about my kids that I do." "She cares about my kids, but she just isn't* smitten *the way I am!"*

- **Parents sometimes worry about the influence of their *stepkids* on their kids.** A dad growing up with three brothers, now raising his three sons, finds his kids' "jungle-life" antics boy normal and fun. His partner, a mom with two younger and gentler children, never realized what it would be like having her kids exposed to her stepsons' *roughhousing* day-in and day-out.

- **Sometimes parents have to step in and protect their kids.** When stepparents are harsh or overly critical, it's the parent's job to protect their kids. This can be a very difficult and painful decision but a crucial one for kids' well-being. Aligning with your children's needs against your partner will likely involve relationship fallout that will take thoughtful repair. If it cannot be repaired, protecting children may require leaving the relationship.

Once you've become a parent, a new relationship and a new family structure doesn't change the indelible and amazing role of *being the parent*. This is what it means when you say, "I have children."

BECOMING A TEAM

You've brought a new partner into your life, your children's lives. You're creating a *home*. You've joined the fray for better or for worse. Now let's focus on the two of you as a team.

> ### Helpful Tips for Building a Strong Team Around Kid Issues
>
> Successful stepcouples find ways to do a *collaborative cha-cha* rather than a *polarization polka*. What dance you end up doing together is much more about *how* you talk about your differences than whether you have them.
>
> - **Use your tool kit of great communication tools** when you need to make adjustments or do repair work. *Calm yourself*. Take a breath, take a break. *Listen*. Seek first to understand. *Switch out of defensiveness*. Stay on the high road. Balance five positives for each negative. Cherish one another. *Repair the hurts*. A heartfelt apology really helps.

- **Notice even the tiniest positive changes.** All parents are sensitive about their parenting. Parents in stepfamilies often feel hopeless about being able to measure up to their partner's expectations. An encouraging word, an acknowledgment of the effort they and their kids are making, will go a long way. Likewise, stepparents often feel very discouraged, and they often don't get much appreciation from their stepkids. Parents can acknowledge when stepparents do something for their kids, or when they hold back from being authoritarian and practice patience with frustrating kid behavior.

- **Turn toward one another gently as often as possible.** A "struggling" partner or child may need even *more* warmth and connection. Withdrawing affection is *never* a good solution. Notes of appreciation or silly drawings in a kid's lunchbox? Texting a heart to a partner for "no reason"?

Even couples in flourishing stepfamilies occasionally find themselves tugging against each other over parenting issues. For stepparents, building family-like relationships with children wired to the hearts of other adults is complicated. When stepparents let go of trying to be disciplinarians, an amazing opportunity opens for building warm and enduring relationships with stepchildren. And when stepparent-stepkid relationships thrive, so does the whole stepfamily.

For parents, hear the frustrations from your partner as code language for, *"I'm struggling* right now." If you've ever watched performances on the rings in men's gymnastics, imagine yourself now as strong and capable of holding your kids in one hand and your partner in the other as you work your way through differences. By keeping defensiveness at bay, you'll be more capable of keeping your balance together.

Like so many things stepfamily, this challenge asks you both to dig down deep to understand the conundrums you each face and to keep reaching toward each other. From this refueled place, armed with perspective, you can begin each day as two of the key people who will usher children along their path to adulthood.

Chapter 14

Fourth Stepfamily Challenge: Co-parents Are Part of the Stepfamily

> *"What is best for the child is not always what is most convenient for the parent" [or stepparent]. (Brackets added by authors!)*
>
> —Bonnie Bedford, writer

Co-parents are an inescapable part of stepfamily. For the partner who might want a more typical nuclear-family experience—an adult couple with kids and no other significant influences—this can be quite a challenge!

There's a lot that you (as a new stepcouple) and your co-parent(s) will share—in *all* kinds of weather along the journey. Each of you will find your place in the whirlwind of raising kids across two homes. You'll exchange regular forecasts on the kids' needs and moods: The storms of upsets, illnesses and accidents. The dustups of a forgotten "lovey" or algebra textbook. The constant snowstorms of extracurriculars and activities. Hopefully, you'll stand together in the bright sunshine of graduations and weddings and other celebrations.

Together, this group of adults (parents, stepparents, co-parents) may have hard times with one another. With discipline and generosity, these tangles may remain a tempest in a teacup. Or, if left unchecked, they can erupt into an all-out earthquake that threatens to bury the whole family.

As you begin your lives as a stepfamily, one of your key tasks will be coalescing as a team that respects the co-parents' primary decision-making roles. In time, a step at a time, the ultimate goal is that the parents and stepparent(s) become a fully functioning parenting coalition.

To meet this challenge, you'll both need to bring the best in yourselves to circumstances that could tempt your worst. But, no fear: We've got some routes picked out and the tools you'll need to make this aspect of your stepfamily journey as stress-free as possible.

LET'S REVISIT KIDS CAUGHT IN THE MIDDLE

We've said it before and we'll say it again: The most powerful predictor of a child of separation/divorce's adjustment is the level of conflict between their parents, combined with the quality of parenting. This means that children's physical and emotional health, academic performance, peer choices and general well-being are often a direct result of the skillfulness of the co-parenting relationship.

Kids don't do well when they feel torn between the people they love. Whether it's a noisy war or a silent battle, they feel it and hate it!

Caught in the Middle

(Used with permission of Dawn Braithwaite)

If co-parents are still battling, what can you both do to keep kids out of the middle? So much! First, let's get clear about what's harmful for kids: Hearing their parent or stepparent make snide comments about a parent. Seeing facial expressions that telegraph disgust at the mention of their other parent. Burdening kids with ugly adult information *("Dad is sleeping with his boss."*), or leaking bitterness (*"Don't count on her showing up on Sunday. She lets everyone down."*) or directing children not to repeat something that shouldn't have been said in the first place (*"Don't tell Mom I told you . . ."*). Not good. Period.

You might also want to know that if the adults slip up and put the kids in the middle, you may find that kids try to manage their predicament by telling not-so-true stories as a desperate attempt to make each parent feel "chosen." The solution is: *Keep kids out of the middle.*

No matter what, kids need to feel free to love and want their other parent. Kids should never be the spoils in adults' battles! Recognize that what we're after has to do with how to include a new member on the team, and how to join a team that has an already-established hierarchy and history.

PARENTING RELATIONSHIPS IN STEPFAMILIES CAN BE CONFUSING (AND FRUSTRATING)!

Even now that you're living together, the co-parents remain the CEOs (co-parent executive officers) of their child(ren)'s life. They hold bottom-line responsibility for ALL major kid decisions. In healthy stepfamilies, stepparents *become* contributing members of that team. Effectively joining a team takes skill and time. So, generally, in the first year or two of ramp up, until new agreements are made about how the parenting coalition will function, co-parents usually need to continue as chief communicators regarding the kids

Helpful Tips for Maintaining Constructive Co-parenting Communication

Nothing is more important for parents raising kids across two homes than clear and effective communication. Here are some tips that will help:

- **Communicate directly with each other**—*not through the kids*. Successful co-parents, even highly conflicted ones, communicate constructively, respectfully and succinctly. Use short emails, texts, quick phone calls or other agreed-upon methods.

- **Talk with co-parents before including partners.** Stepparents may expect and even need to be included in adult conversations about kids. But adding them to the communication thread (cc'ing on emails or text, for instance) without checking with the co-parent can become a surprising hot button.

- **Don't believe everything you hear from a child:** Young children are famously bad reporters, *especially* if they think it's their job to manage a tense relationship between their parents.

- **Use curiosity over accusation** when approaching your co-parent about a concern. So instead of, "*I can't believe you let your stepson beat up our daughter!*" Try, "*Effie sounds like she's struggling with your stepson. She mentioned an incident of hitting. Can you help me understand what's happening?*"

- **Use B.I.F.F.* to guide email communication.**

    Brief: Limit to 200–300 words per subject. No commentary, criticism, attributing bad motives or dragging up unpleasant past.

    Informative: Stick to *information*, neutrally presented. "*I have a request about bedtime calls. I sure want you and the kids to connect. They love it and I know it's really important to you. But bedtime is not working on my end, both kiddos are ending up out of bed multiple times afterward. I think it's just hard for them to settle after talking with you. Can it work to call before 7:30? That way bedtime can be calmer. Thanks for considering.*" Note Brianna's clear and firm request without attack or criticism. And her thank you!

Fourth Stepfamily Challenge: Co-parents Are Part of the Stepfamily

Firm: Be clear and answer questions directly. *"Sure, that works"* or *"No, that doesn't work for me."* Or offer a reasonable alternative. *"I'm often not in from work until closer to 8 pm. Would sometime in the morning work better?"*

Friendly: Try for a tone you might use with your boss or any respected third party.

(*Credit for BIFF goes to Bill Eddy. You can find his books in the resource section. Look for his work at the High Conflict Institute in the Online Resources section.)

Helpful Tips for Building a Two-Home Parenting Coalition

Leave your first-time-family mentality behind in your next-time-family parenting coalition. If you, as a stepcouple, strain to operate as if your family starts and stops at your front door, you'll precipitate some serious unintended consequences. You'll both have to hold the door open to the influences and impacts of a co-parent. This is where first-time-family history either visits with or collides against stepfamily. Let's break this down:

- **Stepfamilies often have a complicated power structure.** In most stepfamilies, the areas of negotiation for major kid decisions occur between the co-parents, not within one household.

- **Kid-related decisions made by co-parents often have consequences** for finances, time, resources and emotional impacts on the new stepfamily—including the nonvoting stepparent. This can cause tension when interests and needs diverge among the adults across the children's two homes. Stepparents who immediately start pushing for subtle (or not so subtle) changes to how co-parents have operated will contribute to rising temperatures. You'll need some endurance and considerable patience. Team development is not an overnight event.

- **The stepcouple is in charge of implementing decisions in their own home.** The catch comes when the co-parent has strong wishes (for instance, no ears pierced before age 14) that a stepparent does not agree with. This is a classic opportunity for that "stuck insider" dynamic to rear its head for parents—only this time, they're stuck between a co-parent and a partner! Holy cow, how do people do this without losing their minds?

What to do? Well, ideally, all the adults can (do what?) *slow down*, hold their fire, adjust their expectations, find ways to respect each other and bend a bit. Easier said than done sometimes, but nevertheless, *this is possible*. In the meantime, decisions that have a lasting impact on kids belong in the purview of co-parents. So, stepparents, deep breath. Swallow hard. Soldier forward.

How long does this take? You can bet it can take at least good year or two! (Sometimes lots more.)

In the early months and years, the co-parent outside the stepcouple's home may not want or appreciate the stepparent's input.

Parents, you're in the co-leadership position with your co-parent. *Stepparents,* lie low and stay out of the fray (if there is any). In these first couple of years, think of yourself as a "parenting coalition member-in-training." You're earning your chops as a contributing adult in the children's lives. You are demonstrating your respect for the children's other parent, showing them that you will not usurp their spot, that you will in fact only have the best interests of the kids in mind. You'll provide useful information when asked for and support important joint decisions.

This is your best approach to becoming an important voice at the parent-teacher conference table. This is definitely a situation where you'll catch more flies with honey than vinegar.

> ### Helpful Tips for Building a Stepcouple Parenting Coalition
>
> Like building a relationship with someone who is shy or hurt, you move slowly, and gently, with attention to whether they're opening up or pulling further away. Do what you can to convert power struggles and conflicts into opportunities for respectful discussion and problem resolution. Use your survival kit of communication skills. (Don't leave home without it!) Here's the step-by-step approach:
>
> - **If you haven't met yet**, there's no better time to break that ice if you have a willing co-parent. Ideally, you all seized this opportunity months ago, but for some, a co-parent may have not taken you seriously until you started living together.

- **Read your audience.** A reluctant co-parent doesn't really want to hear about what a great stepparent the children now have. Any news of the stepparent's positive qualities will best come across the two-home wires via children's sharing. Let that be enough until you have signs that there's openness to learn more.

- **Civility and cordiality is key.** Partners, when you cross paths at your stepdaughter's gymnastic meet and hellos are exchanged, and you sense that a few more exchanges about Lilah's floor exercise performance will be appreciated. Go for it!

- **Remember that parents are the experts on their kids.** Parents love to talk about their kids! A well-timed question and genuine curiosity about a stepchild will often be experienced as bridge building by a co-parent. When answering a co-parent's question about the kids, keep in mind that input about their child will be more easily accepted with a kind of deference that says, "I offer this humbly and I trust you'll use it in whatever way will be helpful." Your role as an authority on kids is only granted through relationship development and experience—never taken by force.

Following these guidelines sets the table for a time in the future when all the adults caring for children across two homes problem solve and rally to support and celebrate children. Barbara Kingsolver in her essay "Stone Soup" describes one of these moments for a young soccer player:

"In the catalogue of family values, where do we rank an occasion like this? . . . His own cheering section of grown-ups and kids all leap to their feet and hug each other, delirious with love for this boy. . . . The cheering section includes his mother and her friends, his brother, his father and stepmother, a stepbrother and stepsister, and a grandparent. Lucky is the child with this many relatives on hand to hail a proud accomplishment. I'm there too, witnessing a family fortune."

Tricks of the Trade When Two-Home Family-Life Gets Tricky

Parenting expectations and family rules are common areas of disagreements, stress and tension among adults in two-home families. Do children need both their homes to have the same set of rules? No. That's the good news. Most kids can handle some differences. Life is certainly simpler when the adults can agree on some of the basics like bedtimes, screen time, curfew and so forth.

What to do when you cannot agree? Your best choice is to respectfully agree to disagree. *"We do it differently."* Do not trash the other parent's rules or values.

The younger the children, the more important it is that co-parents set similar goals for building competencies and daily rhythms for kids across both homes. Older children also benefit from coordinated parenting regarding limit-setting while facilitating their increasing freedom. Stepparents who support these plans are doing a huge service to kids and the co-parents.

Parenting-time schedule changes can *stir the pot* or build a cooperative spirit! "If I borrow a cup of sugar, I'm going to bring you a piece of pie." Karen teaches every co-parenting pair this old adage. When asking for favors, return with just a little more sweetness. When your co-parent obliges your schedule-change requests, show appreciation. And when they don't, *accept gracefully.* Using some weaponized version of *"If you cared about the kids . . ."* or *"This is in the best interest of our kids . . ."* only harms and never convinces your co-parent that you somehow know better or have something more important to do with the kids than they do. *Doing unto others . . .* can be a tall order sometimes.

Helpful Tips for Negotiating Family Life Across Homes

Co-parents won't and don't have to agree on *everything*. Here are some ideas:

- **Choose your battles wisely:** Making a big deal about one parent allowing junk food may be more damaging than letting the kids eat chips more often than you'd really like. The more stressed the co-parenting relationship, the more important this guideline is.

- **Respect household boundaries:** Don't make plans for children on the other parent's residential time without express permission. Disciplinary decisions don't extend across homes without clear agreement. Be thoughtful about contacting kids during the co-parent's residential time—be certain you're not disrupting their *other* home life.

- **Requests for schedule changes** should be answered respectfully and in a timely fashion with, *"Sure, that works for us,"* or *"I'm sorry, that doesn't work for us,"* or *"Let me do some checking, and I'll get back to you this evening."*

- **The schedule trumps all:** Collaborative co-parents can negotiate schedule changes in a fair and respectful way. When conflict goes up, the two-home family benefits from the fallback principle that, *when there is a disagreement, the residential schedule will be followed—gracefully.*
- **Children's events are about them!** The last thing you want is to make your kids dread having both their parent—and stepparent(s)—in the same place at the same time. Make enjoying and celebrating children's activities cordially a high priority.
- **At joint events, the *residential* parent is in charge of kids.** Other adults are good "guest parents."
- **Maintain a steady flow of positive feedback:** Give credit where credit is due. Be generous with praise and residential time. Even if your efforts aren't reciprocated, keep depositing the positive building blocks of a cooperative relationship and hope for the best in return.
- **Meet the developmental needs of very young children:** As we discussed in Chapter 6, little ones younger than three years old benefit from very frequent contact with each of their parents and regular communication about their needs.
- **Adolescents in two households need both increasing freedom *and* supervision:** This can be challenging. "*I'm going over to Dad's*" all too easily becomes a cover for unsupervised activities at Dad's or elsewhere! Do try to monitor the whereabouts of teens across households. Schedule changes are managed by *both* the teen's *parents by agreement*—not by a teen. Group text messages about teens' plans that include the teen and both parents can often keep everyone honest and safe.
- **Convenient or not, unless otherwise agreed, the parenting plan rules.** Stepfamily life places new burdens on former parenting plans designed before the family expanded. Work thoughtfully with your co-parent to make adjustments when possible.

The Two-Rules Conversation

"Dad always let me bring my iPad to the dinner table," eight-year-old Everett complained to his mom. "Your rules are stupid! Besides, I hate how Cam gets to set all the rules now!"

"Sweetheart, you are the luckiest kiddo that you have a dad who lets you bring your iPad to the dinner table. And—at our house, all the devices go on the counter during meals. Would you like me to put yours up, or will you be putting it in the basket yourself?"

As Everett reluctantly deposits the iPad in the basket, she tells him, "Just think, when you're the grown-up, *you'll* get to make the rules."

WHY IS BUILDING PARENTING COALITIONS SO HARD FOR COMPETENT ADULTS?

If building a parenting coalition were like forming a work group in a new organization at the office, you know that you'd get into the room, identify your shared goals, set your joint objectives, give everyone a clear role, and come up with strategies. Ready, set, let's go! Get 'er done!

Even that can be hard, as we all know. Sometimes even harder for the adults in stepfamily. Why is that?

The Blurry Boundary with Former In-Laws

It's your residential time with the kids, but they want to go to a sleepover birthday party at their cousin's house. The cousins' mom is your ex's sister. She has made it clear that your new partner is never welcome in her home. This is about the kids, yes, but it's also about the stepparent, and the co-parent and the parent . . . and the grandparents, aunts, uncles, cousins and more.

Your co-parent (yes, I'm talking about your *ex*-husband whom you are still barely speaking to) asks your mother (the children's grandmother) to hem his pants. She agrees. You're gob smacked and incensed because she's *your mom* taking care of *him*. You're pacing around the house muttering about "family loyalty." Your new partner wonders what they've gotten themselves into! Welcome to your life. Lots of relationships, often lots of history, lots to consider.

The Dance of Co-Parents

Most parents have an entrenched way of dealing with each other—for good and bad. Enter the new partner. Sometimes stepparents find themselves sucked into the sinkhole of the first-marriage conflict.

Ugh!

"I Also Married Rocko's First Marriage!"

"I knew when I married Rocko that his son was part of the deal," said Judy. "What I didn't count on was that I also married Rocko's *marriage to Mia*, his first wife!"

Rocko—normally a calm, steady guy, transformed into a raging, verbally abusive person when he interacted with Mia about their son.

"An email from her and he went crazy! They couldn't discuss anything without it turning into a big blowup. I tried just *understanding* for a while. Why did he have such a short fuse with her? I couldn't stand it. I finally told him it had to stop. I couldn't be around it."

Highly cooperative co-parent are waaaay better for kids. Yup. And, let's face it. All that coordination can be hard for stepparents, who can feel like the last to know! And worse, your partner is coordinating with their "ex" about their kids' which adds another layer of outsiderness.

Ursula Wants to Switch Weekends (Again)

Dino and his ex-wife, Ursula, regularly checked in with each other about their daughter's residential schedule. They were easygoing and accommodating when one parent needed to change plans at the last minute. His friendly attitude toward his ex was something Dino's new partner, Kimberly, admired about him.

Eighteen months later, Kimberly was frustrated by the constant requests by his ex to change the plan. "Please ask me first, before you tell her 'yes,'" she said. He told her he would. No problem.

And then . . . he didn't! Kimberly had planned a romantic weekend away with Dino when he dropped the news that—change of plan—his daughter would be coming for the weekend. Kimberly was *furious*. "I thought we agreed that you would ask me first!"

"I promise I'll do better," Dino said. "I get it. I blew it again."

Kimberly's temperature dropped and she sighed. "Thanks for understanding." She was thoughtful. "I have a guess. You want to have a peaceful relationship with your daughter's mom so you try to give her a yes. Did I get it right?"

"That's exactly right," he said. "I don't want to be one of those divorced couples who are always picking at each other. She's my daughter's mom. I want peace between us for her sake. So—I'll definitely try, but I might slip up. What happens then?"

Kimberly gave him a mischievous smile. "Every slip-up means you make me a romantic dinner at home. And you owe me a spa weekend in the mountains for cancelling on this weekend!"

He grinned back. "Deal!"

Mom vs. Stepmom

Moms and stepmoms often have some of the most emotionally fraught relationships. Many factors can contribute to this "perfect storm." Despite changes in women's roles, many women's identity and self-esteem are still tied to whether they feel like they're a good mom. Some moms carry deep bitterness about being separated from their children as a consequence of divorce. Their gatekeeping and micromanagement may be an attempt to circumvent the grief of living in a situation where they have to miss their kids.

Often, from the kids' mother's point of view, the stepmom is an interloper who is spending the time with her children that she believes in her heart of hearts should be *hers*. She may feel jealous and insecure and threatened by you, the stepmom. If you swoop in with big gifts for her kids, or trips to Disneyworld, or activities Mom would disapprove of, it's like you're poking a finger into that sore spot.

Sometimes, though, you have to learn by goofing.

Fourth Stepfamily Challenge: Co-parents Are Part of the Stepfamily

Fran Makes an Innocent Mistake

Fran had been struggling with fourteen-year-old Annie, trying to be patient with the girl when she was rude and rejecting. One afternoon when they happened to be alone together in the house, Fran took out her makeup kit and offered to give Annie a makeover. Annie loved it and she asked Fran to show her how to use mascara and eyeliner herself.

"I want to keep it on to show my mom!" she said, excited.

Ben dropped the kids off at their mom's house. Annie said, "Look, Mom! Fran gave me a makeover!" She ran inside to take a selfie to send her friends.

Annie's mom pulled Ben aside. She was furious with him. "How *could* you allow this?! You know I have a no-makeup rule until she's 15!"

What to do? Fran was deeply disappointed and *mortified* at Annie's mom's response to something so innocent (or so she thought). She could also see she had inadvertently put her stepdaughter in a terrible bind with her mother. Both Annie and Ben were now caught in the middle. With considerable thought (and some teeth gnashing) Fran decided to take the high road and *apologize.*

She wrote a simple note to Annie's mom saying, "*Ben shared your concern with me. I am SO very sorry. I promise you it won't happen again.*" She also said to Annie, "Oh dear. Looks like I got you in big trouble with your mom. I'm so sorry. We'll find some other fun things we can do together."

"This was a tough one," Fran said to her best friend, "But respecting Annie's mom's rules come first, for Annie's sake."

Moms do often have a hard time trusting stepmoms with their kids. If you're the stepmom, you might take it personally, as if you're unworthy until proven worthy. Not fair! On the one hand, it's really wonderful if you can have a warm and caring relationship with your stepkids. That's best for the kids and for your stepfamily. On the other hand, it can be threatening to a mom when another woman becomes a confidante to her children. If you have a heart-to-heart with a stepdaughter about first dates or teach a son how to tie a tie, then some moms might feel like you've usurped her rightful place as their mother.

Here's what you shouldn't do: Make it into a power struggle for kids' affection. That will just get ugly, and it's bad for kids, your sweetie and you. No one wins, especially the kids.

It might help to keep in mind that your stepkids' mom is probably frightened, feeling protective, and missing her kids when they're away from her. So, consider yourself on a very prolonged job interview. Hopefully, in time, you too will become a trusted part of two-home family parenting coalition.

BOTTOM LINE

Bend graciously where you can.

Stepparents Often Bring New Resources

Sometimes, stepparents, as outsiders who care deeply ("intimate outsiders") bring a different set of information and a different point of view that can make important contributions to their stepchildren. If only co-parents could appreciate the importance of another caring adult in their children's lives sooner rather than later.

A Clearer-Eyed View of Kids:
The Gift of the "Intimate Outsider"!

During their weekly email exchange about the kids, Ben and Rebecca agreed that Luke needed to focus more on reading homework. He was doing fourth-grade-level math, but his reading was behind where it should have been for a third grader. The co-parents agreed: No video games or TV until reading homework was done.

When Ben informed Luke, he stomped up to his room and slammed the door. A while later, Fran knocked on his door.

"I hated reading when I was your age," she confided, standing in the doorway. "It made my head hurt. I couldn't see the words right." Luke looked up at her, angry scowl turning to curious stare. "I figured I was just stupid."

Luke looked at his feet. Fran could see a tear rolling down his cheek. Fran went on to explain how her fifth-grade teacher figured out that she had dyslexia. "There are lots of reasons why kids have a hard time reading," she said. "You're a very bright boy. And I know you love when Dad reads you the Harry Potter books. But maybe it hurts your head when you try to read them on your own?"

Luke nodded. "I get frustrated. The letters move around."

"You might have a special brain that learns differently," she said. "Why don't we tell Dad about this. He and your mom can find someone who can help you figure this out."

Luke looked hopeful.

"Really?"

"Yes!" she said, smiling. "Lots of people have special brains! There's lots of things you can do to be a better reader!"

He jumped up and gave her a spontaneous hug. "Thanks, Fran," he said.

Ben spoke to Luke's mom on the phone that evening and told her about Fran's conversation with Luke. They agreed to have him tested for learning disabilities.

"I can't believe we might have missed this!" Rebecca said.

"I know!" Ben agreed.

"So he just told you about having a problem with seeing the words?" she asked.

"Um, actually he told Fran. She's dyslexic, so she wondered if that was what was going on."

Silence on the other end. And then, "Oh. Well—that's good, I guess. Tell her thanks."

DADS AND STEPDADS

In the last few decades, shared residential schedules have become more common, but dads in many places still have significantly less time with their children than moms do. This creates a particular vulnerability for a dad's relationship with his kids.

Dads and Stepdads Seem to Have It Easier

Dads and stepdads generally have an easier time with each other than moms and stepmoms. Of course, easier doesn't mean no conflict, ever. If you're the dad or the stepdad (or both!), it may help to know that children who make the best adjustment have a positive, engaged relationship with *both* dad and stepdad regardless of the residential time spent with each. Those children most at-risk are close to neither one.

Father-Child Relationships with Less Residential Time

If you're a dad who doesn't have much or any residential time with your kids, it may be easy to lose connection with them. Father-daughter relationships can be especially vulnerable. When kids become teens, their social lives and activities ramp up, and it can be even harder to get on their schedule when you're a dad.

Please, don't give up! If you're starting to feel like *"What's the point?"*, then we can assure you that the point is the kids need to know they matter to *both* their parents. If your teen is pushing you away, step in closer to let them know you're committed to a relationship. You could try making a point of showing up at track meets whether you get much attention for doing so or not. Every time you show up for your kiddo you're making a deposit into the bank of healthy emotional development, and it will pay dividends in your future relationship with them.

BOTTOM LINE

*All children—teens, young adults, adults—notice when their dad hangs in and wants to know them, spend time with them and participate in their lives. It may be early adulthood before they have the maturity to say, "**I love you. Thank you for coming to my track meets**," or, "**I appreciated all the birthday cards**," or, "**It meant a lot when you texted for no reason but just to check in**," and so forth.*

> ## Helpful Tips for Involving a Parent with Significantly Less Residential Time
>
> Some kids feel they lost a parent in the separation/divorce. This can be prevented! Parents and stepparents can both help make sure kids have secure, loving connections with both their parents. Dads especially are vulnerable to losing contact with their kids.
>
> - **Moms and their new partners** can facilitate regular, meaningful, *stress-free* contact between their kids and dads. If possible, try to be generous with extra time. See it as a good thing, and not as disrespectful or threatening to you. It's really, really good for kids to stay connected to their dads.
>
> - **Dad's new partner can help.** No one would blame you for wanting your sweetie to yourself. Kids can be a handful. But for the kids' sake, and also for the mental health of your partner, choose the high road and encourage him to reach out to his kids. Support him in having time alone with his kids, even if you feel like the outsider when it happens. In the long run, this will be so much better for your sweetie, and therefore, for your couple relationship.
>
> - **Use technology to connect.** Dads and kids can have both planned and spontaneous video calls to do homework, read bedtime stories. Include dads in special moments, like when a daughter pins on her corsage for prom, or a son opens college acceptance letters. Even if you're a continent away from the kids, you can create an everyday connection with a cell phone and a good app.

Loyalty Binds for Re-partnered Dads

Dads who don't have much residential time, and who are living with a new partner and her kids, may feel especially torn. If this is you, you might feel guilty that you have a stronger everyday relationship with your stepchildren than you have with your own kids. You may feel pulled to give up on your co-parent relationship.

Please remember that kids always need their parents—both of you. They are *not* better off without you!

As the nonresidential co-parent, you might also be feeling that when you do see your kids, it's fraught with anger, resentment, sorrow and other difficult feelings, so therefore it's not worth it—too hard on everyone. Or maybe they're sending you the message that your time with them is inconvenient, an unwelcome intrusion in their lives. If possible, try to hear your kids' frustration *and also* let them know that while they might rather be at home or hanging out with their friends, you want to be part of their lives. Try to hang in there with them and look for ways to connect and enjoy one another.

You might want to keep in mind that if you and your new partner have a child, your kids might feel replaced. They might feel abandoned physically, emotionally and financially by you. Do try to stay engaged with your co-parent about helping your kids. If your co-parent knows you're committed to being in the kids' lives, they could be an ally in helping you strengthen your connection to them, which will help the kids in the long run.

> **HAZARD** ⊗ Dads in this position often go quite silent with both their partners and their kids. Some handle their pain by withdrawing from children from the first marriage. *Please, please, reach out for help with the grief, the loyalty binds, the shame* and stay connected to your kids. Your kids need you. Stepparents and moms, *please step up and help!*

Karim Feels Doubly Alone

"I miss Alika every single day," says her dad, Karim. He and Alika's mom divorced when she was four years old, and his ex-wife moved to another state for work, so he rarely gets to see his child. Now he's remarried to Evie and they have a newborn. "When I play with Evie's kids, or hold our new baby, I am thinking of Alika at that age. It's like I'm not here and I'm not there. Every month when the child support check goes out, Evie grumbles that we could sure use that money for our kids. I feel torn in two as a dad and inadequate as a provider."

CARING FOR OLD RELATIONSHIPS WHILE FORMING NEW ONES

Separation and divorce often require renegotiating longstanding relationships with your co-parent's grandparents, parents, aunts, uncles, your own family, plus the friendship and community networks from the first family.

Typically, moms have more residential time with kids, which leaves paternal grandparents vulnerable to being excluded from children's lives. It can really help to remember that *more* love and positive connections for kids is a good thing. Research shows that children are strengthened by close connections to grandparents, extended family and key adults. Stepparents are also clearly important. The main takeaway is that maintaining connections helps kids.

Successful stepcouples integrate new relationships *without cutting off old ones*. You can expand your family without chopping off limbs from the kids' family tree.

Treading Sensitively Pays Off

Ben's mother, Vivian, had known Ben's ex-wife, Rebecca, for 15 years and they had always been close. A few weeks before her 65th birthday, she popped a party invitation in the mail to Rebecca.

Rebecca wisely emailed Ben with news of the invitation and asked what he thought.

"I know you and Mom are close, but it will be tense," he wrote.

"I agree," Rebecca replied. In fact, she and Fran had just had a run-in around the makeup incident with Rebecca and Ben's daughter, Annie.

Rebecca called Vivian and said she wouldn't be able to make it and suggested that she take Vivian out for a special birthday lunch that would also include the kids.

Five years later, at Vivian's 70th birthday celebration, family relationships were much warmer. Fran, Rebecca and Ben all came, much to Vivian's pleasure and the children's delight.

Relationships among parents, co-parents and stepparents can evoke intense reactivity. For kid's sake, it's imperative that stepfamily members find the best in themselves, even in circumstances that pull for the worst. All the expanded family members play a role in, and are affected by, how everyone takes care of already-existing family members while integrating new members into a family system.

· · · · · · · · · · ·

Karen often says, "World peace begins one family at a time." Learning to dig down deep, cultivate your skills and grow your compassion for one another creates an environment of healing. When you respectfully resolve the conflicts that you can, build the relationships that are available, and expand your love as far as you can stretch, you move your family's world closer to *peace on earth*.

Someone's got to do it. Why not you!

Chapter 15

Fifth Stepfamily Challenge: Building a Shared Culture That Respects Differences

"The secret to blending families is ... there is no secret. It's scary and awesome and ragged and perfect and always changing."

—Mir Kamin, award-winning blogger

If you think "blended family," you might expect that all you have to do is combine the folks in your two families—your metaphorical blueberries and bananas—whirl them around in the blender and *voila*! A smooth-running stepfamily in one easy push of a button.

Not going to happen!

Becoming a stepfamily is more akin to two strangers from different countries falling in love and then leading their (willing and unwilling) family members to a new land with the hopes of founding a new country called "stepfamily." One group may arrive with a fleet of canoes filled with kids, dogs, goldfish and baggage of extended family, co-parents and the like. The other may similarly lead a fleet of canoes, or paddle over with a much smaller group, or come in a kayak built for one.

Despite the strangers' love and high hopes, it's hard to understand one another or get along in the new land of stepfamily. Cooperation is really hard when there are so many personalities and individual needs, not to mention differences in daily habits, family traditions, rituals, beliefs and even languages. Your clan hears "privacy" and "dinner" and "quiet" to mean one thing, and theirs assumes something very different. A million other small and large differences require a lot of diplomacy and tact, which are not skills people have right away. Uh oh.

Remember "middle ground"? Middle ground refers to *the way we do things*—the pathways of connection that deepen over time with mutual experience. Middle ground becomes a sense of "home" for those who share it. The exciting news is that over time you can build a shared middle ground as a stepfamily. The hitch is that when you're first getting started forming the new country of stepfamily, parents and kids import their already firmly established middle ground. If you were the one in the solo kayak, you're going to be greatly outnumbered when it comes to having a voice about what your new stepfamily middle ground will look like and feel like. And it will be disappointing at times that it's not the couple who have the established middle ground. Parent is on the inside; stepparent is on the outside. If you both have kids, then you both have both these experiences at times when your beloved's middle ground with their kids comes to the fore—and it's foreign territory for you.

Over time, the new stepfamily middle ground will take root. You'll learn one another's languages and come up with your own shared words, jokes and favorite recipes for turtle soup. No one gives up their old middle ground—you just add new elements to it and adjust to changes to some of your old ways of feeling "home." Some adjustments will be easier to tolerate and accept than others, and some will be quite welcome and delightful. So you don't blend. You keep what makes each of you unique. And from that you create something new together.

The chapter starts with a wide-angle lens of a key stepfamily task: building a shared culture while honoring your differences. We'll then then drill down into three specific areas of middle ground that form a stepfamily's sense of "home":

- **How you live**—everyday habits and routines

- **How you celebrate**—traditions and rituals for holidays and special occasions

- **Who you are**—important ethnic, class and family values

Then we'll take a look at money challenges for stepcouples. Throughout, we'll point out ways to slowly, respectfully and sometimes playfully bring your stepfamily together while you honor the differences between your clans.

Fifth Stepfamily Challenge: Building a Shared Culture That Respects Differences

BOTTOM LINE

*In a stepfamily, new middle ground—a new **stepfamily culture**—must be negotiated and developed slowly over time while continuing to respect and honor already-established ways of doing things.*

UNDERSTANDING THE CHALLENGE

Let's start with some basics. Creating anything meaningful with a new group of people involves a lot of getting to know one another. Building a stepfamily culture, you'll find yourselves doing lots of what Patricia calls "*learning by goofing.*" Here's why:

Differences Abound

Moving in together raises the question of "whose home?" We all enter love relationships longing for that feeling of home. However, in a new stepfamily, what feels like "home" to one part of the family can feel uncomfortable and even upsetting to another. While many of us talk a good game about appreciating differences, the actual experience of colliding with intimate others over things we hold as givens does not feel like home. Here's a story Patricia often tells about an apparently simple tuna fish sandwich:

A Tuna Fish Moment

Imagine that you are my stepdaughter. You have already been dragged through a deluge of changes you didn't ask for. You grew up eating your tuna fish pure, unadulterated by "things." No celery, no onions and certainly no weird herbs. You like your tuna mixed with plenty of *real* mayonnaise on two slices of nice soft white bread.

I don't know this about you, so I make you a healthy Papernow tuna sandwich. I chop up two sticks of crunchy celery and mince a bit of tasty parsley. Concerned that your tuna does not get lost in a sea of fatty goo, I added just a dab of low-fat mayo. I present my creation to you on two pieces of lovely toasted whole wheat bread. Yum!

You reluctantly take a bite. What are the chances that you are going to say, "Thank you, Patricia, for introducing me to a new kind of tuna fish sandwich"? Much more likely you will blurt out, "YUCK!" Or, perhaps you will simply leave my carefully prepared masterpiece sitting uneaten on your plate.

The very best outcome would be for Patricia to say, "Oops. Another goof! I guess we just learned something new about you, me and tuna fish sandwiches." Still, how easy would it be for a harried stepparent to see this child as ungrateful and rude? Like the sandwich with unexpected "things" in it, early stepfamily life is often full of these "tuna fish moments." They occur at the most unanticipated times, often in the context of activities that we fully expect to be comforting and uneventful. They may register as constant small jolts or major earthquakes. The frequency for the unsuspecting family member can be stunning!

"Learning by Goofing" Is Part of the Process

". . . givens are not givens" write John and Emily Visher, pioneer stepfamily therapists.

Holy cow! How can we make our family feel like *home i*n a place where givens are not givens? Knowing that "tuna fish moments" are a normal part of becoming a stepfamily can help make an "ouch" a little less personal and turn it into a "goof" that you learn from.

You and your beloved may have had lots of thoughtful conversations before you moved in together about values, bedtimes, money, discipline, hopes for the future and so forth. Even so, it's likely that you probably never talked about tuna fish, or how loud is too loud when kids are watching a movie, or how to decide who gets the last slice of cake. We sometimes don't even have words for many of our assumptions, core underlying values and habits of daily living.

Oh—until someone *violates* what someone else thought was a *no brainer.* Then there's an (often totally unexpected) spike of discomfort, or even irritation. Sometimes there *are* words—sometimes surprisingly harsh words.

Extended Family (and Dear Friends) Are Part of Your Middle Ground

No family or stepfamily is an island. We're all steeped in a wide web of extended family, friends and community. In your stepfamily, the parent-child middle ground is woven into this wider web, which means birthdays and holiday rituals for one parent and their children may have included relatives or neighbors before. But now in your stepfamily a celebration, with "family and friends" is a different group for each part of the family. Complicated.

> ### Some Helpful Tips to Begin Stepping Your Way Through Differences
>
> - **Do talk ahead of time about money, values, bedtimes, discipline and so forth.** Right now, the job is just to get to know each other and to notice and start learning about your differences, not try to *eliminate* them. Smoothing out the wrinkles will require living together for a while. Sometimes for quite a while.
>
> - **Expect "tuna fish moments."** There's bound to be lots of "learning by goofing."
>
> - **Take a breath!** Disappointed expectations can be upsetting. You want to respond with a mild *"Oops, another one!"* rather than making it into a federal case. Remember that first mantra from Chapter 4, take a breath? Pull it out of your tool kit and have it ready. You're gonna need it. A lot.
>
> - **Curiosity is a powerful pathway to connection.** When you smack into differences, ramping up your curiosity may help you transform frustration into fascination. *"Tell me about that... I'm curious why ... Can you share with me what you were thinking?"* If your internal conversation slips into, *"That's ridiculous,"* you are likely on your way to making things worse.
>
> - **Give everyone a voice.** Outsider stepparents are often the voice for change. Parents and their children are often the voice for continuity. Children have surprisingly particular thoughts about familiar things (*"But we have to eat cookies after we open the stockings!"*). Changes are accepted more easily if everyone is part of the conversation and—within reason—has a *say*.

HOW YOU LIVE, HOW YOU CELEBRATE, WHO YOU ARE

You'll likely find yourselves wrestling with three main areas of differences that need to be negotiated: (1) everyday habits and routines (*"This is how we live"*), (2) holidays and special occasions (*"This is how we celebrate"*) and (3) beliefs and values rooted in ethnic, class and religious traditions (*"This is who we are"*).

Everyday Habits and Daily Routines: "This is How We Live"

Families develop their own particular habits, rules and routines that, over time, become woven into "how we live." For Ben and his kids, macaroni and cheese on Wednesday nights was a comforting reminder of "home," *"just like we've always done it."* For Fran, "healthy food"—salads, lean protein, and lots of vegetables—was just as basic. For one side of the family, having familiar stuff everywhere feels homey. For the other, clean uncluttered spaces are "basic." In one home, the hubbub of noise and kids shouting from room to room feels caring and friendly. In the other, "basic decency" means everyone is careful never to interrupt without first saying, *"Excuse me."* For a parent, kids' friends may be welcome without asking parents first. For their partner, not getting permission first would be "disrespectful."

Knock First or Just Walk In?

> When Lucien and Sabina first moved in together, their four boys ranged in age from 9 to 13. Lucien's sons were accustomed to barging in to each other's rooms and sharing clothes, sports equipment, school supplies and even friends. Sabina's boys expected people to knock before coming in and ask before borrowing their stuff. They had separate friends. What one set of siblings experienced as easy and intimate felt intrusive and disrespectful to the other.

Lucien and Sabina, unfortunately, found themselves arguing (a lot) over whose kids were out of line. In fact, the first step was for the adults to help both sets of boys be curious and respectful about the other's "culture." Realistically, this isn't as simple as it sounds, though. It will take many reminders for Lucien's sons before "knocking first" and "asking first" will become automatic.

Familiar *Things* Are Part of How We Live

Familiar things are important part of the fabric of daily living. Sometimes, pulling even one thread out of the familiar and cherished fabric can provoke an unexpectedly intense response.

Fifth Stepfamily Challenge: Building a Shared Culture That Respects Differences

Shiny New Dishes or Familiar Family Plates?

Ellie, a new stepmom, decided to surprise her family with a new set of dishes to replace the mismatched set her husband had taken from his first marriage. But when Ellie served dinner on them for the first time, her nine-year-old stepdaughter shrieked that she "hated" the new plates and then burst into tears. Those old, chipped dishes were a remnant from the time her parents were still together. Ellie had had no idea she was messing with something so central to her stepdaughter's sense of "home."

Familiar *routines* are an important part of feeling at home. Over time, families develop a familiar rhythm for when and how and where life happens. You can think of it as background music that you don't really tune in to until the rhythm changes for some reason. When your family expands to become a stepfamily, you can expect that treasured routines that comfort one side of the family may feel down right disturbing to the other.

> **Helpful Tips for Managing Differences in Daily Routines**
>
> - **Slow and steady.** Driving too fast toward "feeling like a family" ups the chances that you'll miss important landmarks and increases accident rates! Moving slowly, changing just a little bit at a time, as inconvenient and awkward as it may feel, usually works much better. Read on.
>
> - **Respect kids' needs for the familiar.** We can support children's adjustment by maintaining routines like bedtime rituals, continuing to serve favorite foods and honoring children's wishes to hold on to familiar items. Double sets of kids may need double sets of dishes for a while!
>
> - **A few changes in rules at a time.** Successful stepfamilies agree upon, *at the most*, two or three *realistic* changes in rules and routines that help the family function *well enough*. They live with the rest while the children adjust and everyone gets to know one another. Rules that ensure safety and civility come first. In double stepfamilies, try to equalize the amount of change being asked of each set of children.

- **Two sets of rules may work best for a while.** One parent manages the bedtime routine with their team of kiddos while the other parent manages theirs.

- **Keep it positive.** Positive feedback goes a long way to reinforce change and make everyone feel better about the process. Gentle reminders will actually change behavior faster than criticism and nagging.

- **Be realistic.** You may have to accept that there will always be places where the two families stay different.

BOTTOM LINE

Successful, mature stepfamilies are less like an evenly woven wool blanket and more like a patchwork quilt. There will always be some patches that are quite specific to each side of the stepfamily, and some areas that are co-created. That's what the fabric of a healthy stepfamily looks like!

Holidays and Special Occasions: "This Is How We Celebrate"

For some stepfamilies, creating new family rituals can bring everyone together. We'll share some ways to do this successfully. Meanwhile, we want you to know that in many stepfamilies, at *just* a moment when you're *most* expecting togetherness, things sometimes fall apart. This was the case for Sarah and Martin.

Where's My Menorah?

Sarah and Martin were excited about the first Hanukah that they would be spending in their new home with their combined three elementary-school-aged children. In Martin's family, his daughter, Lydia had always loved lighting her own menorah. Sarah's kids shared a tradition passed down from Sarah's grandfather of lighting a family menorah as a group standing right next to each other. For their first Hanukah together, Martin and Sarah decided to start a new family tradition. They would get each of the kids their own matching menorahs with their names on them.

Fifth Stepfamily Challenge: Building a Shared Culture That Respects Differences

Lydia arrived from her mom's for the first-night candle lighting and immediately noticed that her menorah was not on the table. She was excited to open the present waiting for her. But she was taken aback when she saw the new menorah. Then she saw her stepsisters' matching ones. She went numb.

Sarah's kids were confused as well. "Where's Grandpa's menorah?" they asked their mom.

"And where's mine?" Lydia asked tersely, pushing the new menorah away.

Martin, in his excitement, failed to notice that his daughter was tearing up, happily pointing out that now everyone in the family had matching menorahs.

Lydia crossed her arms and started to cry. "I want to go back to my Momma's."

Oops! What happened? As Sarah and Martin discovered, in a stepfamily, each side of a stepfamily brings its own vivid sense of *exactly* how holidays, birthdays, graduations and other life cycle events "should" unfold, woven out of a wealth of sequences, cadences, smells and tastes that have gathered shape and meaning over a history that the new family group does not share. Holidays also come packed with emotionally laden hopes and expectations. They can generate intense expectations for *togetherness* with anticipation of making special memories. They often evoke intense disappointment when the expected does not happen. What to do?

One way through is to find holidays for your stepfamily where neither family has any stake in "the way we do things." Neither Martin nor Sarah's first families had celebrated *Tu Bishavat*, the Jewish tree-planting holiday. They involved the girls in creating a new ritual for their new family, which included going out together to the nursery to pick out a fruit tree. Together they picked a spot to plant it in the yard, and they took turns watering it and saying the prayer. Over the years, it became a cherished new stepfamily holiday tradition. (At the next Hanukah, though, they brought out the *familiar* menorahs.)

Ethnic, Class and Religious Differences: "This Is Who We Are"

Middle ground in this area often has roots that go back generations. Your sense of identity feels like more than just your personal habits or preferences. It's how you see yourself and the roles you take on in relation to others. We all absorb a sense of identity through our particular cultures, and gender, age, religion and other social influences have subtle and not-so-subtle influences. "Who I am" can feel non-negotiable. In the words of Popeye: "I yam what I yam!" In your stepfamily, it can get a little more complicated.

Whose Job Is It?

Giuliana grew up in a big Italian family with grandparents, aunts, uncles and cousins. As a girl, she was raised to cook, serve and take care of the men. She took great pride in doing this well. When her own young-adult sons came over on weekends, she lovingly cooked big beautiful dinners. She insisted on doing all the clean-up and happily packed up the leftovers for them to take home. They often brought their laundry for her to do while they visited, which she folded beautifully for them to take with them.

Bret came from a middle-class Irish family that valued hard work and independence. He'd raised his own children, a boy and a girl, to do chores around the house, assist in cooking dinner and, now that they were adolescents, to clear the table and take turns washing dishes. Each child had also learned to do their own laundry.

Bret felt Giuliana was "spoiling" her sons. He certainly didn't want her doing the same with his own kids. Guiliana felt he was rejecting her efforts to be nurturing.

As you can see in this story, cultural differences often feed into parenting challenges!

MONEY ISSUES

Money fights are incredibly common in any couple—stepcouples included. How much credit card debt are you each comfortable with? What are your spending priorities? Where do you want to bring your finances together—or not—in your stepfamily? What happens when one set of kids has more or less money than the other? How can you handle upset feelings when some kids get cell phones and cars and are headed to private colleges while the other kids in the family can't afford those things? How are you thinking about and planning for your estate when you die, and who gets what? Extended families and already-established agreements with co-parents often also play a big part in terms of college costs, allowances, inheritances, birthday gifts and more.

"How Do You Buy a Car?"

Fran grew up in a working-class family. She never bought anything unless she had saved enough to pay for it on the spot. Carrying no credit card debt had been passed down as a basic tenet of managing money well. Fran always did careful research before she made purchases, took good care of her things and kept them for a long time. Ben had grown up in an upwardly mobile middle-class family. As his parents had, he used credit to purchase a new car every few years, pay for family vacations and make other major purchases. When Ben announced that he was going to trade his two-year-old car in for a new one, with a car loan, of course, Fran was appalled. To her mind, his car was perfectly fine and he was being wasteful and financially irresponsible! Many (many) conversations later, they decided that Ben would keep his car for another two years, and then finance half of it.

Helpful Tips for Handling Money in Stepfamilies

- **One pot, two pots, three pots, mixed pots?** Some stepcouples pool all their funds: the "one pot" solution. Some couples use a "two pot" model. They keep their money entirely separate, each paying a share of joint bills from their own accounts and paying separately for their own kids' expenses. Others use a "three pot" model. They have a joint account to pay for shared expenses and separate individual accounts for their own personal and/or child-related expenses. There's no right way to do it.

- **Do what works.** It may take lots of conversations with your beloved to help you both get clear on what works for your relationship and stepfamily. No right; no wrong. Just curious and honest about what you need. You might like the togetherness of jointly making all spending decisions about kids. Or, you might find that intrusive. Often agreements with a co-parent need to be considered.

- **Be sure to update legal and financial agreements.** Stepfamily relationships change a *lot* over time. What seemed right in year one may seem very different in year four or five. You may want to put a date in your calendar app to remind you to look at your money agreements at least every couple of years.

- **Think about college aid formulas.** As soon as the "married" box is checked, most college financial aid formulas count the resources of *both* members of the couple, even if the stepcouple have agreed that only the parent will contribute to college expenses. This is a situation where an ounce of prevention is worth a pound of cure.

- **Start planning ahead.** Life insurance policies? Long-term disability insurance? How can you plan for the future financial health of your stepfamily when you're incapacitated or gone? You might be wise to talk to an estate planner or financial planner who specializes in next-time families.

BOTTOM LINE

No one money management plan is best. *What's important is finding agreements that* **work***. And then changing them over time to meet your evolving needs. What feels right in the early stages may not be the best fit several years down the road.*

Fifth Stepfamily Challenge: Building a Shared Culture That Respects Differences

THREE WAYS TO MAKE CONNECTIONS OUT OF DISCONNECTIONS

In your backpack of essentials for this journey, you may have brought along a sewing kit. If so, good planning! It really helps to stay on top of the small tears in the fabric of your stepfamily. Repair them before they get bigger. Here we're going to show you how to put in a few strategic stitches that will reinforce the seams of your stepfamily and will prevent major rips in the future. *A step in time saves nine*, and so does a *stitch* in time! Here are three key strategies for strengthening the fabric of your relationships as you figure out the best ways to manage the stretching that's asked of everyone in everyday stepfamily life.

Make a Family Question Jar

Curiosity can transform disconnections into connections. *"Help me understand what happens when . . ." "Can you share with me what you were thinking?" "Tell me more about . . ."*

One fun way to do this is to make a "family question jar." Place a jar in a public place in the home to collect "curious questions." Ask each family member to contribute at least one or two questions. If the kids don't volunteer right away, don't despair! The adults can simply start stocking the jar. Then take turns choosing a question to launch conversation over dinner. Here are some examples:

- If you could eat lunch with your favorite movie character, who would you eat with? What would you eat?

- If you could wake up tomorrow with a super power, what super power would you want? How would you use it?

- If you could be any animal in the world, what would it be? What would you like about being that animal?

- How are you like your mom? How are you like your dad? (This question can be asked of all family members, including adults and children. Including children in this question acknowledges that they have an equally important parent outside the household.

- What was the best thing that happened for you today? What was the least favorite thing that happened?

Questions can be funny or serious. The idea is to start building a family habit of curiosity. When Luke, who went to Methodist Sunday School, got the knack of curious questions, he asked Fran, who was Jewish, "You mean, you've *never* had a Christmas tree before? Where did Santa put the presents?"

Sharing Family Stories

Even though it may take years before stepfamilies have enough experiences together to build their own collection of stories, you can start sharing your family stories with stepfamily members.

How you tell these stories matters. If you say, *"I wish you could have seen Luke's face when the Jell-O spilled on his head! Lemme show you what he looked like!"*, the listener feels included. If you say, *"You had to have been there,"* the listener feels excluded. A little sensitivity and extra effort goes a long way.

Fran and Annie Revisit That Cake

Several years after moving in together, Fran and her stepdaugher Annie were out to dinner together. Over a shared piece of chocolate cake with ice cream, Fran said, "Birthdays when I was growing up were really special. My mom would always bake us each our favorite cake from scratch. Mine was carrot cake, with gobs and gobs of cream cheese frosting and colored sprinkles on top. My brother Charlie's was vanilla with lemon frosting. My little brother, Frank, who I adored, liked chocolate with lots of layers of chocolate frosting and shaved chocolate bits on the top—just like *you*, Annie."

"My grandma and I once made a carrot cake to take to school for a bake sale," Annie said. "It was a really funny story, because my grandfather loved carrot cake so he snuck downstairs and ate a big piece of it. Me and grandma were so mad! And he tried to pin it on Dad!" The two laughed.

"What was your grandpa like?" asked Fran, treasuring the girl's warm memories of Ben's father, who'd passed away years before she and Ben had met.

Fifth Stepfamily Challenge: Building a Shared Culture That Respects Differences

Children especially love to hear when their stepparents have made mistakes. They relish your stories about how you figured your way out of a crazy situation. Kids also love to be asked to tell their stories. They love when you give them your full attention and enjoy them. This is true for children of every age! Any time you can offer focused, gentle, loving attention, you'll put another strong stitch in the fabric of your relationship.

Doing Fun Things Together

The key word is *fun*. Are we having *fun* yet?

Establish family game night and learn a game together that's new to everyone. Organize short fun projects to do together—raking leaves into a pile *and* jumping in. Plan excursions together—stomping in puddles after a rain, or having a picnic in the park. At home, set aside movie-and-popcorn time. Creating fun times together may seem obvious. But it can take some skill.

It may take a few tries to find activities that are fun for everyone. Remember that for Fran, Ben and his kids' Scrabble games exposed her spelling difficulties. Keep looking!

Also keep in mind, not all children will *come to the party*, for complicated reasons we've already discussed—loss, change and loyalty binds. You are looking for that "sweet spot" of just enough togetherness without pushing too hard.

WHEN "US" TIME BECOMES A STRUGGLE

Adjusting to change, finding your way through differences and riding through missed expectations takes energy. Sometimes, providing some down time increases everyone's staying power in the long run.

Use One-On-One Time to Lower the Intensity for Children (and Outsider Stepparents)

Many a stepfamily vacation or holiday celebration sours when a child suddenly reaches their "family time" limit. When crankiness, irritability, withdrawal or what looks like "oversensitivity" begin popping up, kids may be needing more focused parent-child time. Breaking the family-time stride to respond to an unsettled child actually helps children strengthen and lengthen their togetherness muscles.

Likewise, stepparents may also reach their limits for "we" time, especially when family activities belong *only* to the other side of the stepfamily. Stepcouple alone time helps. So does some stepparent "away" time.

․․․․․․․․․․

Stepfamilies don't start out feeling like "home," but they will eventually—inevitably—develop their own culture, with patterns, rhythms and flavors. These things will emerge over time through shared experiences, through negotiation and with creativity.

Once you take the pressure off your stepfamily to "blend," you can look for ways to honor differences and forge stronger connections with respect and curiosity. The citizens of the new stepfamily country have rights and responsibilities, and it's up to all of you to decide "who we are" in this moment and who you will be together through the years. The couple takes the lead, but stepfamily thrives when everyone is included and valued.

By the way, in your stepfamily, many people will continue to hold dual citizenship. Just because you are together now doesn't mean the old country of first-time family is unimportant. Ultimately, a new stepfamily's sense of "home" will be a passport stamped with lots of experiences—some shared together, some created before you were together and some provided as blank pages for new adventures.

Chapter 16

. . . .

A New Wrinkle: Gray Recouplers

"It's impossible," said Pride.
"It's risky," said Experience.
"It's pointless," said Reason.
"Give it a try," whispered the Heart.

—Author unknown

So maybe you had this fantasy that stepfamily would be a snap for you because your kids are grown and out of the house now. With childrearing duties, co-parenting agreements and residential schedules behind you both, it would be just you two lovebirds playing house in your undies, doing what you want when you want.

Bliss!

Um... reality check! You may discover that even if you have young adult and older adult children, you'll all still face challenges that are stunningly similar to younger stepfamilies.

If you're in a stepcouple that began in later life— fifties and older— you're in good company. "Silver surfers" are the fastest-growing demographic using Internet dating sites. While divorce has gone down for every other segment of the population, it went up for your cohort. That means there are more "gray recouplers" starting on the stepfamily journey every day.

You'll find that most of the issues we've already covered in *The Stepfamily Handbook* apply to you. In addition, because you stepped on to the path with kids already grown and out of the house (or almost out of the house), your particular pathway will also have some different twists and turns.

For instance, you may all be looking, sooner rather than later, at the extra complexities involved when stepfamilies engage in decision-making about elder care and estate planning, or perhaps manage illness and dementia as a stepfamily.

Also, unlike younger couples, gray recouplers are more likely to see cohabiting as a preferred alternative to marriage rather than a step on the way to marriage. Committed gray recouplers are also more likely to be "Living Apart Together" in a committed relationship. In fact, rates of LAT couples triple in people over 55!

So let's open up *your* part of the map now and see where you've been, where you're going, and how we can help you get to a healthy, thriving stepfamily while avoiding twisted ankles, getting separated from your loved ones or losing direction.

HOW STEPFAMILY CHALLENGES UNFOLD FOR LATER-LIFE RECOUPLERS

Keep in mind: Once a parent, *always* a parent. And that's why those same five challenges show up for couples who come together in midlife and beyond.

First Challenge: Young Adult and Older Adult Children Struggle with Losses, Loyalty Binds and Change

Many relationships formed in later life do indeed deliver love at last. And many adult children are delighted to see their parents find new love. However, quite a few are not. *"Why can't they be happy for us?"* you might wonder. *"Don't I deserve love?"*

As in younger stepfamilies, the happy new couple is thrilled. But even for adult children, Mom's or Dad's new partner can make some painful losses and loyalty binds felt—and lead to some hard changes. Here is the story from the point of view of an adult daughter, Kayla.

Mom's Love Is a Loss for Kayla

Jenice and her new husband, Jamie, were both in their sixties, both previously divorced. Jenice's daughter, Kayla, was having a hard time with her mom's new relationship. A teacher like her mother, the forty-two-year-old was unhappy at having to share her mom. Ten years earlier, when Kayla's parents had divorced, Kayla began spending almost every afternoon with her mom. For those first few years, Kayla and Jenice would have supper with each other then sit at the table grading papers together. After Kayla married and had kids, her mom was there to help out. She'd take the kids overnight a few times a month so that Kayla and her husband could be alone together.

Then Jenice started dating Jamie.

"I didn't recognize her!" said Kayla. "She was like a smitten teenager—not like my *mom*. And Jamie is *always* there when I bring the kids over. I feel like I've lost my mom. And my kids have lost their grandma. The worst is, she doesn't get it. I'm an adult. It's embarrassing that it's so hard. But it is!"

Jenice was disappointed in her daughter's lack of support for her new relationship. *"I don't get it. She should be happy for me,"* she said sadly.

Age doesn't change the fact that adult children feel a sense of loss when their parent turns toward to a new partner. And it doesn't change the truth that kids at every age need their parents to understand them.

Loyalty binds can be very tight for adult children. Kayla's parents' separation was mostly amicable. Nonetheless, the end of a long marriage was painful for everyone. Because her daughter was an adult, Jenice felt she could confide in her about the marital problems that ended the relationship. Being privy to parental discord is just as corrosive for older children as it is for younger ones—especially daughters. Like many adult daughters in this position, part of her wanted to hear every detail. And most of her didn't want to hear a thing. Her mom's disclosures put Kayla smack in the middle of her parents' divorce. Like younger children, adult kids just want the people they love to be okay. When Jamie came on the scene, Kayla found herself worrying about her dad's feelings about a new man in Jenice's life.

Second Challenge: Insider/Outsider Positions Are Intense. And Stuck

Late-life stepparents enter as outsiders to adult children *and* grandchildren. Parents are stuck insiders—(much) more connected to all these folks.

> *Feelings About Grandkids*
>
> Jenice loved having her daughter and her grandchildren in her home whenever possible. Jamie tried to be polite. But for him, they were unwelcome intruders—not the romantic "just us" he had imagined. Jenice found her sweetie's distant behavior with her daughter's family "offensive." And terribly disappointing. "They're my family!" she said. "What's your problem?"
>
> "They're not mine!" was his reply. Jamie's kids lived in another state. When they visited, their positions reversed. Jenice liked them, but she couldn't wait for them go home so she could return to their now-familiar couple routines and have her beloved all to herself.
>
> "We fight like clockwork when the kids are around," she said sadly.

Extended family and in-law relationships add another (thick!) layer to insider/outsider positions. Gray recouplers come with long-established extended-family and in-law relationships from previous marriages. While younger stepfamilies form after an average marriage of about eight years, late-life recouplers inherit decades-long family and friendship networks. Intimidating if you're the new person coming in.

> *Kids Aren't the Only Ones With Loyalty Binds*
>
> A few months into their relationship, Jenice and Jamie attended her mother, Rose's, 85th birthday party. Jenice looked forward to introducing her new love to the family. Jenice's brother, Tom, and her ex, Eric, had been "like brothers," for more than thirty-five years. During the party, Tom and his wife barely acknowledged Jamie. "We just felt weird," Tom said later. Brothers-in-laws have loyalty binds, too! The whole situation was awkward for everyone and

painful for the new couple.

Jenice's mother had also been very close to her son-in-law. Indeed, for many decades, Eric had been another son to her. For the last twenty-five years since Jenice's father died, Eric had looked after his mother-in-law—putting up storm windows, pruning trees and installing grab bars in the bathroom. So when Rose met Jamie, she also was decidedly cool. As she said to Jenice later, "I just couldn't quite make the trip so fast."

Because Jenice was among family, *she* felt connected and cared about. After the party, though, Jamie was distant and withdrawn. "Your family is rude!" he said tersely. Jenice, who had fully enjoyed herself, was deeply disappointed. And offended. Another fight.

We've said often in *The Stepfamily Handbook* that *time* is the master ingredient in the recipe for thriving stepfamilies. But that's a bittersweet truth for gray recouples. Aware of the sand running out of their hourglasses, these couples often feel more urgency to move ahead quickly into coupledom. They don't feel like they have all the time in the world to take it step by step.

The reality is that nothing can replace time when it comes to stepfamily adjustment. Even with older couples. Families need to adjust to the changes that come with introducing a new partner. Partners and parents still need to figure out how to be a team with compassion and empathy for their stuck insider/outsider positions. They need time to grow trust between them so they can appreciate each other's efforts and struggles and gifts.

Slow and Steady Wins the Race

Jenice went alone to the next few family events. After some encouragement from his sweetie, Jamie reached out to Tom and invited him for a beer, saying, *"I really don't want to step on Eric's turf, but I'm serious about your sister and I'd like to get to know you because you're her people."* Slowly, over time, both Tom and Jenice's mother warmed to her new love.

Third Challenge: Parenting Tasks Divide Parents and Stepparents

Parents want more love and care for their kids. Stepparents want more limits! At every stage of life, children need emotional support from parents. At times, some will also need physical and financial support. That can be quite a surprise for partners who expected active parenting to be over at this later stage of life.

Let's note also that although adult kids are grown, they often aren't gone! Parents are no longer helping with homework and chauffeuring children around. However, crushing student loan debt, the high cost of housing, downturns in the economy and other cultural and social factors have increased the likelihood that kids will boomerang back into the basement or their old bedroom after going away to college or living on their own for a few years. Parents may see this as *"providing needed support."* Stepparents may feel it's an intrusion and call it *"indulging slackers."*

"Indulging" or "Supporting"?

Jamie wanted to buy a car for his 30-year-old son, who was struggling financially. Jenice accused Jamie of coddling his son. She'd been hoping they would spend that money on a romantic Bahamas cruise. Jamie shot back that Kayla took advantage all the time of Jenice's free babysitting. She could pay a sitter and then Jenice would have more time for him.

After they calmed down, they both chuckled a little as they realized they were both still involved parents, and always would be.

Fourth Challenge: Building a New Culture While Respectfully Navigating Differences

Late-life recouplers face the same challenge of finding middle ground while navigating a multitude of differences. It can be complicated by the fact that as people grow older, they tend to get more set in their ways.

As gray recouplers begin to develop daily routines together, celebrate holidays together and learn about the other's cultural, social and religious traditions, they often run smack up against different values. Even without kids living with them, finding middle ground is complicated for older couples. At this life stage, separate ground is now decades in the making and has deep root systems that spread across generations of extended family and friendship networks. *"This is how we do things,"* becomes, *"This is how we've ALWAYS done things."*

More on Insiders and Outsiders

Jamie and his first wife and children, and now grandchildren, had a three-decades-long tradition of gathering with their longtime neighbors for Christmas Eve dinner. Every year, Jamie's adult kids came in from out of town for this family and neighborhood reunion. Since his divorce had been friendly, Jamie and his ex-wife both attended. In the new couple's first year together, Jenice was, of course, also invited. However, she found herself feeling very alone sitting with a group of women who spent the entire evening talking to Jamie's ex-wife.

That night's fight was another painful one for the couple. Jenice wanted Jamie to understand why she never wanted to do that again. Jamie shook his head in disbelief. "You're asking me to give up something I've done for years. I won't!"

Fifth Challenge: Co-parents Are Still Part of the Family

Co-parents will always be part of your stepfamily, even when the kids are grown and there's no more negotiation around residential time or child support. Your paths will all cross at graduations, weddings, births of grandchildren, funerals, holidays, family reunions and more. Former spouses who learned to cooperate for the sake of kids have often, by now, made a lasting peace with each other during these events. They might even be affectionate. A new partner often feels like a "super outsider."

The entry of a new partner after a long marriage can be especially evocative for former spouses. As for younger stepfamilies, do take these things a step at a time. Yes, you may feel a sense of urgency because you have only so many years left. But let's not spend those years with kids (and friends and extended family) caught in the middle.

Triple Trouble: Fraught Father-Adult Daughter Relationships and New Partners

All these challenges can be especially intense with one particular subgroup of late-life recouplers: Older dads with young adult and older adult daughters. This is especially true if a daughter had a strained or distant relationship with her dad, often one that extends back to childhood. Sometimes Dad was never around because of work. Sometimes he was a better parent to a son, leaving his daughter to her mother. Add that post-divorce relationships between dads and their female children sometimes deteriorate much more than father-son relationships do.

Now Dad has fallen in love. Dad's expectation that his daughter will open her arms to his new beloved, *"When he was never there for me,"* opens the door to a deep well of loss and an unleashes a flood of grief and anger.

In a few of these more fraught late-life families, daughters and dads actually had a very close relationship, often partly because the marriage was cool. Now suddenly Dad is head over heels in love, a wrenching loss for these daughters. A third pattern is the classic loyalty bind, where a daughter becomes ever more protective of her mother, now alone in later life, who has to bear her ex's newfound happiness.

Three Broken Hearts

> Don was brokenhearted as he approached his 65th birthday party. His sweetie, Vera, was incensed. Don and Vera had been together for three years. While Don's two sons and their families had immediately RSVP'd and offered to help, his daughter, Amelia, refused to have any part of it. Amelia announced that she, her husband and their three children would not be attending.
>
> This was the last straw for Vera. Amelia had never accepted her, and, to Vera, had never made an effort even to get to know her. She was *done* being insulted and dismissed by the thirty-seven-year-old who, in Vera's opinion, was behaving like an immature teenager.
>
> Don was miserable that his wife and his daughter were so upset with each other. He had no idea how to fix the mess. One of his sons tried to intervene. Amelia told her brother, "He was always there for *you*. He went to every one of your games. He never came to a single one of mine. Even when I was captain of the basketball team. And now he wants me to watch him adore Vera in a way he *never* adored either me or Mom. No way. I'm done."

If this situation sounds familiar to you, there are some particularly helpful things you can do to ease the tension. The first is, let go of "blending." You've heard this one before. But here we mean literally, completely. Vera and Don need to know that Amelia will not be ready to make a relationship with her dad's new love until Don has repaired his relationship with his daughter.

If you're the dad, you'll need to invest in a lot of one-on-one time reconnecting with your daughter. Try reaching out by text or email or phone *("It seems like something isn't going well between us. I want to understand better.")*. It might take a few tries! You're likely going to need to listen to some tough stuff about how much your daughter has missed you. And, if she's in a lot of pain, she may not be able to say it very graciously or kindly. Your daughter will not need excuses or explanations from you. She'll need your best attempt at getting to know her and letting her know what you DO understand *("I am really seeing that I wasn't there for you. I'm getting it. Tell me more.")*.

And Dad and daughter will also likely need some fun easy "just us" time together. Maybe a lot of it, without your sweetie present.

Meanwhile, concentrate on deepening your couple relationship *without pressuring dad's adult daughter to be part of it*. All this means that dads in these couples are especially stuck insiders. New partners are painfully stuck outsiders, sometimes for a very long time. You'll both need each other's comfort and understanding.

If both Don and Vera can hang in, working on parallel tracks for now (dad-daughter and stepcouple), it is very likely that slowly, over time, Amelia will become more open to Vera.

HAZARD ⊘ Partners may want to say, *"Me or them."* Cutting off relationships with children to ease the pain for a new partner is not the answer. Children will always need their parents, even adult children. What the parent *can* do is comfort their partner and offer care and closeness.

ELDER CARE AND ESTATE PLANNING

If you haven't yet passed the fifty-year mark, then you might not have given much thought to how you'll divide your estate and who you'll want making medical decisions for you if you're incapacitated. Younger stepcouples often feel that they can procrastinate on these decisions for a while (not a good idea, by the way!). Older recouplers don't have that luxury.

Who will take care of Dad? Will it be his second wife, and will he stay in their home or go into assisted care? Who will pay for it? Will his daughter take him in and care for him in her home? Where will her stepmom fit into that scenario? And who's in charge of caregiving and end-of-life decisions? Will Dad be buried beside his deceased first wife (his children's mom), or will his new wife arrange for a plot where she can be buried beside him some day?

To avoid a landslide of conflict and hurt feelings, every stepcouple needs to engage in thoughtful advance planning. That means wading into these conversations sooner rather than later. Start by writing down everyone's wishes. How will you divide up your estates if one partner dies? Will yours go to your kids and mine go to mine? Will all of it go to whichever of us survives? If we're not legally married, and the home belongs to you, will I have move out if you die first?

For gray recouplers, these issues often come front and center very early in the relationship if a partner has health issues early in the relationship—or comes into the relationship with health problems. Suddenly, adult children, new partners and stepsiblings are scrambling to figure out how to deal with Dad's deteriorating health well before they've had time to build the reservoir of trust and understanding needed to address these issues. It may be hard to face these delicate conversations so early in your relationship. But we highly recommend that you start talking and thinking them through together.

Jamie's on the Hot Seat

Jamie didn't live near his three adult kids, and he wasn't particularly close to them, but he let Jenice know before they married that he planned on leaving his estate to them. She was not happy. "Don't you trust me to give your kids their due?" Jamie assured her that it had nothing to do with love or trust. It was just his feeling that this was the right thing for him to do as their dad. Jenice pointed out that his youngest son was always hitting Jamie up for loans that were never repaid. "You know he'll just fritter his inheritance away," she said.

"Then he will," Jamie said.

Although it was hard for her to hear that Jamie's kids were his priority, after many long and difficult conversations, Jenice acknowledged that Jamie had to do what he felt was right. She appreciated that he took his responsibility as a parent seriously. She liked that about him. His decision also freed Jenice up to divide her estate (which would consist mostly of the proceeds from her home) equally between her two children. After Jamie moved into her home, Jenice changed her will to stipulate that he could live in it as long as he wanted after she passed.

A couple of years later, when their relationship had matured more, Jamie changed his will to leave Jenice a quarter of his estate. He named his only son as executor and told his children about the new estate plan. They received this news unenthusiastically. To them, their stepmom was still a virtual stranger. Thinking about having to share their inheritance with her rekindled resentment about having to share their dad with Jenice. When Jamie informed them that Jenice would have legal power of attorney to make medical decisions for him, it only made feelings worse between him and his kids and his wife and his kids.

Jenice had decided that Kayla would be her health proxy. Jamie thought he should have that role, since she was his. "I'll tell them in front of you that I want them to consult with you and get your input," said Jenice. "But Kayla will have the final say." Jamie came around to the idea after a few months, saying, "I would never want to get between you and your kids."

HAZARD ● **Plan ahead for everyone's sake!** We have seen many a case where "steps" who had a tolerable or friendly relationship before the death of a parent, but were suddenly at one another's throats over estate plans that were absent, poorly conceived or a total (unpleasant) surprise.

Seeking guidance from an attorney, an estate-planning professional and/or a mediator is often a great idea. Your early attention to end-of-life financial planning, living wills, healthcare directives and durable power-of-attorney is an investment in long-term stepfamily health.

* * *

Finding love in later life is a gift. Many couples delight in the fruits of their hard-won life experience—maturity and patience and the ability to deeply appreciate another person amid the potent possibilities of love and intimacy. The couple's new relationship will present complexities for children of every age, grandchildren, extended family and community. The combined stepfamily tree now sprawls across generations. If the middle ground has become a thicket too tangled to navigate, Living Apart Together allows many couples to build a nourishing intimate relationship while maintaining separate homes where they can keep up their cherished routines, traditions and relationships. For later-in-life recouplers, *a step at a time* protects, honors and treasures the years of history woven into each part of the stepfamily's legacy.

Chapter 17

Coming Apart with Kids on Board: Thoughtful Endings for Stepfamilies

"Opportunities to find deeper powers within ourselves come when life seems most challenging."

—Joseph Campbell, American mythologist and writer

The stepfamily journey isn't a sure thing. Some will finally come to a place in the path that starts to widen out and feel like easier, even easy-, going. They'll look back and marvel at where they've been and the good place they've come to. Others, though, will need to end their journey and leave the trail. We've included this chapter even though we hope you won't need it.

We wish we could say "love conquers all." Sometimes, no matter how in love you were and how willing, prepared and diligent you were, your stepfamily comes apart. Just so you know, the divorce/separation rate for stepfamilies is only slightly higher than it is for first-time families. In case you are among those who decide that this just isn't going to work, this chapter will help you end well.

A note about language: Not all couples in stepfamilies marry. However, just for simplicity, we'll be using the word "divorce" here to talk about a split, whether you were married or not.

If you're feeling lost right now, that's understandable. Most maps don't chart this territory. Some of the landmarks might look similar to a first-family separation/divorce. Others will remind you of any respectful breakup with no kids in the picture. And as you'll discover, there are some unique aspects to bringing a stepfamily to a healthy close.

BEING THOUGHTFUL ABOUT KIDS—OF ALL AGES

The average length of a first marriage is around eight years. For a second marriage with children, it is five to seven years. Five to seven years is a small percentage of your life, but it's a significant percentage of children's lives. In fact, for some kids, the stepfamily "home" holds the majority of their lifetime memories. All the wisdom you might have heard about protecting kids in a first-time family divorce applies here—plus some:

Protect Kids from Conflict

We've said it over and over again. Adult conflict and tension are toxic for children. You may feel the urge to confide in young adult and older adult children. You do need support. But NOT from the kids—of any age. Many stepkids may have already been through this with a first, and sometimes second or third, divorce. This is the place for the adults to present a united front of mutual respect and calm. This is the most crucial thing you can do as a couple to help children come through well.

"It's My Fault"

Kids may feel guilty about the breakup. Especially since the adults in stepfamilies often fight about children.

Mixed in with guilt can also be a whole range of other feelings, including relief if the end of the stepcouple ends a conflict-filled family pressure cooker. Sitting right alongside may be grief and considerable worry about losing a beloved stepparent or cherished stepsiblings.

Telling kids the news of your decision begins another transition. As with other transitions, your job is to walk next to kids and help them feel safe in the changing terrain.

Helpful Tips for Breaking the News to Kids

These guidelines apply to children of all ages. Together, your goal is to be reassuring.

- **Deliver the news together, as a couple, if possible.** *"We've decided to end our relationship and that means we've decided to live apart."* Doing this together tells kids, *"We're doing this ending together. We'll work together to support you."*

- **Keep the explanation kid-level.** Explain the separation simply, without blaming each other. *"We're not able to love each other the way both want and need. So it's better for us to be apart now."* If one person is leaving the other, this is *not* information to share with children. Tell your best friend, your therapist or your hairdresser. NOT the kids!

- **Stay "low and slow."** Lowering the register of your voice and slowing *way* down will help you stay grounded and emotionally connected to your kids and stepkids during this difficult conversation.

- **Keep it brief.** Children, especially younger ones, will listen for about 45 seconds. Stick to a few *short* sentences. Then lean back and listen.

- **Expect follow-up questions.** Kids will have more questions as the news sinks in. They may start to ask for more details about what happens next. *"Will we have to move? Will I see my stepbrothers again? Who gets to keep the family cat?"*

- **Check in periodically.** Remain available. Initiate conversations over the next weeks and months that invite children to share their thoughts and feelings. *"Sweetie, how's your heart feeling about all this?"*

- **Provide information that is useful to *children* when *they're* ready to hear it**. Kids benefit from knowing what's going to change and what's not and when things will happen. *"In February, we're going to move into a new home and your stepdad and his kids will stay here. And we'll try to set up regular times for you to see them, and for his kids to see us."* For the things you're uncertain about, reassure with, *"We haven't figured that out yet, but we will and we'll let you know."* Then do follow through.

- **If there has been conflict and tension, acknowledge its impact, without blame.** "We're aware that things have been really tense around here sometimes. That makes a lot of kids feel like it's their fault. Wrong! It was our job to be respectful and not say mean things, and we didn't do our jobs well. We know that made things hard for you. We apologize. We hope living separately will make things easier for everyone."

- **Convey confidence that that the grown-ups will manage the process.** "It's our job to do this as peacefully as possible." "You can tell us if we mess up." If kids complain about tension, *thank them* and try to do better. *Make no excuses.*

Endings are never easy. Everyone is exhausted, nerves are frayed, stress is often high. A lot is being asked of adults at a time when their emotional resources may be low. Here are some ways to help kids through that leave them feeling protected and connected:

Helpful Tips for Supporting Children Through Stepfamily Endings

Divorce is painful for you as a couple. Restructuring the family (again) is tough for kids. As the adults going through the logistics of separating and the emotions of ending a much-hoped-for intimate partnership, you're likely a bit overwhelmed. So, do your best to siphon off enough bandwidth to support the kids. Keep it simple: Gently urge kids to talk, listen and love. Here are some helpful details:

- **Help kids talk.** Some kids may need help putting words to their feelings. "*Some kids feel really surprised. Some don't. I'm betting maybe this is part a surprise and part not?*" "*Lots of kids think it's their fault when there's a divorce. Any chance some part of you thinks that?*"

- **Mirror back what you see and hear:** "*Sounds like you're worried. Want to say some more?*" "*You look sad. Did I get that right?*" "*Makes sense to me that you're mad. This is hard.*"

- **Keep the door open:** "*Say some more.*" Stay curious: "*Tell me more.*" "*Help me understand more about that . . .*" Some of the books in the

> resource section may be helpful. (Please read them yourself first to see if they're right for your kids.)
>
> - **Talk to co-parents.** Just as you told them when you first started dating and getting serious, they need to hear about what's happening now. Not all the details—you can keep those private—but the basics *that will impact children*.
>
> - **Maintain regular routines.** Kids do best when their lives are not upended dramatically. Keep daily life as stable and steady as possible. Continue to provide *authoritative* (warm, caring and moderately firm) parenting.
>
> - **Agree to be friendly and warm to all kids.** If you're mad at your partner, please don't take it out on their kids.

POST-DIVORCE STEP RELATIONSHIPS

> *Children are 100% responsible. Parents [and stepparents] are 150% responsible.*
>
> —Cedar Barstow, Right Use of Power Institute (Brackets added by authors.)

Post-divorce step relationships vary tremendously, from continued warm connection, to occasional friendly meetings, to total disconnection. If you share a child, that's a whole different story. The relationships among steps who have neither genetic nor legal ties to bind them together after a split will require proactive efforts to hold on to important connections. Generally, that effort has to be initiated by the adults.

Keeping Stepparent and Stepsibling Connections

Stepparents are often disappointed that their stepchildren don't reach out to them after a split. *"I keep waiting,"* one stepdad said, somewhat bitterly. *"I put so many years in. Ballgames and rides to camp and nights up late helping with term papers, not to mention paying the mortgage and putting food on the table. And now, nothing."*

If this is your situation, remember that *you* can reach out. Your former stepkids might not realize you miss them or think about them. Try sending a friendly or funny text or a short email to let them know they're in your thoughts and heart. Meet for coffee or show up for one of their games. Mail a card or make a "just seeing how you're doing call."

A stepchild may not be ready to reconnect with you. It's natural for children of all ages to feel protective of and loyal to their own parent. They may need time. You can let them know you get it, and that you're supportive. For instance, *"I know your Daddy is hurting right now. You're his daughter. Of course you want to support him. And you and I have a ten-year relationship. You're in my heart and in my bones. So if and when you're ready, I'm here."*

In almost every case we know of, kids eventually do reach back, even if, at first, only for an annual birthday chat. Invisible lines of connection. Shared history. Where the heart is concerned, everything is possible.

Stepsibling Relationships

Relations among stepsiblings may be anywhere from very close, to basically friendly, to quite distant, to openly antagonistic. Our suggestion is to talk with kids about how much connection they want with one another. Again, kids, especially if they're young, will need to rely on the adults to help make this happen. Keep disconnecting your own hurt feelings from the children's needs. Kids get attached. It may seem easier for you to make a clean break, but your kids may still value or treasure step relationships.

When Adults Forget What It's Like to Be a Kid

After Olivia's dad and mom divorced when she was 9, her dad, Vic, remarried Dana a couple years later.

"This is your new family now," he told his daughter when he introduced her to Dana's two daughters, Shayla and Shana, ages 4 and 6. Olivia, who shared equal residential time with her mom and dad, at first felt replaced by these new little girls who lived with her dad most of the time, rode on his shoulders and called him "Papa Vic." But her dad kept making special "just us" time, and she began to feel more relaxed about the two new "little sisters." Although she didn't like her stepmom at all, to her surprise she began to enjoy being a big sister. The little girls adored her, and Olivia looked forward to spending time with them.

The new marriage lasted about two years. Olivia knew her dad and stepmom were fighting. It gave her a feeling of dread in her stomach. One day her dad picked Olivia up from school and broke the news: Dana and the girls had moved. Dana was filing for divorce. Her dad was very upset.

"Will I ever get to see Shayla and Shana again?" Olivia asked.

"No, Honey. They moved out of state. I wish it had worked out, but they're gone."

Olivia wrote her stepsisters a letter and drew them a picture of herself waving goodbye with tears in her eyes. Her dad mailed it for her. The letter came back unopened.

Five years later, Olivia still thinks about Shayla and Shana. "I never got to say goodbye," she says. "They were my *family*!"

Healthy letting go and relationship ending is possible—even for kids. Helping children say good-bye and express their love and grief is important. So, if you know that remaining connected is not possible or is not going to happen, help children through a tough ending that honors the past relationship.

UNTYING THE LEGAL KNOTS OF STEPFAMILY

Coming to cooperative agreements regarding the separation is best for everyone. If a couple is legally married, there will be some legal documents involved. But in most cases, what stepfamilies need exists outside the legal system: Guidance for how to support the bonds that have been forged in step relationships.

Step Relationships Exist Outside Any Legal Protections

The laws in most states don't acknowledge the emotional bonds of stepparent-stepchild relationships. In first-time families, both parents have rights. In the U.S., most stepfamily divorce agreements only address property settlement. Stepparents who never formally adopted the kids have no parental-like rights in their stepchildren's lives. For stepparents who spent years caring for stepchildren, this can be heartbreaking for both the adults and the kids.

When the adults are committed to maintaining relationships, even though it may mean additional time away from a parent, regular times for stepparents and stepchildren (and stepsibs) to get together can be really important for kids. It might be a dinner once a week, an overnight once a month, attending children's events and so forth.

Stepfamilies *can* create their own plans for stepparent-stepchild relationships. You might need a skilled mental health professional or mediator to help you create a family document that reflects commitments made by parents and stepparents and that guides these connections into the future.

Before Initiating a Court Action, Consider Alternative Dispute Resolution (ADR)

Alternative dispute resolution (ADR) methods resolve disputes (including divorce) without costly or adversarial litigation. ADR professionals provide support to settle differences and co-create durable agreements for adults who prefer *collaborative* and *respectful* methods for handling conflict. More respect in coming to agreements generally leads to far less conflict once you push back from the table and move forward in your life. Two regularly used nonadversarial methods are:

- **Facilitative mediation.** A highly trained, neutral mediator assists the couple through decision-making about finances, inheritance, property settlements and parenting/stepparenting arrangements. Karen, for instance, mediates parenting plans (stepfamily plans) with couples. She works with financial colleagues who mediate the property settlement portions. Both adults may also hire their own lawyers for legal education and consultation and to prepare court documents. Others may use websites to prepare the final documents needed for the legal step of the divorce.

- **Collaborative divorce.** The couple contracts to work together constructively and fairly to reach resolution without court action. Each member of the couple retains a specially trained collaborative attorney. Other professionals are often part of the team to provide expert advice on children's issues, post-divorce co-parenting, financial analysis and so forth.

Choosing Litigation and Initiating Court Action

Mediation and collaborative law do have some limitations if the relationship is actively violent, or if either member of the couple is unable or unwilling to participate in good faith, or if a partner suffers from serious personality problems. These situations often require attorneys and the courts to step in to ensure safety and to facilitate the divorce process through to completion.

If you decide to use the court system to end your relationship, our best advice is to find an attorney who is skilled in, and committed to, *constructive* resolution. In other words, not someone who wants to start a war with your soon-to-be ex. That will put your family (and your money) through a paper shredder!

Other Things to Think About

Stepparent financial support of stepchildren: In most U.S. states, stepparents have no legal financial responsibility for stepchildren, unless they've adopted them. Nonetheless, stepparents may want to continue to support stepchildren. This will be an issue to decide in mediation or between the couple. The agreement will exist outside the formal legal system.

Connections with extended family: Stepfamilies often include other significant relationships with stepcousins, aunts and uncles, grandmas and grandpas. By now, these steprelatives have often been woven into the fabric of children's lives. It's up to parents to remain open to relationships that matter a lot to kids.

Celebrations, milestones and special occasions: In an ideal world, stepfamilies who have grown to love one another will continue to celebrate special moments together—award ceremonies, graduations, weddings and other life-cycle events. When adults come out the other side of their hurt, the bonds of connection can be honored and memorable "family" experiences can continue.

Making the decision to stop, to give up, to end relationships for which you had so much hope is painful. Hope often dies hard and love often burns strong, *until it burns out*.

Even if the journey ends, you have deepened your capacity to love, to stay *in it* and to find a glint of light in the dark moments. How you go forward from this point will make a tremendously important impact on everyone's healing. Here are a few final guideposts to follow as you bring your stepfamily to a close:

> Care for the children's hearts.
>
> Grieve the ending with as much grace as you can muster. Have compassion for the complexity that finally got the better of you both.
>
> Be as sweet as you can to yourself and to each other.

In the words of A.A. Milne's Winnie the Pooh: "How lucky I am to have something that makes saying good-bye so hard."

CONCLUSION

Stepfamilies Over Time

"Every moment and every event in every person's life on earth plants something in their soul."
—Thomas Merton, theologian, mystic, poet

"Is this normal?"
"How long should this take?"
"What happens next?"
"Are we there yet?"

Every stepfamily wants to know if they're on the right track and not walking in circles or heading into a patch of poison ivy. It can be very comforting to have a panoramic view of where you are and where you're going. This chapter gives you just that. It's called the Stepfamily Cycle—a model of development Patricia created to help answer these questions.

You can think of the "stages" of the Stepfamily Cycle as "signposts" or "stations"—interpretive signs along the trail—that you can refer to if you're not sure how (or if!) your stepfamily journey is progressing.

THE STEPFAMILY CYCLE

You may be one of those who is riding straight through the stages of the Stepfamily Cycle in linear sequence. Or not. Some are able to skip some of the boggier areas. Others have to hit every one of them. Chances are you'll breeze past a few important trail markers and get held up at others. You might have to turn around sometimes and go back to pick up a missed turn or a lost tool. Lots of stops and starts and a few wrong turns, bruised feelings and goof-ups figuring out how to do it are normal for this journey.

Stay hydrated with a sense of humor! Keep up your strength with a trail mix of solid skills, a better understanding of the territory, and a commitment to walk at a pace everyone can manage!

EARLY STAGES: GETTING STARTED OR GETTING STUCK

The Early Stages of stepfamily begin with the already-established relationships sitting solidly between children and their parents and between co-parents. As fantasies of blended bliss dissipate under the reality of next-time family architecture, couples often start to feel pulled apart by the first markers of potentially divisive challenges.

Disappointment starts to intrude in the face of kids' and co-parents' lukewarm or negative reactions to the new couple relationship and stepparents' irritation with stepkids. It's easy to get mired in the mud here. With your good map in hand and a solid dose of hope, persistence and skill, you can start to see the light toward the end of the Early Stages.

Fantasy: *"This Will Be So Wonderful for All of Us."*

You might have started this journey with a spring in your step, thinking, *"We're in love! We will finally have the family we've both been waiting for."* *"I love you, so of course I'll love your kids."* *"You love me so of course you'll love my kids."* *"The children will be as thrilled as we are!"* You wouldn't be alone in imagining these things.

Some may experience a bit of a crash and burn as all that luscious early-relationship sexual energy is confronted with the realities of living under one roof. Others pick themselves up, dust off their skinned knees and say, *"I guess we're learning something about what we've walked into here!"*

Immersion: *"What's Wrong with Me (or You or the Kids)?"*

As you and your sweetie move from dating to getting serious to moving in together, you may find yourselves starting to feel *immersed* in those five stepfamily challenges. You're experiencing insider/outsider roles, kids' feelings of anxiety and loss, loyalty binds, co-parents complications, plus differences in parenting styles, and you're trying to make a home where everyone feels comfortable.

Especially if you leaped into stepfamilydom looking forward to the promise implied in "blended family," you might be feeling awfully lost. With the right map in hand, you can move out of doubt and into darkness.

Some couples stay here for a very long time, constantly feeling like they're losing their footing, feeling ashamed and resolving to *"do better"* in reaching for. . . the impossible. In this place, it is easy to see those knotty dilemmas and painful glitches as failures. When that happens, lots of folks find themselves tucking their feelings under the rug. But it can get awfully bumpy under there! Rates of avoidance are very high in stepcouples for a very good reason. It's scary to talk about these things, and hard to talk about them well.

Know that it's never ever too late to start embracing those challenges and move forward together, one step at a time.

Awareness: Acceptance and Curiosity

"We're starting to get it! It's not that something's wrong with you, or me. Or the kids. Or my ex. It's that we live in a stepfamily!"

Something really nice happens in this stage of the stepfamily journey—keep an eye out for this signpost. *Awareness* starts to kick in. You begin to embrace the realities of stepfamily rather than strain against them.

You're starting to discern the difference between things that signal trouble and things that are simply telling you, *"This is happening because we live in a stepfamily—there just are insiders and outsiders!"* Stepparents may now be shifting from, *"I'm invisible, what's wrong with me? (Or my partner)?"* to *"Gee it's really painful when nobody looks at me. I could sure use a hug."* Parents may be shifting from, *"I can't make everyone happy, what's wrong with me?"* to *"I feel so torn. I need you to understand. I need support, too."* Accepting rather than straining and struggling to shape yourselves into a first-time family is the final exam here. You start to have more clarity, compassion and genuine curiosity about the journey!

It's becoming easier to take a breath, feel a bit calmer and maybe even find a spark of confidence. *"We're OK. We're just hiking a hard stretch! We'll get there if we just stay on the trail."* You're starting to recognize the boulders and gullies that are part of the landscape you've entered. You may even be finding that sometimes boulder scrambling can be fun.

If you're still feeling like, *"something's wrong with me,"* you've gotten bogged down in the doubt of Immersion. Time to take a breath and take a good look around. See if you can line up the things that are bothering you with any of the five challenges in part III. That may give you a way forward.

You're solidly in Awareness when you know that the challenges haven't gone away and that the terrain hasn't changed. But you're starting to give yourself (and everyone else) a break.

MIDDLE STAGES: REORGANIZING FAMILY RELATIONSHIPS

You're on your way as a stepfamily. Now in the Middle Stages, you'll see two signposts: *Mobilization* and *Action*. In the Middle Stages you are starting to more openly engage with the different colors, shapes and textures you've each brought to your stepfamily. You'll also begin to start stitching together new patterns of coexistence and cooperation. As you move toward creating your own "stepfamily quilt," these will sit right next to the patches of what's unique about each of you.

Mobilization: Airing Differences

This is the spot in the journey where some, or all, folks in the family begin declaring more openly what they like and don't like. Often disagreements start to be expressed in some areas, while others take much longer. Some family members (often a struggling outsider stepparent or an unhappy child) may lead the way. At first it may seem they're upsetting the apple cart. But usually they're waving a signal flag for everyone else: *"Hey, Guys. There are some things we need to pay attention to here!"*

Some of us are better than others at just getting our feelings *out there*. Some remain stuck in Immersion with no voice for their feelings. Others suddenly burst into Mobilization with big, not terribly gracious, blurts.

It's not unusual to find yourselves fighting more at this stage as you engage more directly with each other about what hurts, what's hard, and what you need more of and less of. The trick will be to keep the fights comparatively short and reasonably constructive.

If you're fighting a lot, with no resolution, it's a sign you're stuck in Mobilization. Time to backtrack to Awareness. Go back to your survival kit, flex your muscles and start exercising those five skills from Chapter 4: Take a breath, listen to understand, switch out of defensiveness, look for five positives to each negative. And, especially important in this stage, *repair the hurts*!

BOTTOM LINE

You are starting to appreciate that being a stepfamily means you're not going to be a team that gets close through easy agreement. You're going to get close by being kind to each other, learning how to express your differences (gently) and by hanging in there with each other.

Kids who had no words until now may be finding their voices as well. *"I hate my stepmother."* It may not always be pretty, but your handy-dandy decoder ring (user instructions in Chapters 6 and 11) will help you read their signals more clearly and give you the clues you need to help kids feels more grounded. (The Children's Worksheets in appendixes A and B are a great way to help kids put their feelings into words and share them with you and each other in a safe way.)

Action: Building Shared Stepfamily "Middle Ground"

In this stage, patches of middle ground are starting to form. Maybe you've all found a few fun things you really like to do, a few foods you'll all eat, or a few creative ways to divide up household chores. Over time, these areas of shared ground spread and grow. So does your sense of connection with each other. Differences also remain. But you might notice you've been making more space for your different parenting styles and your different ideas of "what's good food." These things are less a source of conflict and more just part of "who we are." You've been *learning through goofing*, getting better at laughing with each other when that happens. Yay!!

If things are going well, stepparents are slowly becoming part of a "parenting coalition" across households. Co-parents and stepparents are increasingly working together as a team to discuss concerns about kids, to support each other and to honor the unique contributions they're each making.

You might notice that you've forged some of these shared ways of doing things through active negotiation. Other "ways we do things" are emerging naturally over time as you walk together on this path.

In your eagerness to get to this place of feeling you're an "us," watch for any signals that you're rushing it. Remember how Ben and Fran learned that in immediately jumping into spending their Friday nights "all together," they accidentally skipped over the kids' need to be "just with dad" on their transition night. Likewise, Sarah and Martin had excitedly made new matching menorahs for all the kids. They learned rather quickly that their "cool new idea" had left each of their children feeling unhappy. They wanted the familiar experience of doing it like they always had before. *"Why does everything have to be different?"* Ben's daughter, Annie, got sullen and distant, leaving Fran feeling like a bump on a log. Martin's daughter, Lydia, fell apart. Both families read the signposts, backtracked and slowed down.

Lesson learned: Middle ground in a stepfamily is best planted slowly. A step at a time.

Here's how the middle ground of food unfolded in the Papernow/Goldberg family. Notice that this is a story about shared ground forming over many, *many* years.

The Papernow/Goldbergs and Food

In year two of the Papernow/Goldberg stepfamily, Patricia's daughter went through the kitchen pointing out, "Papernow, Papernow, Papernow" (organic whole grain cereal, skinless chicken, fish, skim milk, nonfat yogurt, lowfat mayo and the entire fruit and vegetable bin). And "Goldberg, Goldberg, Goldberg" (sugar cereals, white bread, steak, two-percent milk and *"real"* mayonnaise).

In year four, her daughter, now age 16, began inching out of her fervent vegetarianism and adding fish to her diet. In year five, she added chicken and *even*, occasionally, red meat. Over the years, Patricia's husband *slowly* converted to lowfat cheese and skim milk, and he began eating fruit. In year six, Weight Watchers drew him into the lower "point" values of whole grains, nonfat yogurt and chicken.

Seven years later, Papernow food and Goldberg food had become *almost* indistinguishable—*except* for the vegetable bin, which, twenty-three years down the road, remains *entirely* Papernow territory. The refrigerator still has both lowfat and "real" mayo sitting right next to each other.

LATER STAGES: THE "WE" OF MATURE STEPFAMILIES

Congratulations! You made it to the Later Stages' signposts: *Contact* and *Resolution.* You're starting to feel like you're a "we" instead of an "us and them." At last! Your couple relationship is now solid and secure. Stepfamily challenges will likely still come up, but they're less extreme and threatening than they once felt. The temperature swings can be less dramatic.

That "stepfamily quilt" of yours is also starting to feel more whole. All the pieces are now being held together by comforting strips of new middle ground.

Some stepfamilies enter the Later Stages within a few years. For others, a bunch of larger boulders, a few wrong turns or a poorly stocked tool box may have made it a longer, harder journey.

Contact: Intimacy and Authenticity in Step Relationships.

Your couple relationship has now become a reliable sanctuary for connection and caring. Stepparent-stepchild relationships have stabilized. The bonds in some stepparent-stepchild relationships have gained considerable strength and warmth. Others may remain comparatively distant.

With children who were 8 or under when you started, stepparents may have moved into an *autho*ri*tative* (warm and moderately firm) parenting role with some of their stepchildren.

With stepkids who were already teenagers and older when you started your journey together, stepparents may now enjoy warm, caring relationships that leave limit-setting to the parent. Stepchildren with extremely tight loyalty binds may be a lot more civil and even sometimes friendly. (Again, no signs of failure. Just a part of being a stepfamily.)

A rewarding, "intimate outsider" role may now be emerging for stepparents with some or all their stepchildren. By this time, stepparents know their stepchildren very well and have come to care deeply about some of them. *And* they also often remain less reactive than parents. This combination can open the way to a very special mentoring role for stepparents, especially around touchy issues like boyfriends, sex and career planning. It may come several years down the road with struggling early-teen girls , and much earlier with children who were more available from the start.

Resolution: Holding On and Letting Go

As you enter the Resolution Stage, there's a growing sense of "we-ness"—deepening layers of shared history, more and more aligned values and increasingly reliable nourishing connections in many, if not all, your step relationships. You can feel yourselves (finally!) relaxing into easier, cooperative functioning. Often there is considerable closeness and warmth in at least some stepparent-stepchild and stepsibling relationships.

The real honeymoon comes much later in stepfamilies, but it's here now and it's real and it feels really good. In many stepfamilies, parent-child relationships do remain stronger than step relationships. Normal! It's just the way stepfamilies are made.

You may find yourselves facing some of your familiar stepfamily divisions as you encounter college financial decisions, graduations, weddings and grandbabies. Time to dust off that tool box of communication and problem-solving skills. You've got this! And because you now have much more solid and secure relationships all throughout your mature stepfamily, these glitches can often be worked through much more quickly than they could at earlier stages.

Family events may now bring everyone in the extended stepfamily "village" together. Most hopeful, stepfamily relationships keep growing and changing. Sometimes, even many years down the road, new grandchildren, weddings or the illness of a child can provide an opportunity for mending previously fraught stepparent-stepchild, or co-parent–co-parent, or stepparent–co-parent relationships. As author George Elliot wrote: "It's never too late to be who you might have been."

HOW LONG DOES IT TAKE?

Everyone wants to know how long this journey will take. From our experience and from some of the research, "faster" families move into forming some areas of more solid middle ground in the Action Stage within a couple of years. They then need a couple more years to feel that solid family-wide sense of "we-ness" of the Later Stages.

"Slower" families may get stuck in the doubt and sense of failure of the Immersion Stage and get caught in chronic conflict in Mobilization. Or some have raced too quickly into Action and find themselves hurtling over a cliff.

All these folks will need to inch forward, or trek backward, to Awareness in order to get themselves back on the path to thriving stepfamilydom.

"Faster" families move into the Later Stages within a total of about four years. Struggling stepfamilies may need a lot more time. Don't despair though. Even fifteen years down the road, a good map can move things along.

"*Any tips on speeding things up?*" you're wondering.

Qualities of Successful Stepfamilies

Paradoxically, the stepfamilies who get there faster actually focus more on s*lowly* building family and walking step by step rather than racing forward. Here are some more things that allow stepfamilies to unfold more easily and with less struggle:

- **Successful stepfamilies let go of trying to "blend" early on.** Some begin with a more realistic map of the territory. Others adjust their course quickly: "*We learned really early—it didn't work when we tried to discipline each other's kids! 'To each his or her own' worked a LOT better, especially in the first few years.*"

- **Successful stepcouples tend to bring better interpersonal skills.** Stepcouples who move more quickly to "resolution" are *not* thrilled by their challenges! They get hurt, disappointed and angry. But they're able to air their differences more kindly and more constructively. They repair their goofs fairly quickly and find their way back to each other.

- **Parents practice *authoritative* parenting.** Both warm *and* firm. Kids thrive with this kind of parenting. Thriving kids equals happier stepfamily!

- **Stepparents concentrate on *connection not correction*.** They don't become disciplinarians of the partner's kids until or unless they have taken the time (often lots of it) to form solid, caring relationships with them. They absolutely avoid *authoritarian* (harsh and firm) parenting. Meanwhile, they are warm, friendly and interested in their stepkids.

- **Some travelers may be in better emotional shape for this trip.** Lighter baggage, fewer old emotional injuries, can make the climb easier. In succesful stepfamilies, those who do have a bum knee and old hurts are able to find ways to heal them enough to move a new way and strengthen new muscles.

The optimism of the human heart, along with a good map and some solid skills, will let you build your thriving stepfamily—one step at a time. You undertook this adventure with two hearts leaping. With equal parts kindness and determination and with your trail guide in hand, you can navigate this landscape together.

Take a look around.

No matter where you are on your journey, the truly amazing view isn't *out* there. What's amazing is resting your eyes on the people who are walking beside you, hearts open, hiking sticks in hand.

The stepfamily journey has likely been, and will continue to be, different for each of you. As you walked side by side—to varying degrees—you are becoming beloveds. Despite some challenging climbs and a few potholes, the promise of love shared and family expanded can be with you every step of the way.

APPENDIX A

MY FAMILY

A Worksheet for Children

DIRECTIONS for CHILDREN: Complete the following phrases and discuss with your family. *You don't have to answer anything you don't want to.*

DIRECTIONS for ADULTS (and other listeners): *Listen* to each child's answers. *NO explaining or convincing. Only:* "Gee that sounds tough." "That sounds fun." "Tell me more." "Help me understand more about that."

1. List your family members and one thing you like to do with each other:

2. **We argue a lot about**

3. **One thing I would change is**

Appendices

4. I really like when we

5. I wish they knew this about me

National Stepfamily Resource Center *Smart Steps: Embrace the Journey* **Child Handout**

Used with permission from Dr. Francesca Adler-Baeder

APPENDIX B

CHANGES IN MY LIFE

A Worksheet for Children

DIRECTIONS: FOR CHILDREN: Complete this sheet and ask your family to listen as you share. *You don't have to answer anything you don't want to.*

DIRECTIONS for ADULTS & other listeners: Help all family members *listen* to the child's answers. *NO explaining or convincing. Only*, "Gee that sounds tough." "that sounds fun." "Tell me more." "Help me understand more about that."

My parent's decision brought change into my life.

Mark each with √ if there have been a *few* changes.

Mark √√√ if there have been many changes.
Two checks if in-between.

Home _____

Family _____

School _____

Church _____

Parents I live with _____

Other people I love with _____

Rules _____

Time together _____

Time alone _____

Friends _____

Food _____

Money _____

Fights _____

Feelings _____

The best change for me:

_____

_____

_____

_____

_____

_____

_____

_____

The most difficult change for me:

How I feel about these changes:

National Stepfamily Resource Center *Smart Steps: Embrace the Journey* **Child Handout One**

Used with permission from Dr. Francesca Adler-Baeder.

APPENDIX C

CHOOSING A THERAPIST

Whatever you're struggling with, or whoever you're worried about, there are times that getting a good family psychotherapist involved makes a huge difference! Unfortunately, although some therapists have some training in supporting healthy post-divorce relationships, very few therapists receive any training about stepfamily. As a result, many simply don't know how different stepfamilies are from first-time families. Therapists who inadvertently apply first-time family principles to your next-time family may not only be misleading for you, but can actually lead you down the wrong path, creating more problems, not less.

Especially given the lack of available good training, it is perfectly acceptable to tell a counselor that it would be really comforting to you if they would read this book or Patricia Papernow's *Surviving and Thriving in Stepfamily Relationships* (the latter written for both clinicians and stepfamily members).

> ### Choosing a Therapist for Your Stepcouple or Stepfamily
> - **If you'd like some help for your couple relationship, a stepfamily-informed therapist** can deepen your understanding of your very different positions and help you reach for each other and comfort each other (versus drive each other nuts).

- **If you'd like help for your whole stepfamily, be sure the therapist is willing to meet separately with each of your family's "subsystems."** Many family therapists are trained to insist on seeing a whole family together. It may *seem* like a good idea to get everyone in a room to hash out your difficulties. But this is often actually destructive in stepfamilies.

- Stepparents and parents will likely need a safe place to hear each other's struggles with insider/outsider pulls, discipline, etc., *without children present*. Children need to be able to say, *"I hate my stepparent"* and feel heard by their parent. Only a sainted stepparent can be present for this.

- Skilled stepfamily therapists work first with the stepcouple, or with each parent with their respective kids, and/or with just siblings, perhaps combined with stepsiblings. After connection is solid in those relationships, then work can proceed with the whole family, and in stepparent-stepchild relationships. Like everything stepfamily, a step at a time saves nine!.

- **Lowering the tension in the co-parenting (ex-spouse) relationship may be key.** A skilled therapist or divorce coach can meet with co-parents together using a carefully structured agenda focused on kids. If conflict is high, it's particularly important to work with a skilled conflict manager to keep the focus on the kids and to help each parent feel safe.

Sorting Out When a Child Needs Individual Therapy

An "unruly" or depressed child is often like the canary in the coal mine alerting everyone that there are family dynamics that need attention. The "fix" often lies with the adults, not in the child. That said, especially for children caught between high-conflict co-parents, or who were struggling with a particularly intense loyalty bind or dealing with a compromised parent, a skilled therapist can provide a safe place to help a child sort through their own feelings and learn some helpful coping strategies. Here are some key criteria:

- **Children live in their families, not in the therapy room.** Child therapists will be most effective *if they also work with parents, and, often, with stepparents.*

- **An uninformed child therapist can easily align with a child's pain,** becoming outraged at a parent's lack of empathy or a stepparent's distance, leaving children feeling more alone, and adults feeling even more helpless. You want a therapist who will recognize normal stepfamily challenge, who can hold compassion for both adults and kids and provide skillful evidence-informed guidance.

If your child is showing alarming changes in mood change or behavior that persist, if they aren't sleeping, if eating patterns are changing drastically or if school performance precipitously drops or peer relationships take a noticeable change, please consult your child's healthcare provider for health concerns. *Then,* try to find good help from an expert in stepfamily!

Making Your Own Therapy a Priority

Stepfamily challenges can be intense. Having a good map and learning some solid skills can help immensely. IF you find that you are continuing to get really upset, or you find yourself regularly shutting down and withdrawing, it can often be helpful to get some good individual therapy. You'll never love being a stuck outsider or a torn insider, but healing "old bruises" can help you find the resources to meet your challenges.

RESOURCES

BOOKS FOR ADULTS ABOUT STEPFAMILIES

Anne Burton, Editor. *My Father Married Your Mother: Dispatches from the Blended Family.* Norton, (2007). Essays by writers about stepfamilies, including authors Barbara Kingsolver, Andrew Solomon, Susan Cheever, Roxana Robinson and others.

Ron Deal and Gary Chapman. *The Smart Stepfamily: Seven Steps to a Healthy Family.* Bethany House, (2012/2014). Christian-focused, evidence-based book about stepfamily.

Ron Deal and Gary Chapman. *The Smart Stepdad: Steps to Help You Succeed.* Bethany House, (2013). Christian-focused, evidence-based book about stepfathers.

Diane Fromme. *Stepparenting the Grieving Child: Cultivating Past and Present Connections with Children Who Have Lost a Parent.* Merry Dissonance Press, (2017). An excellent compassionate, and practical resource.

Patricia Papernow. *Surviving and Thriving in Stepfamily Relationships: What Works and What Doesn't.* Routledge, (2013). Written for both stepfamily members and clinicians and hailed as the classic in the field.

BOOKS FOR ADULTS ABOUT CO-PARENTING AFTER DIVORCE

Constance Ahrons. *We're Still Family: What Grown Children Have to Say about Their Parents' Divorce.* HarperCollins, (2004). The author of *The Good Divorce* interviews the now-adult children in her first book. Lots of wisdom here.

Karen Bonnell with Kristin Little. *The Co-Parenting Handbook: Raising Well-Adjusted and Resilient Kids from Little Ones to Young Adults through Separation and Divorce.*

Sasquatch Books, (2017). (First version available on Audible.) Parents will discover how to move from angry, hurt partners to constructive co-parents. Chock full of strategies to help resolve day-to-day issues.

Karen Bonnell with Felicia Malsby Soleil. *The Parenting Plan Workbook: A Comprehensive Guide to Building a Strong, Child-Centered Parenting Plan.* Sasquatch Books, (2017). (Complementing videos that support the book available on Karen's YouTube channel.) A roadmap for creating a plan that leads to successful co-parenting and well-adjusted children.

William Eddy. *So What's Your Proposal? Shifting High-Conflict People from Blaming to Problem Solving in 30 Seconds.* Unhooked Books, (2014). Solid practical guidance.

Robert Emery. *The Truth about Children and Divorce: Dealing with the Emotions So You and Your Children Can Thrive.* Meredith, (2006).

Jeffrey Wittman. *Custody Chaos, Personal Peace: Sharing Custody with an Ex Who Is Driving You Crazy.* Penguin, (2001). An extremely practical guide for co-parents.

HELPFUL BOOKS FOR ADULT RELATIONSHIPS

Janice Abrams Spring. *How Can I Forgive You? The Courage to Forgive, the Freedom Not To.* HarperCollins, (2004). Excellent book about recovering from an affair.

John Gottman. *Why Marriages Succeed or Fail: What You Can Learn from the Breakthrough Research to Make Your Marriage Last.* New York: Simon & Schuster, (1994).

John Gottman. *Seven Principles for Making Marriage Work: A Practical Guide from the Nation's Foremost Relationship Expert.* Harmony Books, (1999/2015).

Sue Johnson. *Hold Me Tight: Seven Conversations for a Lifetime of Love.* Little Brown, (2018).

Douglas Stone, Bruce Patton, and Sheila Heen. *Difficult Conversations: How to Discuss What Matters.* Penguin, (2010).

BOOKS ON PARENTING SKILLS

Bayard & Bayard. *How to Deal with Your Acting-Up Teenager.* Evans, (1998).

Robin Deutsch and Jenifer Marshall. *7 Things Your Teenager Won't Tell You—And How to Talk about Them Anyway.* Ballantine, (2011). Fabulous, practical, wonderfully written book about parenting teens.

Adele Faber & Elaine Mazlish. *How to Talk So Kids Will Listen and Listen So Kids Will Talk (20th anniversary edition).* Scribner, (2012). Also available in audiotape, and in videos by Adele Faber.

Howard Glasser, Joan Bowdidge, and Lisa Bravo. *Transforming the Difficult Child Workbook: An Interactive Guide to the Nurtured Heart Approach.* pubisher, (2008.)

Dan Hughes. *Attachment Focused Parenting: Effective Strategies to Care for Children.* Jessica Kingsley, (2012). (See also his website below.)

Dan Siegel. *Parenting from the Inside Out: How a Deeper Self-Understanding Can Help You Raise Children Who Thrive.* Penguin, (2004).

Dan Siegel & Tina Bryson. *The Whole-Brain Child: 12 Revolutionary Strategies to Nurture Your Child's Developing Mind.* Bantam, (2012).

BOOKS FOR CHILDREN ABOUT STEPFAMILIES

Please Note: This list has *not* been vetted by us. Children's books about stepfamilies tend to be either horrid or very good. *Please read them before giving them to children!* Let us know what you think!

http://www.readbrightly.com/books-about-blended-families/ List of books with descriptions
https://www.barnesandnoble.com/b/books/family-growing-up-kids/stepfamilies-kids/_/N-29Z8q8Ztxo Barnes and Noble's list of books about kids and stepfamilies.

Julie Johnson. *How Do I Feel About My Stepfamily.* Franklin Watts, Ltd., (1999).

Julie Leibowitz. *Finding Your Place: A Teen Guide to Life in a Blended Family.* Divorce Resource Series, (2000).

Debbie Glasser and Lisa Cohn. *The Step-Tween Survival Guide: How to Deal with Life in a Stepfamily.* Free Spirit Publishing, (2008). This one is well-reviewed.

BOOKS FOR CHILDREN ABOUT DIVORCE

Please Note: *Unlike the stepfamily titles, these have been vetted by knowledgeable professionals.*

Danielle Lowry. *What Can I Do? A Book for Children of Divorce.* Magination Press, (2001). Offers resources to help children understand and sort out feelings they face over divorce. Appropriate for ages 8-12.

Jeanie Franz Ransom. *I Don't Want to Talk About It.* Magination Press, (2000). Illustrated by Kathryn Kunz Finney, this storybook explores the range of emotions that children are likely to feel when the subject of divorce is first brought up. Appropriate for ages 4-8.

Judith Aron Rubin. *My Mom and Dad Don't Live Together Anymore: A Drawing Book For Children of Separated or Divorced Parents.* Magination Press, (2002). Allows kids to express their feelings through art. Appropriate for ages 4-12.

ONLINE RESOURCES FOR ADULTS

Academy of Professional Family Mediators: https://apfmnet.org/find-a-mediator Find mental health professionals and lawyers in your areas who have training in conflict resolution.

Arthur Becker-Weidman www.center4familydevelop.com Resources for parents of adopted and foster children and for clinicians who want to help.

Karen Bonnell www.coachmediateconsult.com Resources for separating, divorcing and co-parenting teams! Child-centered parenting plans. Stepfamily. Podcast, articles videos.

Gesell Institute https://gesellinstitute.org/collections/ages-and-stages-pamphlets Strongly recommended for further study of children's ages, stages, and healthy development:

High Conflict Institute www.highconflictinstitute.com Training and consultation to identify and manage complex high-conflict situations in family, (including divorce and co-parenting), business and legal settings.

Dan Hughes. www.danielhughes.org Excellent resources (including cd's and books, videos, and professional training) for attachment-based parenting.

International Academy of Collaborative Professionals (IACP) www.collaborativepractice.com
Find lawyers, co-parent coaches, and mental health professionals and skilled mediators. Practitioners listed throughout the US and around the world. Contacting mental health professionals who are collaboratively trained, is an excellent resource for stepfamily referrals.

National Stepfamily Resource Center www.stepfamilies.info One of the few online sources of evidence-based info about stepfamilies. Check out their Resource page for excellent interactive video program for stepfamilies.

Patricia Papernow www.stepfamilyresources.com and www.stepfamilyrelationships.com Radio interviews, video clips, and a list of Patricia's current workshops.

Colby Pearce. http://securestart.com.au/colby-pearce Excellent resources for foster and adoptive parents, and for clinicians working with reactive attachment disorder.

RESOURCES FOR THERAPISTS, C0-PARENTING COACHES, PARENTING COORDINATORS, GUIDANCE COUNSELORS AND MEDIATORS

American Family and Conciliation Courts www.afccnet.org Devoted to creating resources that lower conflict in families. Their conferences provide excellent training in post-divorce mediation, parenting coordination, and conflict resolution.

High Conflict Institute www.highconflictinstitute.com Training and consultation to identify and manage complex high-conflict situations in family, (including divorce and co-parenting), business and legal settings.

National Stepfamily Resource Center www.stepfamilies.info Excellent, evidence-based, 10- to-20-minute video modules for helping professionals.

Patricia Papernow. *Surviving and Thriving in Stepfamily Relationships: What Works and What Doesn't* (Routledge, 2013). Written for both stepfamily members and clinicians. "The classic in the field." www.stepfamilyrelationships.com/

Patricia Papernow, "Recoupling in Mid-life and Beyond: From Love at Last to Not So Fast." *Family Process*, 57(1), 2018, 52-69 (March, 2018). DOI: 10.1111/famp.12315

Patricia Papernow "The Remarriage Triangle: Working with Later-Life recouplers and their Grown Children." *Psychotherapy Networker,* (January/February, 2016) pp. 49-53).

Patricia Papernow. *Therapy with couples in stepfamilies.* In A. Gurman, J. Lebow and D. Snyder (Eds.) *Clinical Handbook of Couple Therapy, Fifth Edition.* Guilford, (2015), pp. 467-488.

Dan Siegel. *Mindsight.* Random House, (2010).

Smart Steps: Embrace the Journey. Smart Steps is a 6-session educational program for stepfamilies (couples *and* kids). Each lesson is clearly laid out, step-by-step, with handouts and supportive materials. Each session includes separate tracks for adults and kids, bringing them together at the end. Evidence-based, beautifully designed, and proven effective for a wide range of ethnic groups, educational levels, and distress. Available from the National Stepfamily Resource Center http://www.stepfamilies.info/smart-steps.php

ACKNOWLEDGEMENTS

ac·knowl·edg·ment
The action of expressing gratitude;
The desire to share deep appreciation.

Karen would like to recognize the generosity of my professional "trust": Anne Lucas, Elise Buie, Chris Mills, Gary Direnfield, Kyle Hopps, Joe Shaub, Shelley Chambers, Kristin Little, Felicia Malsby Soleil and this is just the beginning of a long list of pros to whom I'm indebted. So many collaborative colleagues in my own backyard and around the world have contributed their wisdom to this book and their talents to the ever-growing web of family-centered dispute resolution—they've shared in the conviction to show up again and again, to learn more, teach a bit and write it down!

And to the parents who have given me the honor of working with them as they transitioned out of intimate partnerships and white-knuckled their way from parents-together to co-parents raising children together-apart—thank you. With renewed hope, you invited me back into your lives months and years later to meet your new loves with the promise of another chance at thriving family—wanting to get it *right* for your kids, to honor your co-parent's place and successfully navigate your stepfamily transition. Thank you.

It was this latter wave over the last ten years that inspired me to reach out to Patricia and say, "Let's do a *handbook* together." Patricia has culled her experience for a depth and knowledge about stepfamily that is unrivaled. She shares easily, laughs at herself regularly, draws a tough line when it's important, and has become my writing-sister-on-the-opposite-coast through the thick-and-thin of birthing a book. Patricia, dear one, thank you.

And without friends who cheer from the sidelines this could never have happened. Kate Bell, Anne Maxham, and Linda Wolff your check-ins, love and support meant so much.

Patricia would like to recognize all of the stepfamilies I have worked with over the years. Their perseverance, courage, and heart stays with me always. And: My daughter, Dina—your deep soul has always been there, now growing into such a grounded, confident young woman. My husband, Steve, who I adore, who gives the best hugs in the world, and who shares me with my work. I am grateful to my three stepchildren, Becky, Adam, and Jaimi, and their partners, Dave, Angie, and Ally, and their wonderful (seven!) kids. You welcomed me into your hearts and homes from the start. Pam and Phyllis, my two stepdaughters from my first marriage, who started me on this whole adventure more than forty years ago remain in my soul. To my friends and colleagues who have accompanied me on this journey—thank you for your warmth, your wonderful support, your tireless editing, your amazing smarts, and your great good giggles—Beverly Reifman, Mona Fishbane, Betty Pristera, Rob Garfield, and so many others.

And last, but not least, I want to acknowledge Karen Bonnell. We came together as total strangers and have managed to integrate our two overlapping but very different areas of expertise, and our wildly opposing writing styles with incredible collaborative spirit, deep respect, and great good humor. Hurrah! I am honored and grateful.

And together we'd like to recognize... the incredible women who have accompanied us as midwives as we birthed this project. Kathryn Campbell (kathryncampbell.com), whose artful eye and design talent have created a book that's lovely to hold and read. Laura Markowitz (lauramarkowitz.com), you were a disciplined conductor bringing our two writing voices into harmony, and Karen Taylor, our copy editor—thank you for your eagle eye. Thank you to all three of you for being an integral part of our team.

AUTHOR BIOGRAPHIES

Karen Bonnell, ARNP, MS, is a board-certified clinical nurse specialist with more than thirty five years of experience working with individuals, couples and families. Her private practiced is dedicated to working with couples across the spectrum from premarital preparation, to navigating divorce, to co-parenting across two homes, to resting into stepfamily. As a divorce and co-parent coach, Karen had dedicated her work to resolving conflicts thoughtfully—one person, one couple and one family at a time.

Karen has served on the board of King County Collaborative Law and was a founding member of the Collaborative Professionals of Washington. She is a member of the International Academy of Collaborative Professionals and Academy of Professional Family Mediators. She regularly presents on topics related to divorce, child-centered parenting plan development and co-parent coaching, as well as advanced communication skills.

Karen is the author—with contributions by Kristin Little—of *The Co-Parenting Handbook: Raising Well-Adjusted and Resilient Kids from Little Ones to Young Adults through Divorce or Separation;* and—with contributions by Felicia Malsy Soleil—*The Parenting Plan Workbook: A Comprehensive Guide to Building a Strong, Child-Centered Parenting Plan.* Both books are available through your favorite booksellers.

Karen lives on the eastside of Seattle with weekends spent in her cabin nestled in the foothills of the Cascade Range. Her two adult children and her granddaughter are her daily inspiration for the beauty of love, forgiveness and trust in the capacity of family in all its forms. In her free time, you'll find her exploring national parks and hiking trails with her point-and-shoot camera.

You can reach Karen at Karen@coachmediateconsult.com.

Dr. Patricia Papernow is widely recognized as one of the world's foremost experts on "blended families." She is nearing four decades of working with, learning about, and teaching others about stepfamily relationships.

Dr. Papernow's most recent book, *Surviving and Thriving in Stepfamily Relationships: What Works and What Doesn't*, consistently receives rave reviews from both stepfamily members and helping professionals. She is the author of several dozen articles and book chapters on stepfamilies, and she is frequently interviewed as a stepfamily expert by national and local media. Her first book, *Becoming a Stepfamily*, remains a classic in the field. Dr. Papernow is the 2017 recipient of the Distinguished Contribution to Family Psychology from the American Psychological Association Couple and Family Therapy Division.

Dr. Papernow is the Director of the Institute for Stepfamily Education. She is a psychologist dividing her time between clinical work teaching and consulting to other therapists. She is the mother of an amazing young woman with a child on the way. And she is a stepmother to three married stepchildren with seven step-grandkids between them, as well as to two stepdaughters from her first marriage. She is an avid (some would say rabid) gardener. She lives with her husband in Hudson, Massachusetts. Her website is www.stepfamilyrelationships.com

Made in the USA
Monee, IL
02 June 2020